WITHDRAWN
UTSA Libraries

The Strategic Development of Multinationals

Also by Marina Papanastassiou and Robert Pearce

THE TECHNOLOGICAL COMPETITIVENESS OF JAPANESE MULTINATIONALS
The European Dimension

MULTINATIONALS, TECHNOLOGY AND NATIONAL COMPETITIVENESS

Also by Robert Pearce

MULTINATIONALS AND TRANSITION (*with Julia Manea*)

GLOBALISING RESEARCH AND DEVELOPMENT (*with Satwinder Singh*)

INTERNATIONAL ASPECTS OF UK ECONOMIC ACTIVITIES
(*with Peter J. Buckley*)

GLOBAL COMPETITION AND TECHNOLOGY

PROFITABILITY AND PERFORMANCE OF THE WORLD'S LARGEST
INDUSTRIAL COMPANIES (*with John H. Dunning*)

THE GROWTH AND EVOLUTION OF THE MULTINATIONAL ENTERPRISE

THE INTERNATIONALISATION OF RESEARCH AND DEVELOPMENT BY
MULTINATIONAL ENTERPRISES

THE WORLD'S LARGEST INDUSTRIAL ENTERPRISES (*with John H. Dunning*)

US INDUSTRY IN THE UK (*with John H. Dunning*)

The Strategic Development of Multinationals

Subsidiaries and Innovation

Marina Papanastassiou and Robert Pearce

© Marina Papanastassiou and Robert Pearce 2009

All rights reserved. No reproduction, copy or transmission of this publication may be made without written permission.

No portion of this publication may be reproduced, copied or transmitted save with written permission or in accordance with the provisions of the Copyright, Designs and Patents Act 1988, or under the terms of any licence permitting limited copying issued by the Copyright Licensing Agency, Saffron House, 6–10 Kirby Street, London EC1N 8TS.

Any person who does any unauthorized act in relation to this publication may be liable to criminal prosecution and civil claims for damages.

The authors have asserted their rights to be identified as the authors of this work in accordance with the Copyright, Designs and Patents Act 1988.

First published 2009 by
PALGRAVE MACMILLAN

Palgrave Macmillan in the UK is an imprint of Macmillan Publishers Limited, registered in England, company number 785998, of Houndmills, Basingstoke, Hampshire RG21 6XS.

Palgrave Macmillan in the US is a division of St Martin's Press LLC, 175 Fifth Avenue, New York, NY 10010.

Palgrave Macmillan is the global academic imprint of the above companies and has companies and representatives throughout the world.

Palgrave® and Macmillan® are registered trademarks in the United States, the United Kingdom, Europe and other countries

ISBN: 978-0-230-55133-6   hardback

This book is printed on paper suitable for recycling and made from fully managed and sustained forest sources. Logging, pulping and manufacturing processes are expected to conform to the environmental regulations of the country of origin.

A catalogue record for this book is available from the British Library.

A catalogue record for this book is available from the Library of Congress.

10 9 8 7 6 5 4 3 2 1
18 17 16 15 14 13 12 11 10 09

Printed and bound in Great Britain by
CPI Antony Rowe, Chippenham and Eastbourne

To
Augustina and Chrissa
and to
Jonathan and Katie

Contents

List of Tables and Figures	ix
List of Contributors	xi
Acknowledgments	xii

1. Subsidiaries, Innovation and the Strategic Development of Multinationals — 1
   Robert Pearce and Marina Papanastassiou

2. Creative Transition and the Role of MNE Subsidiaries in Host-Country Industrialization — 21
   Robert Pearce and Marina Papanastassiou

3. Strategic Internalization and the Growth of the Multinational Firm — 43
   Marina Papanastassiou, Robert Pearce and Fragkiskos Filippaios

4. Technology Sourcing in Multinational Enterprises and the Roles of Subsidiaries: An Empirical Investigation — 57
   Dimitris Manolopoulos, Marina Papanastassiou and Robert Pearce

5. Strategic Heterogeneity in MNEs and the Integrating European Economy — 78
   Dimitra Dimitropoulou, Robert Pearce and Marina Papanastassiou

6. To 'Almost See the World': Hierarchy and Strategy in Hymer's View of the Multinational — 98
   Robert Pearce and Marina Papanastassiou

7. Individualism and Interdependence in the Technological Development of MNEs: The Strategic Positioning of R&D in Overseas Subsidiaries — 115
   Marina Papanastassiou and Robert Pearce

8. Multinationals and National Systems of Innovation: Strategy and Policy Issues — 138
   Robert Pearce and Marina Papanastassiou

9	Externalization and Individualism: MNE Laboratories' R&D Collaborations *Robert Pearce and Marina Papanastassiou*	163
10	Funding Sources and the Strategic Roles of Decentralized R&D in Multinationals *Marina Papanastassiou and Robert Pearce*	186
11	Globalization of Technology and the Movement of Scientific Personnel in Multinational Enterprises in Europe *Marina Papanastassiou, Robert Pearce and George Anastassopoulos*	204
12	Multinationals and Economic Development in the Era of Globalization *Robert Pearce and Marina Papanastassiou*	216

References 230

Index 244

List of Tables and Figures

Tables

2.1	Roles of subsidiaries in the UK	26
2.2	Relative importance of sources of technology in MNE subsidiaries in the UK	31
2.3	Summary of hypotheses	35
2.4	Regressions with subsidiaries' sources of technology as dependent variable	36
3.1	Summary of hypotheses	50
3.2	Regression tests of knowledge sources accessed by MNE subsidiaries in UK: home-country samples	52
4.1	Relative importance of sources of technology in MNE subsidiaries in Greece	66
4.2	Variable description	68
4.3	Regressions with sources of technology as the dependent variable	71
5.1	Determinants of US FDI in Europe 1981–2001	91
5.2	Determinants of Japanese FDI in Europe 1981–2001	92
5.3	Determinants of intra-EU FDI 1981–2001	93
7.1	In-house R&D as a source of technology in MNE subsidiaries in the UK	121
7.2	Sources of R&D used by MNE subsidiaries in the UK	123
7.3	Anticipated changes in size of R&D laboratories of MNE subsidiaries in the UK, by industry and home country	125
7.4	Regressions with anticipated changes in size of R&D laboratories as dependent variables	126
7.5	Roles of R&D laboratories of MNE subsidiaries in the UK	128
7.6	Evaluation by MNE subsidiaries in the UK that do not have an R&D laboratory of reasons for not having one, by industry and home country	131
7.7	Evaluation by MNE subsidiaries in the UK that do not have an R&D laboratory of factors that could influence them to set one up, by industry and home country	132
9.1	Extent of collaboration between MNE laboratories in the UK and other scientific institutions	168

9.2	Types of R&D involved in collaborations of MNE laboratories with other UK scientific institutions	174
9.3	Reasons for collaboration of MNE laboratories in the UK with other scientific institutions	178
9.4	Nature of collaboration with UK universities of MNE laboratories in the UK	180
10.1	Roles of MNE laboratories in the UK	194
10.2	Sources of funding for MNE laboratories in the UK	196
10.3	Regressions with sources of laboratory funding as dependent variable	197
11.1	Proportion of scientific personnel of subsidiary laboratories that come from home country of MNE	206
11.2	Roles of home-country scientific personnel in MNE subsidiary laboratories	207
11.3	Frequency of movement of host-country personnel to other scientific laboratories	209
11.4	Reasons for movement of host-country scientific personnel to other institutions	212
11.5	Regressions with movement of scientific personnel as dependent variables	213

Figures

8.1	Global Innovation Strategy	143
8.2	National System of Innovation	147
8.3	Basic Research	150
8.4	Applied Research	154
8.5	Product Development	156
8.6	Adaptation	158

List of Contributors

Marina Papanastassiou – Copenhagen Business School

Robert Pearce – University of Reading

George Anastassopoulos – University of Patras

Dimitra Dimitropoulou – Council of Economic Advisors – Greek Ministry of Economy and Finance

Fragkiskos Filippaios – University of Kingston

Dimitris Manolopoulos – Athens University of Economics and Business

Acknowledgments

The papers we include here have been written between 1996 and 2009. They were, in the nature of the academic process, written for a range of different purposes and in response to varied stimuli. They reflect, therefore, different areas of our interest and, in the case of four papers, different collaborative contexts. Our first acknowledgment is then to these co-authors for the distinctive contributions and insights they have provided. But for us, over this period, a fascination has been the way in which our seemingly quite diverse research agendas have both evolved organically from one to another and fallen into place as parts of a wider coherent perspective in our work. The first and last chapters of the book were written to put into place the two 'overview' contexts we would now like to impose on our work. Firstly, that the studies become part of a much wider narrative in International Business that perceives immense strategic restructuring of MNEs as they respond to basic changes in the global economic environment over the past 40 years or so. Secondly, that this restructuring of the *global* strategies of MNEs defines and refocuses their interaction with many *national* economies. This is at the core of wider public debates about the value of MNEs. Thus a subtext of our work (taking prominence here in Chapters 6 and 8) now is that trying to understand what the MNE really is and what it really seeks to do has crucial value in improving the formulation and articulation of debates on MNEs and globalization.

Against this background we have benefited enormously from two rather different modes of scholarship. Firstly, the very wide range of detailed studies that have contributed to the generation of important knowledge of the specific areas that our own work has addressed. Secondly, the analytical approach that has projected the concern with the wider picture of MNEs; their relationship to the reformulation of the global economy and the implications of their position in it. With every acknowledgement to the many researchers and authors whose work we have benefited from enormously in the former mode, we would here wish to express our gratitude to three scholars who have helped both of us in ways far beyond their defining contributions to the latter mode.

Firstly, we acknowledge in memory John Dunning and Neil Hood. To have lost John and Neil is a great personal sadness to us. A concern that we now share is that our profession and discipline may be losing the invaluable type of example that they showed us. Intellectually their awareness of the need for scholarship to understand the full picture of international business and its context, and to see its purpose as feeding knowledge back into that wider perspective, must not be lost. Also the generosity of spirit showed by these two gentlemen, as well as the many acts of personal support and kindness we both received from them, is something we must not, and will not, forget.

Happily we are still able to benefit from the considerable wisdom and support of Tamir Agmon. Tamir's wide-ranging reading and notable ability to rediscover unfairly forgotten foundation texts of our discipline have, for us, helped shine valuable light into and around the incremental minimalism of much of the current literature.

A vital supportive presence through the whole process of generating this collection has been that of Jill Turner. Jill not only typed the four completely new papers here (Chapters 1, 5, 9 and 12) but also the first versions of many of the earlier ones. One of the most difficult tasks in completing the book has been finding and renovating some of these early works. Jill has performed this immensely frustrating exercise of 'electronic archaeology' with all her usual patience and support. We are, as always, extremely grateful to Jill's calm efficiency – which we have not always matched or merited!

The authors and publishers are grateful to the following for permission to reproduce copyright materials.

Elsevier for D. Manolopoulos, M. Papanastassiou and R. Pearce 'Technology sourcing in multinational enterprises and the roles of subsidiaries: an empirical investigation' in *International Business Review* Vol. 14 (2005) pp. 249–67.

Elsevier for R. Pearce and M. Papanastassiou 'To 'almost see the world': hierarchy and strategy in Hymer's view of the multinational'. *International Business Review* Vol. 15, No. 2 (2006) pp. 151–65.

Blackwell for M. Papanastassiou and R. Pearce 'Funding sources and the strategic roles of decentralized R&D in multinationals'. *R&D Management* Vol. 35, No. 2 (2005) pp. 89–100.

Chapter 7 is a slightly revised and expanded version of a paper originally published in J. Birkinshaw and N. Hood (eds) *Multinational Corporate Evolution and Subsidiary Development* Macmillan Press (1998).

Chapter 8 is an expanded version of a paper originally published in A.T. Tavares and A. Teixeira (eds) *Multinationals, Clusters and Innovation: Does Public Policy Matter?* Palgrave Macmillan (2006).

Chapter 11 was originally published in M.D. Hughes and J.H. Taggart (eds) *International Business – European Dimensions*, Palgrave (2001).

We dedicate this book to Augustina and Chrissa Economou and Jonathan and Katie Russell, the youngest members of our respective families. We wish them the freedom and happiness to develop their undoubted talents to the full.

1
Subsidiaries, Innovation and the Strategic Development of Multinationals

Robert Pearce and Marina Papanastassiou

The central force driving the views of the Multinational Enterprise (MNE) in the papers that now comprise the core of this book is that of heterogeneity. Thus our view of the processes of globalization, that have conditioned the evolution of the MNE over the past 40 years, is that they have allowed these firms to leverage to greater competitive advantage the differences between locations. This has resulted in MNEs generating heterogeneity in their own increasingly internationally-networked operations. It has also meant that countries (or discrete policy-defined regions within them) have also learnt the benefits of generating differentiated sources of comparative advantage (increasingly deriving from specific institutional and policy arrangements, such as those constituting national systems of innovation).

In our analyses of these forces in the competitive evolution of MNEs we have focused most decisively on the roles played by individual subsidiaries and those strategic needs and motivations that are encompassed by them. This investigation can be seen to operate at two levels. At the broader level we address the organizational transformation of the MNE from a portfolio of very similar subsidiaries (created in the image of the parent company's competitive advantages and product range[1]), each targeting the local market of its host country, into a networked structure in which subsidiaries accede to a much more differentiated status. The essence of this change is that the economic characteristics that have the most decisive influence on location decisions of MNEs (i.e. the relevant location advantages; Dunning 1977, 1993a, 1998, 2000; Dunning and Lundan, 2008) switch from those relating to demand-side factors to those supply-side endowments that can support a subsidiary's competitive position in its MNE's international networks. Thus the broad perspective is of subsidiaries that pursue an *individualized* position in the internationally-oriented competitive capacities of its parent MNE group. The precise form of this position, and thus the subsidiary's specified role within the heterogeneous strategic needs of an MNE's global competitive agendas, should then reflect clearly perceived sources of comparative advantage of host locations.

At a second, more precisely focused, level of analysis the studies included here have tended to emphasize an interest in that dynamic component of the diverse strategic scope of MNEs that relates to renewal and extension of the firm-level sources of competitiveness (i.e. ownership advantages: Dunning, 1977, 1993a, 2000; Dunning and Lundan, 2008) that underpin their international success and expansion. Of course our work is predicated on an understanding of the crucial importance of the effective implementation and balanced integration, coordination and evolution, of a wider range of competitive needs. Notably the need to build supply networks that can maximize the returns from mature sources of current competitiveness (technologies, organizational practices, successful established goods and services) is acknowledged and addressed. Nevertheless, in line with other crucial strands in understanding the organizational evolution of MNEs over the past quarter century, we see the internationalization of the pursuit of competitive regeneration as having become the most challenging and influential analytical frontier.

This brings into play an important set of new location advantages (LAs), in the form of those relating to countries' (or sub-regions') attempts to create dynamic sources of comparative advantage. Since the aim of these policies of potential locations is to underpin their own economic development this element of our analysis allows us to raise the vital political-economy issues of how the participation of MNEs (with their wider global competitive perspectives) affect the success of this. Thus we perceive the essence of the contemporary MNE as providing subsidiaries with *individualized* roles that reflect and are derived from distinctive characteristics of their host locations, but which are then operationalized through *interdependencies* with other affiliates elsewhere in the interests of the global competitiveness and performance of the parent group.

The predominant focus of our analysis of the competitive organization of the contemporary MNE has, therefore, been on the roles played by subsidiaries in innovation and the ways this is supported by a range of dispersed R&D laboratories. The modeling of this decentralized and heterogeneous competitive structure of the MNE is, however, radically different from that perceived and analyzed in early discussion of these firms as important agents in the global economy. It is, therefore, useful to provide a backdrop to our view of the current stage in the evolution of MNEs through a brief review of how, and in response to which external and internal forces, their competitive nature has been reconfigured during, in effect, the era of globalization.

Early thinking in response to the perception (Hymer, 1960/76) of a need to move from macro-level analysis of foreign direct investment flows to a micro-level understanding of the firms undertaking such investment, focused on the sources of their ability to do so, ownership advantages (OAs), and the factors (LAs) that determined the use of these competitive advantages in specific foreign locations. In the pioneering thinking along these lines the views of OAs and LAs provided a modeling of what was soon distinguished (Caves, 1971, 1982) as a horizontally-integrated MNE. Here an initial concern to explain the *emergence* of an MNE, rather than its subsequent competitive *evolution*, led logically to a view of OAs that were generated in, and therefore reflected the economic conditions of, the home country of the putative international firm. This perception of the home-country origins of OAs received its most precise and detailed early exposition in the first stage of Vernon's original product cycle model (Vernon, 1966).

Then, in a complementary fashion, the second stage of the product cycle model provided clear insights into the LAs that were likely to drive the firm's preliminary moves into international production. Here, Vernon suggests, overseas production, based around the now mature OAs, will emerge when foreign economies begin to achieve levels of income and market characteristics that provide significant demand for the firm's goods. Where, as was likely at the time of these analyses, supply of these markets through trade was severely constrained by natural (transport costs) or policy (tariffs) factors then localized production became the logical competitive response.[2] Later in the development of the theorizing it was such a view of the horizontally-integrated MNE, with its intra-firm transfer of competitive advantages, that exemplified Buckley and Casson's (1976) analysis of internalization decision processes.

We can now see the organizational structure of the MNE that is implied by these early economics-based analyses as that of a *multi-domestic hierarchy*. This perspective immediately provides a much more significant analytical position for the *subsidiary* than had the parallel economic theorizing. Thus the international expansion of the horizontally-integrated MNE is now perceived as having been implemented through market-seeking (MS) subsidiaries, whose role is to utilize their parent company's competitive advantages (OAs) to compete specifically for the local market of their host economy. In a manner later designated as part of an MNE's multi-domestic strategy (Porter, 1986) each such subsidiary is one of a multiplicity of very similar units, each fighting an essentially independent competitive battle in its isolated domestic market. At this stage in an MNE's response to international competition each subsidiary is part of a portfolio of MS operations, whose individual performance is not expected to influence, or to be influenced by, the performance of sister units.

It was, of course, constraints on trade that caused the extensive growth of MNEs in the early post-war years to be implemented in the form of multi-domestic hierarchies. Though transport costs were a persistent component of this it was tariffs and other policy-based constraints that had been most influential. In the established industrial economies the high levels of protectionism inherited from the recession policies of the 1930s received an extra stimulus to MS investment with the improved growth performance of the immediate post-war decades. Alongside this the pursuit of import-substitution industrialization in potentially important developing economies created a further protectionist context for the geographical expansion of firms beginning to explore new competitive horizons.

Whilst the multi-domestic subsidiary operates independently of other subsidiaries it is innately hierarchically dependent on its home-country parent company. This reflects another of the defining characteristics of this stage of MNE emergence; i.e. the centralized home-country generation of the sources of firm-level competitive advantages (product cycle model stage one) that provide the ability to expand internationally when needs dictate (product cycle model stage two). Crucially, in the light of future developments, it is then implicit in this view that initial R&D and innovation were exclusively centralized in the home country of the nascent MNE.

The most decisive hierarchical control that the parent company possesses, as the provider of the potential sources of competitiveness to subsidiaries, is, of course, in which countries such MS operations are established. Whilst such hierarchical control can also extend to close monitoring of MS subsidiaries' performance (beyond the options of closure or major managerial restructuring) some degree of operational autonomy may also be plausible. Thus MS subsidiary management may be able to usefully adapt products and processes to better respond to local needs and potentials. Though this does then represent a degree of subsidiary-level individualization this is normally very context specific and certainly not perceived (by subsidiary or parent) as any attempt to contribute to extensions of group-wide competitiveness.

In retrospect we can suggest that the multi-domestic hierarchy provided MNEs with acceptable levels of profitability without needing to approach optimized levels of productive efficiency. We can discern both internal and external sources for this eventually vulnerable and unstable set of circumstances. Firstly, the MNEs that moved into prominence during the first two decades after World War II did so from, what would come to seem, very strong positions in terms of OAs. Up to the apotheosis of the multi-domestic hierarchy, in perhaps the mid-1960s, the international expansion of business had been led by a relatively small number of firms from a small group of home economies, with the US as the predominant source. The strong possession of competitive advantages by these pioneering international firms provided them with degrees of market power that diminished the pressure to pursue optimized efficiency.

The second factor, external to the firms themselves, was that they exercised their sources of international competitiveness in the multi-domestic context dictated by high levels of restraints on trade. This then precluded, as a systematic strategic option, the possibility of using highly cost-effective production in one location to supply markets in other countries. The corollary of this was then that the multi-domestic MS supply of subsidiaries' domestic markets was protected from imports as a source of competition and could thus usually secure profitability from less than fully efficient use of their companies' strong OAs.

This view of the multi-domestic scenario can thus be seen to indicate three specific sources of productive inefficiency. Firstly, many of the national markets that could support a positive contribution to an MNE group's profitability were nevertheless not large enough to allow full realization of optimal scales of production in the industrial technologies of that time. A second problem endemic to the MS strategy was that discerned, early in the analysis of MNE behavior, as 'inappropriate technology transfer'. Thus where MNEs set up MS production facilities, and the parts of the product range supplied to particular markets, was determined by the demand pattern of the host economy. Often the input needs implied by the mature and standardized technologies relating to these goods differed significantly from the factor availabilities and production capabilities of host countries. This would, in the absence of significant subsidiary-level adaptation, generate cost-inefficiencies in supply. Finally, these various sources of market power (including absence of internal competition from other subsidiaries of the group) are likely to allow for X-inefficiency, in which the productive potentials of available OAs are not fully realized.

It was the exposure of these sources of subsidiary-level vulnerability, in an increasingly competitive globalized environment, that led to the first systematic restructuring of MNEs' strategic organization. Here we can distinguish two parallel sets of forces that began to undermine the market power that had provided inefficient MS subsidiaries with viable levels of profitability.

The first of these comprised a group of factors which intensified international competition and thereby removed the trade protected context of the multi-domestic hierarchy. These developments included, the effective implementation of multi-lateral trade negotiations (pioneered in the 1960s by the Kennedy Round of GATT); moves towards regional integration schemes (already becoming operative in Europe); the refocusing of industrialization strategies in many developing countries, away from protected import substitution towards export orientation; improvements in cost-effectiveness of freight transport; technological developments in established and emerging industrial sectors that increased the 'transportability' of intermediate goods and final products. Goods produced inefficiently in a particular market could then no longer compete with lower-cost imports produced more efficiently elsewhere. Such newly importable goods could, of course, be those of rival firms (including those that had previously opted out of the market by not producing locally). Crucially, from the point-of-view of MNE restructuring, they would logically also include goods previously produced inefficiently by the MS subsidiary but now more competitively supplied by a more efficient sister subsidiary elsewhere.

This first set of forces can, therefore, be seen as a fundamental change in the LAs conditioning the position of subsidiaries, with this resulting in a much more competitively intense *international* context in which MNEs seek to secure profitability from their OAs. The second source of increased competition was then the relative weakening of the OAs possessed by key players in many globalizing industries. We already noted that an aspect of the multi-domestic hierarchy had been the hegemonic status of quite a small number of MNEs from a very limited set of home countries. In many sectors, especially those high-growth industries based around major new technological potentials, the global competitive environment was further intensified by the emergence of many significant new MNEs from an ever growing range of home countries. This meant that in this now extensively changing era of globalized competition the OAs possessed by the MNEs, old and new, were less decisively powerful than those that had been exercised by subsidiaries in the protected multi-domestic era. This again meant that MNEs could no longer tolerate any inefficiency in the use of the OAs they did possess, and needed to adopt reformulated global strategies that allowed them to optimize the value they obtained from such competitive advantages.

Indeed another aspect of the way the new MNEs conditioned the intensification of global competition was by basing their initial international expansion around the pursuit of productive efficiency. Thus, from the start, the international location decisions of many of these new MNEs were taken in pursuit of low-cost sources of supply for now open global markets. The perspective adopted by these firms was of a globalized market, most parts of which could be supplied through trade, so that the key driver of their geographical expansion was the need for cost-effective production.[3] Of necessity this mode of internationalization was soon adopted by the majority of MNEs in sectors with global competitive horizons. *Efficiency*-seeking thereby replaced *market*-seeking as the dominant strategic imperative of firms aiming to maximize global profits from their well-established mature goods. This had, indeed, been predicted by Vernon in the third stage of the product cycle model, suggesting relocation of supply of standardized goods to low-wage locations.

This move towards an efficiency-seeking (ES) imperative means subsidiaries begin to produce specified limited *parts* of the group's product range for *international* markets rather than targeting a much more extensive set of goods at their host-national market. In terms of subsidiary evolution, therefore, this role change from MS to ES means a major rationalization[4] of the subset of goods to be supplied, with these now to be mainly exported into markets already created by the MNE. The aim of the rationalization process is then for the subsidiary to focus on supply of goods whose input needs, defined by an already standardized and successful technology, matches as closely as possible the available factor proportions (essentially sources of static comparative advantages) of its host location.

This restructuring of the subsidiary role should now overcome all three of the sources of inefficiency endemic to the MS role. Firstly, in the way suggested above, it would overcome the problem of inappropriate technology transfer. The MNE is now allocating roles to subsidiaries in ways that reflect its knowledge of global input heterogeneity, so that the goods produced in an ES subsidiary now respond to local supply-side, rather than demand-side, characteristics. The subsidiary is still dependent on the stock of centrally-created technology, but now only receives the small subset of this that is appropriate to host factor proportions. Secondly, access to extensive external markets would now allow the subsidiary to fully realize available economies of scale. Thirdly, the ES subsidiary now has to compete for position in the MNE's dynamic network in a manner that the MS subsidiary was, in effect, protected from. The subsidiary location may have been selected as the most competitive, but other similar locations are likely to be available and open to parent company assessment. The subsidiary management will thus be under continual pressure to retain its position in the network by making full use of the potential offered by the host economy. X-inefficiency can no longer be tolerated.

This process of subsidiary refocusing is then a key element in the wider strategic reconfiguration of MNEs, from a *multi-domestic hierarchy* to the internationalized competitive structure of the *network hierarchy*. In the network hierarchy the ability to supply the MNE group's extensive product range competitively to a globalized market is built around a network of ES subsidiaries, each of which is intended to secure cost-effective output of specific goods. For a mature MNE emerging from the multi-domestic era the construction of an effective supply network can involve three facets. Firstly, the process of subsidiary evolution outlined above can provide effective ES subsidiaries through the reconfiguration of previous MS operations. Secondly, new subsidiaries can be created in economies at an early stage of economic development, where low income levels had precluded a viable MS role, but which now become a very competitive source of labor (and other) inputs to ES. Thirdly, it is also analytically possible that previously profitable MS subsidiaries could be closed down if no immediately plausible cost-effective potential can be discerned in the host economy. However, under these circumstances, closure might be considered less than optimal from a wider group perspective. Thus the success of an earlier MS commitment indicates a very significant market which the MNE hopes to supply *mainly* through trade. But closing a very visible subsidiary, with negative implications in the host economy, might meet strong local resistance (to imports) from both consumers and government. A continued role for the subsidiary needs to be found.[5]

Clearly the position taken by an ES subsidiary is innately an individualized one, from which it makes its distinctive contribution to group competitiveness. However, the sources of this individualism are external to the subsidiary deriving, as we have seen, from the competitive juxtaposition of OAs provided by the parent company and LAs defined by aspects of comparative advantage of the host economy. Though the potentials of this juxtaposition need to be fully realized by local management the pure-ES subsidiary does not possess (and is not innately motivated to generate) unique in-house knowledge or skill capacities.[6] In a similar way the execution of its supply role involves the subsidiary in interdependencies with other parts of the global-supply network of which it is part. But this too is externally mediated from a higher-level in the MNE hierarchy which secures the integration and coordination of the network.

Thus the formulation of the network hierarchy remains predicated on centralized innovation, and the home-country generation of the OAs that allow the MNE to achieve international competitiveness. Where and how these group-level sources of competitiveness are utilized is a decisively centralized hierarchical decision. This hierarchical power can be exercised at two levels of decision making. Firstly, the broad configuration of the network; where ES subsidiaries exist and what they supply. As we have suggested this would involve elements of network restructuring over time, emphasizing again that the emergence of internal competition is a source of efficiency gains. Secondly, the effectiveness of the coordination of the network on a 'day-to-day' basis, allowing for changes in demand patterns to be reflected in output of particular subsidiaries. Implementing this also provides the scope to monitor subsidiary performance and thus to signal potential cases for reconfiguration.

However, as the organizational development of the MNE proceeded into the last third of the 20th century it became clear that whilst the focus on an efficiency-seeking imperative was necessary it was not sufficient to secure the full needs of strategic competitiveness (Pearce, 1999a).[7] Thus alongside the challenges and potentials of the increasing freedoms of international transfers offered by globalization another set of forces were driving changes in MNEs' competitive environment. As already indicated these comprised a considerable speeding up of scientific progress and technological change and a very significant widening of the locations from which this derived. This meant that alongside the ES imperative of using their mature sources of *current* competitiveness in the most effective way MNEs also recognized, as an equally decisive strategic priority, the knowledge-seeking (KS) need to access and operationalize new technologies in pursuit of the medium- and long-term regeneration of their competitiveness. Generating internationalized perspectives on this, by tapping into distinctive knowledge sources in different locations (i.e. responding to technological heterogeneity), became a crucial theme of MNEs' strategic development in recent decades.

Building a global organizational structure to address this widening range of strategic priorities involved two distinctive, but closely related, components. Firstly, the emergence of a new type of innovation-oriented subsidiary, categorized here (as elsewhere in much recent literature) as a product mandate. Secondly, a vast expansion in the scope and extent of decentralized R&D units in MNEs.[8]

The product mandate (PM) subsidiary obtains from its parent company full responsibility for innovation and sustained evolution of key parts of the group's internationally-competitive product range. At the core of this is, therefore, the KS need to build-up unique and distinctive subsidiary-level competitive capabilities, in a way that would have been innately alien to the performance of the MS or ES roles. This provides the PM subsidiary with a distinctively individualized position and capacity in both its parent group's current competitiveness and those creative and dynamic scopes from which it is expected that this competitiveness will be renewed and revitalized. The core of this subsidiary-level individualization will then reflect a process of strategic internalization,[9] in which the subsidiary will secure preferred access to creatively distinctive attributes of the host economy. These attributes may be drawn fully into the subsidiaries as in-house capacities (e.g. in an R&D laboratory or powerful market research team) or contractually accessed through collaborative arrangements with host-country institutions (e.g. universities).

We can then see the LAs that attract KS commitments of PM subsidiaries as being elements of the host-country's national system of innovation (NSI). The pursuit of sustained economic growth has, in recent decades, led many countries to seek to generate a strong and distinctive science-base and to use an increased commitment to education and training to build-up a supply of talented and ambitious creative human capital. But, of course, for this policy to work effectively as a basis for successful international competitiveness the defining elements of the emerging NSI (e.g. stock of technology; ongoing research programs; ability to derive new product perspectives from the local customer base) need to take on very distinctive characteristics. Thus the pursuit of knowledge-based growth has led to extensive technological- and market-heterogeneity as central characteristics of the international environment faced by MNEs. Internalizing strong and distinctive elements of these localized creative competences into a PM subsidiary has the potential to allow this operation to generate new goods and services that contribute to international competitiveness for both the MNE and the host country.

Alongside the emergence of PMs the growth of dispersed R&D units constitutes a parallel means by which KS MNEs tap into aspects of the differentiated NSIs that now condition their global knowledge environment. One aspect of this is, indeed, to provide one of the defining elements of PM scope. Thus an in-house laboratory provides a core capability in PMs, by mediating the acquisition, communication (to other functions involved in the innovation process) and application, of new technologies (whether sourced from the host science-base or from other parts of the MNE) into original development. But both firms and governments also understand that long-term competitive regeneration will benefit fundamentally from new technological potentials that derive from the expansion of basic scientific knowledge. To pursue such possibilities many countries incorporate a significant commitment to speculative basic research in their NSIs. These precompetitive research agendas will, however, tend to build on areas of established success and reputation so that, again, individual NSIs become differentiated around distinctive scientific specialisms. This means that MNEs, seeking to access top quality basic research potentials in areas of science likely to fuel their innovation, need to tap into such exploratory work in several countries. This has generated a second type of R&D laboratory in MNEs, which focused on pure scientific investigation in a discipline defining a strength of a host NSI.

The emergence of PMs and decentralization of R&D represent only the most visible, and organizationally challenging, manifestation of the *heterarchy* as a new competitive structure for MNEs. Indeed an important aspect of these MNEs' very heterogeneity resides in their continued use of a range of subsidiary types. Crucially, an effective network of ES operations remains subsumed within the heterarchy, with no diminution of the need to maximize global profits from a currently successful product range. Furthermore a significant residual status for a more responsive variant of MS also plays a role, especially as a means of exploring newly opening markets and economies. But here well-established hierarchical control mechanisms can oversee the ES-supply networks and locally-responsive MS operations benefit from a certain degree of autonomy. Thus it is, indeed, the approach to securing greatest value from the dispersed KS facilities that sets the main new organizational challenges for heterarchy. At the core of this, we suggest, is the need to address the organizational problems and competitive potentials of *interdependent individualism* in dispersed KS facilities.

In the case of PMs the process of generating individualized competences from the host-country knowledge-base can only be effectively operationalized through allowance for the exercise of very considerable degrees of subsidiary-level creative autonomy. But this cannot be allowed to result in isolationism. Certainly the unique knowledge that serves to drive the PM's distinctive innovation will be that which it derives from its host NSI. But the ability to perceive the value of this local knowledge, and to internalize and operationalize it effectively, is likely to derive from what the subsidiary already knows; i.e. its base in the MNE's extant technological scopes. This evolutionary interface between a PM's distinctive innovation and its MNE group's existing competences can then benefit from active exchange of knowledge, ideas and questions across this interface.

Whilst the PM's innovation is individualized around original technology and market perceptions generated locally it will be building this onto its group's established technology trajectory.[10] To achieve this supporting technologies and more generalized advice can be beneficially accessed by a PM from other parts of the group. In a similar way important elements of the knowledge generated by a PM may have values beyond its embodiment in the subsidiary's own innovation. The value of these subsidiary attributes to other parts of the group need to be perceived and intra-group transfer mechanisms generated and supported, so as to secure their effective sharing when appropriate.

In an analogous way the value of stand-alone basic research laboratories also needs to acknowledge interdependencies. Thus, while such laboratories do focus on projects that decisively reflect specialized research strengths of the host-country science-base, the value of their results is likely to take on its strongest potentials (ultimately as an input into commercial innovations) when seen in the interactive light of results, or technology stocks, from other laboratories in other NSI. Again the value of individualized investigation can take its most effective form when opened to intra-group interdependent exchange. As with PMs this emphasizes the fact that the success of such pure research laboratories is likely to derive from their embeddedness in two technological and creative communities; those of the MNE and the NSI of the host country.[11]

Securing the benefits of an internationally dispersed and differentiated network of KS operations becomes a defining challenge to centralized oversight in the heterarchical MNE. This certainly requires the center to devolve to PMs and overseas laboratories the initiative for discerning distinctive local learning and creative opportunities and assets, for accessing and operationalizing them, and for beginning the processes of turning them into competitive advantages for the group. Too much HQ intrusion into these processes of localized initiative and individualization would stifle the flexibility and drive needed to secure the fullest understanding of, and contribution from, such dispersed knowledge potentials. But a total HQ abdication of responsibility for oversight and supervision would also carry severe dangers, potentially amounting to creative anarchy and gross irresponsibility in resource commitment. However talented their personnel, and however distinctive their agendas and potentials, PMs and laboratories cannot normally be allowed to pursue projects which have no roots in the MNE's current scopes and which seem entirely tangential to more mainstream expectations of the group's competitive evolution. However confident the personnel driving such radical initiatives might be, it remains implausible that they could derive locally a complete self-contained set of new attributes adequate to secure a successful autonomous breakthrough. Some degree of positioning in, and access to the competences of, its MNE group's technological trajectory seems likely to be essential. In the same vein, one or more decentralized KS units that are aggressively pursuing autonomous agendas (with no interest in generating or discerning potential spillover benefits back to other group operations) would unbalance an MNE's overall creative programs and compromise those facilities that do feel a need to embed their creativity in such network interdependencies.

Clearly the challenge to managing innovation, and to accessing new knowledge scopes generally, in a heterarchy is now one of securing the balance and coherence of interdependent individualism in a rich portfolio of dispersed facilities. Certainly the center no longer dominates the generation of group competitiveness through exclusive home-country performance of R&D and innovation. But it does, we argue, still possess a unique position and role. Thus for an MNE that recognizes the existence and potential benefits of global heterogeneities the challenge is to learn what these are, to access those that seem likely to provide creative values, and then operationalize them successfully to the ends of group competitiveness. This, it is now well understood, cannot be achieved properly without units on the ground that are embedded in those NSI that are providing these opportunities. But for these units to indeed contribute effectively their distinctive localized contributions need to be formulated in ways that ultimately maximize their overall impact on group competitiveness. Spillovers and synergies between such units are key to the dispersal of competitive regeneration in heterarchies, and it remains a unique responsibility of a 'center' to secure this.

Therefore we can now suggest that the source of a continuing hegemonic power in the parent/center derives from its aspiration to be the only point in the MNE group that knows, and hopes to be able to understand and evaluate, what is going on in all the diverse KS facilities.[12] From this it would aim to coordinate an ever-evolving program of KS activities aiming to secure the strategic competitiveness of the group through the medium- and into the longer-term.[13] This involves dynamic and interactive aspects of the programs which, we suggest, may focus around the twin concerns of *coherence* and *cohesion*.

In terms of coherence the concern will be to have a portfolio of ongoing innovative and investigative projects which seems to be sensibly balanced, in terms of overlaps and synergies that are likely to derive and drive sources of logical competitive evolution. This can involve requiring adjustments to ongoing projects (to improve their contribution to coherence) or, indeed, to closure of those that seem to be going nowhere or even to represent a disruptive misallocation of resources. Crucially, though, it also needs an informed willingness to listen to new proposals from ambitious PMs or laboratories. The more completely a center understands the range and content of its current KS networks the more effectively it can evaluate and, where relevant, co-opt the potentials of proposals from its dispersed facilities. The parallel concern with cohesion will then be to secure the benefits of intra-network interdependence and synergies. This not only involves perceiving where these exist but also facilitating their realization through knowledge exchanges. As already suggested this represents a significant motivational challenge, since units that consider themselves to be successful in individualizing their core capacities may be reluctant to either share these with other parts of the group or accept that they may, themselves, benefit from external learning. Overcoming any such isolationist introversion is another key challenge to the center in building the dispersed knowledge dynamism in heterarchy.

In the next chapter we introduce and investigate the process of *creative transition*.[14] The central theme of this sees the emergence of the heterarchy, and its embracing of decentralized innovation and KS, from the earlier exclusive use of hierarchy and one-way technology transfer. The essence of this is then the technological repositioning of those subsidiaries that take on the PM status and its responsibility for accessing and activating host-country creative inputs. In the survey evidence reported (for MNE subsidiaries in the UK) seven sources of technology that could play a role in a subsidiary's operation are evaluated. Empirical tests then relate the significance of these sources to four alternative roles of subsidiaries (one MS, two variants of ES and one KS). The predictions of creative transition would expect a movement away from a central role for transfer of successful established group technologies into MS and ES subsidiaries (hierarchy) towards generation of subsidiary-specific technology competencies in PMs (heterarchy). Thus we can perhaps see the essence of creative transition in the significant positive position of established group technology in the ES role and that of in-house R&D in the KS/PMs. But two other results for the PMs may also reflect important aspects of PM positioning. Firstly, a significant positive result for the tacit knowledge encompassed in the skills of subsidiaries' engineering and other personnel. This, we suggest, helps build the new innovative perspective of the PMs onto the mature base of the MNE's technological and product scopes. Secondly, and to the same ends, the established product technologies of the group (that would probably have conditioned the subsidiary's earlier, pre-creative transition, role) remains positively (though not quite significantly) related to playing the PM role. The points indicate how moving to the product development status of KS positioning is likely to be coherent with the logical technological trajectory of its MNE group.

In Chapter 2 we also relate these views of subsidiary-level dynamics to the development processes of host countries. We thus see the scope for movement from an ES to KS role as a means of embedding a subsidiary in its host-country's development process, and as an escape from the alleged inevitability of 'footloose' migration. Changes in host-country location advantages are indeed accepted as a beneficial manifestation of development. But the higher value these LAs take, with increasingly distinctive knowledge content and creative potentials, serves to embed the PM subsidiaries in the development processes of the host-country as well as the MNE group.

Chapter 3 complements the previous one by focusing directly on the process of strategic internalization.[15] This represents the way in which subsidiaries seek to secure, from the NSI of their host country (here UK), the sources of their intra-group competitive individualization. The results verify the importance of local creative attributes, demonstrating the powerful roles in PM subsidiaries of an in-house R&D unit and (especially for Japanese MNEs) the contribution expected from the tacit knowledge of talented local engineering personnel. Similar aspects of MNEs' dispersed learning processes are investigated in Chapter 4, but from the perspective of a rather different host economy, that of Greece. Here the dominant source of technology used by subsidiaries was the established technology of the group, supporting the position of MS and ES operations. Though a majority of responding subsidiaries in the Greek survey had an in-house R&D unit the evidence suggests that this was most likely to support effective application of received technology in the MS/ES units.[16] Limited use of R&D collaboration with Greek laboratories (universities, etc.) or local firms again suggest less overall prevalence of strategic internalization in this case.[17]

A potentially important context for the exercise of the strategic diversity of the heterarchical MNE is that of an integrating regional community. In Chapter 5 we analyze the determinants of FDI flows into EU economies, using explanatory variables that reflect country characteristics that are likely to discriminate between MS, ES and KS motivations. Applying an expanded variant of the familiar core/periphery distinction we investigate the extent to which the determinants of FDI into different segments of the EU reflect different MNE motivations. Here, in the main, results for MS proxies are weak or even counter-intuitive. Thus we may be looking at MNEs approaching EU competitiveness through ES and KS location decisions. However, though some results can be interpreted as indicative of a low-cost ES orientation in periphery economy operations the broader perspective is of somewhat higher-value-added activity throughout the EU. As might then be expected this appears to have reached a notable commitment to KS in core economies, at least for Japanese and intra-EU FDI. Significantly, however, the results also provide indications of the emergence of some KS activity in peripheral economies (again for Japanese and intra-EU FDI). This can suggest that though MNEs do discriminate between EU locations from strategic perspectives this is by no means static or immutable. In particular there are distinct indications that in peripheral economies a commitment to knowledge-oriented policies and institutions may already attract the more dynamic of MNEs' competitive needs.

The issue of whether MNEs' international segmentation of different functional facets of their value-chain imposes a comparable and immutable segmentation of those economies in which they operate is again central to the discussion of Chapter 6. Here we outline and assess Hymer's view of a strongly hierarchical organizational structure in MNEs that then imposes a global system of uneven development. To generate his view of a system in which a centralization of control in MNEs imposes a similar centralization of control in the global economy Hymer discerns a hierarchical pyramid of three levels. Here level-1 is the apex of the hierarchical MNE pyramid. Located in one of a small group of metropolitan centers level-1 takes hegemonic responsibility for goal determination and strategic planning, and thereby provides the structure within which lower levels operate. Level-2 managers are then seen to coordinate the application of a regional component of the MNE's overall strategic program through level-3 operations. Thus at the bottom of the pyramid level-3 management is limited to routine production and supply operations, the content of which, Hymer indicates, they have no scope to influence. This dependent and static status for level-3 management, it is then suggested, helps to inculcate a comparable lack of initiative and developmental ambition in host-country decision makers.

Our review of the detail of Hymer's analysis firstly draws out the ways in which the processes of competitive development in MNEs have, over the subsequent 40 years, come to allow for much more diffused creative dynamism and associated intra-group restructuring. This can provide scope for a shared *positive* developmental interdependence between, in Hymer's terms, even level-3 MNE operations and their host economies. Intriguingly, though, we then find in Hymer's exposition clear understandings of how the *potentials* for diffused creative dynamism in MNEs could exist. It is, therefore, central to Hymer's interpretation, we argue, that the retention of centralized hegemonic control in the hierarchical MNE structure was a deliberate choice imposed by level-1 decision makers to centralize the benefits from differentiated globalized operations.

In Chapter 7 we look for the first time at the role of decentralizing R&D units in MNEs, here focusing in particular on the association of R&D with different subsidiary roles. The first section of the chapter validates the view of R&D as a key factor in the repositioning of subsidiaries through the process of creative transition. Using evidence from the survey of MNE subsidiaries in the UK we find that those that have acceded to the developmental responsibilities of a PM are more likely to have a laboratory, and to see it as a significant contributor to their technological scope, than those still playing an MS or ES role. This then suggests two very different roles for R&D in subsidiaries. Pre-creative transition R&D would logically support the ability of MS and ES subsidiaries to assimilate and, if needed (most likely in MS), adapt technology transferred to them. Post-transition PMs would place an R&D laboratory at the center of their development processes and as a defining element in individualizing the subsidiary's position. The second part of the chapter elaborates these qualitative aspects of MNEs' R&D in UK.

A central theme of the studies included here is how MNEs build international networks of R&D and innovation facilities in order to benefit from, and respond to, the technological and market heterogeneities of a range of locations. In Chapter 8 we draw these perceptions together in a stylized model of a global innovation strategy (GIS). The differentiated elements of the GIS serve an MNE's needs by accessing and operationalizing specific components of various national systems of innovation (NSI). However, such NSI are generated and supported by government policies to target particular developmental objectives. We thus build on our descriptions of GIS and NSI to address the issues of the ways in which the selective involvement of MNEs' KS programs in varied elements of different NSI affects the ability of these institutions to provide the targeted outcomes. Whereas the MNE GIS participation is likely to strengthen parts of an NSI it can be suggested that this is by no means certain to strengthen it overall or in ways that can specifically contribute to achieving knowledge-based development.

A key mechanism by which MNEs can embed their R&D in an NSI, and secure the aims of strategic internalization, is through collaborative associations with host-country institutions. In Chapter 9 we analyze the results of a survey sent directly to MNEs' R&D facilities in the UK. This provides us with a wider range of R&D units since it can include stand-alone pure-research units that would not have any direct association with a production operation. This type of unit is likely to be very significant in terms of a response to technological heterogeneity, and the MNE aim of tapping into the most distinctive research agendas of an NSI through externalized collaboration arrangements, since its own aims are mainly the development and progressing of speculative pure-science research programs. From this we are able to analyze the extent, nature and content of MNE R&D collaborations with UK scientific institutions as discriminated by the role the commissioning laboratory itself plays in its group's range of strategic needs and objectives. Some of this evidence on the content and positioning of the R&D collaborations provides a basis for addressing issues raised earlier in Chapter 8.

The survey of laboratories also provides the basis for Chapter 10, where we analyze the sources of funding for UK-based R&D units of MNEs. Here the funding sources (mainly the MNE parent company or a subsidiary that hosts the laboratory) would be expected to vary according to whether the laboratory supports (either through product adaptation or development) the competitive positioning of a specific subsidiary or provides inputs to wider group-level knowledge generation. Overall the parent emerges as the leading source of funding, in ways that clearly confirm that whilst knowledge generation and transfer has become a significantly decentralized function in the heterarchical MNE it remains notably driven, supervised and funded from the center.

One clear indication of patterns of R&D laboratory funding reviewed in Chapter 10 is that a key role of the prevalent parent-company funds is to support interdependencies and knowledge flows in MNE networks. In

Chapter 11 an analysis of movement of scientific personnel in MNEs' operations in Europe provides similar perspectives of the flows and reapplication of tacit knowledge embedded in human capital. By separating scientific from managerial personnel this analysis addresses movements that can both enhance performance of R&D in particular locations and also manage the integration of such work into MNEs' creative networks. In a similar way another part of this data distinguishes between personnel movements that serve to facilitate intra-group technology transfer and those that will play a role in R&D performance in a different location. Overall the evidence in this chapter is strongly supportive of the growth of interdependencies and networking in MNEs' decentralized R&D programs.

Notes

1 In their pioneering typology of subsidiary roles White and Poynter (1984) describe such operations as 'miniature replicas', seeing them as 'a small scale replica of the parent'. Elsewhere (Pearce, 1989; Papanastassiou and Pearce, 1999) we refer to these subsidiaries as 'truncated miniature replicas', acknowledging the absence of the more creative and innovation oriented functions of the parent company.
2 Here this facet of Vernon's analysis of international expansion implies the application of a conventional profit maximizing calculus that, in effect, takes account of market characteristics and supply conditions as LAs. But he also indicates the strategic value of penetration of foreign markets by local production, as a means of building an individualized position in these markets (through product and process adaptation) that can at least hold back the emergence of competition (especially new local enterprises with a better knowledge of needs and conditions).
3 The most significant and influential example of this mode of expansion was that of Japanese MNEs into those Asian economies that later were themselves seen as exemplars of export-led industrialization. This type of trade-creating efficiency-seeking FDI was later modeled by Kojima (1978). This analysis was contrasted with the trade-destroying inefficiency of, in our terms, the MS FDI of the multi-domestic hierarchy.
4 Elsewhere (e.g. Pearce, 1989; Papanastassiou and Pearce, 1999) we have categorized this type of ES operation as a 'rationalized product subsidiary'.
5 In already technologically-sophisticated and industrially-advanced economies this new role might not expect to secure the cost-effectiveness of a pure-ES operation, but might build in local attributes that point towards the innovation-orientation of the product mandate.
6 This helps generate the alleged 'footloose' potentials of a pure-ES role. The OAs provided by the group could also be provided to another subsidiary. The LAs might, at some point, become available at a lower price in a rival economy. If that happens the subsidiary itself possesses no distinctive competence that can restrain migration of its role. It is the desire to escape from the vulnerability of such dependency that, we argue later here (Chapter 7),

more enterprising ES subsidiaries manage to build up forward-looking in-house attributes (notably R&D capacity).
7. Here the full realization of strategic competitiveness is perceived to require, in the short-term, cost competitive supply of established mature goods; in the medium-term expansion of the product range through innovation that may embody new technologies available from recent R&D; in the longer-term the pursuit of radically new potentials through a strong commitment to exploratory, precompetitive research.
8. In multi-domestic and network hierarchies the only role for overseas R&D would have been to facilitate technology transfer.
9. In his typology of strategic motivations Dunning (1993a, 2000; Dunning and Lundan, 2008) designates the comparable role of accessing new competitive competences as *strategic* asset-seeking.
10. Innovations that represent a revolutionary break with the group's established technological scope and product range are, of course, possible. However, these are likely to be relatively few and rarely successful. Even if a radical possibility can be perceived from host-country knowledge the innate distance of this from the subsidiary's base in established group capabilities and competences is likely to severely compromise its ability to realize its full potential. Similarly an MNE HQ may resist subsidiary-level innovations that represent a radical break with current technology and products, seeing this as perhaps a dangerous disruption of group cohesion.
11. The implications of this, in terms of sharing benefits and, especially, effects on the host-NSI, are the central theme of Chapter 8.
12. It would, of course, be expected that strong proactive PMs and laboratories would have good information and comprehension of activities in other KS units they interact with or where they perceive potential overlaps and synergies. But resource constraints would inevitably limit this to a relatively small 'hinterland' of associates. Indeed the parent/center might, in a divide-and-rule basis, be quite happy that no rival location would emerge in terms of understanding the group's knowledge scope.
13. PMs would aim to innovate for medium-term competitive renewal from new technologies and market perceptions becoming available. Beyond this the precompetitive laboratories will address the need for exciting new longer-term scientific possibilities.
14. This paper was originally presented at the 1999 conference of the European Association for Research in Industrial Economics.
15. The chapter was originally prepared in response to a call-for-papers (from the *Journal of International Business Studies*) for a special issue to celebrate the 25th anniversary of the publication of Buckley and Casson's *The Future of the Multinational Enterprise*.
16. Though our views of sources of creative transition could suggest that the presence of R&D in those 'low-level' subsidiaries could be a platform for evolution to more ambitious roles.
17. Though in regression tests the use of collaborations with local scientific institutions was significantly positively related to the PM role.

2
Creative Transition and the Role of MNE Subsidiaries in Host-Country Industrialization

Robert Pearce and Marina Papanastassiou

Introduction

A very pervasive characterization of Multinational Enterprises (MNEs) is that their operations are innately 'footloose', with limited embeddedness in individual host countries. From this can be derived the presumption that MNEs are unlikely to be able to provide support for *sustained* processes of national industrial development and growth. Thus many of those host-country characteristics that are normally believed to attract new 'inward investment' are also intended to change as the host economy proceeds through those processes of development whose initiation the MNE's original commitment was designed to be part of.

The most explicit context for this proposition resides in the emergence (through perhaps the last third of the 20th century) of *efficiency-seeking* (Dunning, 1993a; Behrman, 1984) as a strategic motivation of the modern MNE. Thus, activating a growing potential for use of international (or intra-regional) trade as a strategic asset, MNEs increasingly located parts of their productive scope (final product assembly, component manufacture, stages of vertically-integrated manufacturing processes) in particular countries where current input availability (the countries' sources of static comparative advantage) matches the processes' factor needs, so as to optimize cost efficiency. Through the provision of firm-specific sources of competitiveness (product and process technology; management and marketing expertise; international market access) that are not available as effectively in indigenous firms, an MNE's activity increases the effective operationalization of potential local comparative advantage.[1] This plays a positive role in the industrial development that is sought by the host country.

However, success in host-country industrialization is manifest in changes in the rewards expected for local inputs (through, in the case of labor in particular, changes in their characteristics as a result of reinvestment, e.g. in education and training). This breaks the optimizing match between the attributes provided by the MNE and the complementary local inputs that had originally asserted the subsidiary's competitive status intra-group (its cost-effective positioning in the company's supply network). With comparable standardized inputs available in other countries at a now lower cost than in the initial location the MNE is assumed to exercise the footloose option and relocate production to a new site.[2] This scenario therefore sees efficiency-seeking as a self-obsolescing form of support for industrialization, and thus as one that will ultimately hollow-out the bases of the development it helped to initiate.

The key theme of this chapter is that the footloose scenario takes an unduly asymmetrical view of the availability of dynamic and evolutionary procedures. The assumption of pure efficiency-seeking excludes the possibility of subsidiaries changing their scope by their own volition, instead being defined in an immutably static form around those MNE-group sources of competitiveness with which they were initially supplied. Inability to secure adjustment to the factor changes implied by host-country development is thus expected to lead to loss of intra-group competitiveness and to closure. By contrast with this prediction, recent understanding of competitive evolution within MNEs indicates the significant emergence of the potential for individual subsidiaries to take steps to generate differential in-house scopes, which will reflect the upgraded, and increasingly creative and dynamic, sources of host-country competitiveness. This possibility reflects a second strand in the ways in which the contemporary MNE activates globalized dimensions in support of the pursuit of sustainable competitiveness. Thus alongside the need to utilize dispersed networks of supply facilities in order to produce existing goods in the most competitive fashion (efficiency-seeking) MNEs are now also moving towards globalized approaches to product innovation and the generation and acquisition of significant new technologies (knowledge-seeking).

Accession to knowledge-seeking responsibilities (notably as activated in the form of localized product development) represents a highly desirable dynamic possibility that *is* available to the more enterprising and entrepreneurially-driven MNE subsidiaries. It is usually expected to be built around distinctive subsidiary-level technological and creative capacities that are ultimately embodied in new products developed within the facility. These unique competences (that provide the subsidiary with a distinctive competitive status within its group) will themselves derive from the ability to internalize and individualize elements of host-country technology and creative skills (tacit knowledge) that are themselves becoming richer and more valuably idiosyncratic as the local economy develops. It is then possible to assert a dynamic symmetry between the evolutionary potentials available to those subsidiaries that can claim a role in the dispersed creative and learning processes within their MNEs' development programs and the enhanced capabilities that emerge within host countries as the latters' development upgrades their sources of comparative advantage. Far from alienating MNE subsidiaries this scenario sees them as being positively motivated by the potential to access and operationalize those newly emergent (and higher-cost) host-country competences that reflect reinvestment towards sustainable development. As MNEs activate these local knowledge attributes in support of their own development they may, in the process, add dimensions to their commercial effectiveness and provide extra resources for further technological progress, thus reinforcing the sustainability of host-country development.

The perspectives outlined above characterize the contemporary MNE as organizing its global operations as a 'dynamic differentiated network'.[3] This now provides the scope to use geographically-decentralized approaches to securing all the variegated competitive needs of a modern enterprise. At a mainly tactical level subsidiaries with an efficiency-seeking orientation play roles within carefully-coordinated production networks that seek to optimize the competitive supply of the MNE's standardized and mature staple product lines. Beyond this, however, aspects of strategic competitiveness (Pearce, 1999a) require the systematic regeneration of product range and technological scope. Thus a medium-term dimension of strategic competitiveness pursues innovation of new products, encompassing perceptions of new market needs, evolutionary reapplication of existing technologies and the interjection of new technological potentials that are coming on stream from scientific research. To secure the longer-term aims of strategic competitiveness MNEs need a current commitment to the more fundamental regeneration of core technologies (through pre-competitive basic research) that can provide the key bases for eventual more radical innovation.[4]

The remaining sections of this chapter present information from a survey analysis of foreign MNE operations in the UK in order to elaborate on aspects of these companies as dynamic differentiated networks. One aspect of this is, of course, that at a point in time a subsidiary may have a primary focus on one of the number of differentiated objectives that MNEs need to pursue in order to secure all the levels and dimensions of competitiveness discerned earlier. Thus the next section introduces a typology of subsidiary roles and presents evidence on their relative prevalence amongst MNEs' operations in the UK.

The crucial facet of the modern MNE for host countries, we have suggested, is, however, that the status of these subsidiaries need not be unchanging and, indeed, cannot be if they are to be integral with local industrialization and development. They are part of dynamic MNE networks and can gain (or lose) stature within those networks in ways that should reflect the changing quality of local inputs. We argue in section 3 that the defining momentum in subsidiary upgrading is through a process of creative transition (Papanastassiou and Pearce, 1994, 1999), in which they move from dependence on pre-existing parent-group technology to a status which is essentially defined by their own unique knowledge scope, generated from attributes of the host-country economy and science-base. Section 3 thus evaluates seven sources of technology that can be activated within MNEs' UK subsidiaries and derives hypotheses as to how the presence of these may be related to the roles played (as derived in section 2). Regression tests of these hypotheses are reported and discussed in section 4, with section 5 providing conclusions.

In the survey a questionnaire was sent to 812 manufacturing subsidiaries of MNEs located in the UK, which represented all the relevant cases that could be identified from the National Register Publishing Company's *International Directory of Corporate Affiliations*.[5] Satisfactory replies were received from 190 of the subsidiaries.

Roles of subsidiaries

The categorization of subsidiaries used here adopts a variant (Papanastassiou and Pearce, 1999, pp. 24–30; Pearce 1999b) of the scope typology (White and Poynter, 1984; D'Cruz, 1986).[6] Here subsidiaries are differentiated along three dimensions of scope; *product* scope (the extent of the product range produced); *market* scope (the extent of the geographical market area supplied); *functional* scope (how many of the functions that would be operationalized in a fully-mature independent company are available at the subsidiary level).

The first subsidiary type discerned is the *truncated miniature replica* (TMR), whose motivation is the *market-seeking* one of supplying the national market of the subsidiary's host country with all those parts of the parent MNE group's existing product range that are applicable to local demand. In this sense it can be considered a miniature replica of the parent company. In terms of functional scope, however, this type of subsidiary will be severely truncated, with none of the crucial innovation-oriented activities (substantive R&D; creative market research; strategic or entrepreneurial management) that could provide the basis for independent progress and significant embeddedness in the host-country economy. The host-country characteristics that attract TMRs are the size and growth potential of local demand for the MNE's established goods and levels of tariff and other protection that prevent supply through trade.

The expectation is that in most mature industrial economies the conditions conducive to market-seeking TMR-type behavior as a priority in MNEs have declined in relevance. Two developments underpin this expectation. Firstly, the emergence of much freer trading conditions, which expose the inefficiencies likely to be endemic to TMRs (i.e. those traditionally imputed to most import-substituting industrial activity). Secondly, the increasing availability in many of the main host countries of potentially valuable creative inputs (technology; research capacity; provocative new product ideas; distinctively skilled engineers and other personnel), which makes the knowledge dependence of TMRs wasteful from the point of view of overall MNE competitive regeneration. This indicates that hierarchical MNEs, operating through a portfolio of TMRs (a multidomestic strategy in Porter's [1986] terms), represents the archaic structure from which the more flexible and responsive dynamic differentiated network is emerging. It also points to the bases for the two crucial strategic imperatives that we discern in contemporary MNEs, efficiency-seeking and knowledge-seeking. The remaining elements of the typology formalize these motivations at the subsidiary level. Meanwhile the survey evidence in Table 2.1 suggests that, whilst in relative retreat,[7] TMR behavior is still significant amongst MNEs' subsidiaries in the UK.[8]

The scope typology sees efficiency-seeking as the responsibility of *rationalized product subsidiaries* (RPS). These share with TMRs an, essentially dependent, production of goods that are already well-established amongst the MNE's competitive product range and also possess a comparably constrained functional scope.[9] By contrast, however, RPSs will have a much wider market scope but a much narrower product scope than TMRs. Thus RPSs will have emerged in MNEs as the result of a rationalization process in which previously TMR subsidiaries now focus on the supply of a small subset of their previous product range, and export this to wider geographical market area. In general terms this specialization boosts productive efficiency by allowing for full realization of economies of scale and by lowering X-inefficiency by placing the subsidiary in a vastly more competitive environment. The choice of specific location for

Table 2.1 Roles of subsidiaries in the UK

	Roles of subsidiaries (average response)[1]			
	TMR	RPS1	RPS2	WPM/RPM
By industry				
Food	2.56	2.33	1.11	2.67
Automobiles	2.24	2.33	1.65	2.35
Aerospace	2.33	2.17	1.33	2.17
Electronics and electrical appliances	2.33	2.53	1.41	1.96
Mechanical engineering	2.08	2.27	1.33	2.36
Instruments	2.33	2.10	1.33	2.36
Industrial and agricultural chemicals	2.14	2.03	1.48	2.17
Pharmaceuticals and consumer chemicals	2.27	2.55	1.45	1.91
Metal manufacture and products	2.09	1.90	1.22	2.20
Other manufacturing	2.44	1.73	1.20	1.80
Total	2.26	2.24	1.38	2.15
By home country				
USA	2.28	2.24	1.52	2.27
Japan	2.31	2.41	1.32	2.03
Europe	2.13	2.07	1.29	2.09
Total[2]	2.26	2.24	1.38	2.15

Subsidiary roles:
TMR – to produce for the UK market products that are already established in our MNE group's product range.
RPS1 – to play a role in the MNE group's European supply network by specializing in the production and export of part of the established product range.
RPS2 – to play a role in the MNE group's European supply network by producing and exporting component parts for assembly elsewhere.
WPM/RPM – to develop, produce and market for the UK and/or European (or wider) markets, new products additional to the MNE group's existing range.

Notes:
1. Respondents were asked to evaluate each role as (i) our only role, (ii) a predominant role, (iii) a secondary role, (iv) not a part of our role. The average response is calculated by allocating a value of 4 to 'our only role', 3 to 'a predominant role', 2 to 'a secondary role' and 1 to 'not a part of our role'.
2. Includes subsidiaries of MNEs from Australia and Canada.

a particular RPS should then provide a further source of efficiency if the input needs of its production process matches the relative resource availability of the local economy.

It is the scope to use within a RPS precisely those process technologies that require the inputs that represent a current under-utilized source of comparative advantage in the host economy that provide the potential for MNEs to generate a short-term impetus to industrialization processes. However, in a pure RPS, optimized cost-efficiency means combining standardized MNE technologies with undifferentiated host-country inputs with minimal resources having to be committed to the adaptation of either.[10] This means that a pure RPS will not encompass any natural sources of dynamism (pointing towards potentials beyond supply of its allocated products) or be in any sense distinctively embedded in the local economy (its operations can be reproduced elsewhere with equal ease). It is thus pure-RPS behavior that provides the basis for the footloose characterization of MNEs.

In the survey respondents were asked to evaluate two variants of the RPS role. The first (RPS1) related to the supply of final products, whilst the other (RPS2) covered an operation that focused on production of component parts. As Table 2.1 shows RPS1 now matches TMR in overall prominence,[11] but RPS2 is much less prevalent and is thus least significant of the four subsidiary roles evaluated.[12]

A temporary way forward for a RPS that is rendered vulnerable in the fashion suggested above may be upgrading within this cost-driven mode of behavior. Thus the relocation of supply of its original goods to other (lower-cost) subsidiaries elsewhere may be replaced by the allocation to it of responsibility for producing another part of the extant range[13] requiring higher-quality (and higher-rewarded) local inputs. Again, however, neither the newly-transferred MNE technology and supporting capabilities, nor the local inputs would (if this represents merely an upgrading of pure-RPS behavior) require significant alteration in the process. The innate lack of locally-generated dynamism or embeddedness at the subsidiary level is replicated, albeit at a higher level of productivity and in supply of higher-value goods. Ultimately this reformulating of pure-RPS behavior becomes increasingly less viable as a host-country's capacities become more distinctive (i.e. when types of dynamic or created comparative advantage have substantially replaced those standardized inputs that can be routinely applied to extant technologies). The use by subsidiaries of these increasingly differentiated and creative potentials in the host country cannot now support the cost-effective use of existing MNE technologies in a routine RPS fashion, but can be applied in a dynamic and synergistic way with available elements of the group's knowledge scope in order to secure localized product development capabilities.

The logical desire of entrepreneurial management in increasingly mature and well-developed RPSs to secure survival through a metamorphosis to product development status requires the build-up of in-house capabilities (R&D; creative marketing; talented engineering staff) that reflect those increasingly knowledge-based and skill-oriented attributes of the local economy that are replacing the ones that were more applicable to routine cost-efficient production. However, these attributes represent investments in the generation of future supply capabilities, and can be interpreted as overheads that are alien to the current needs of a pure RPS. Yet it can also be suggested that the needs of a MNE that is truly acting as a dynamic differentiated network lead to a selective tolerance for certain degrees of 'impurity' (resource development commitment) that does not relate to the short-term cost-efficiency aim.

Thus dynamic competitive processes emerge *within* the contemporary MNE. The inevitable aim of any forward-looking RPS management, in a host country that is providing increasingly differentiated and creative capacities, is evolution to product development responsibilities. MNE central planners recognize the crucial value of tapping into those dispersed creative potentials that are emerging throughout the global economy, and accept that local subsidiaries are the best means of detecting, accessing and operationalizing them. Balancing the short-term aim of efficient production of existing goods and the longer-term need to regenerate the product range then sets a crucial challenge to planners that are seeking to optimize globalized inputs to both priorities. Profligacy in allowing creative overhead expenditures in too many RPSs may compromise current competitive efficiency. Too little apparent sympathy for decentralized initiative, however, may place most RPS management on the defensive (enforcing a reluctant short-term cost emphasis) and stifle the potential vibrancy of dispersed learning processes.

Ultimately, though, it appears that the interests of MNE groups, individual subsidiaries and host countries[14] can coalesce around the emergence of the third type of facility, the knowledge-seeking *product mandate*. These subsidiaries take full responsibility for the initial development, supply and sustained competitive progress of particular product lines. They may do this for a distinct regional group of countries (as a regional product mandate [RPM]) or for the full global marketplace as a world product mandate [WPM]). Thus the WPM/RPM has an extensive market scope. Its product scope is definitionally indeterminate,[15] but is likely to be quite narrow in practice as these subsidiaries focus on the most efficient regeneration of those elements of the group's range where they have asserted an individualized capability. Clearly the crucially distinctive dimension of the PM is its functional scope, with vital status for a powerful in-house R&D unit (in turn often collaborating with local university laboratories to most effectively tap into the most influential aspects of scientific research), a deep commitment to market research,[16] the generation of a talented process-engineering group and the core drive of entrepreneurial management.

Successful PMs assert an individualized status within their MNE's innovative and supply networks by operating a dynamic and mutually-enriching interface between the group's core competitive competences and aspects of the host-country's sources of created comparative advantage. Such subsidiaries can provide the higher rewards that attract distinctive local inputs away from indigenous enterprises through their ability to combine them with more effective complementary capacities (elements of the MNE's core technologies, management and marketing techniques). For the MNE this provides a unique extension to its product range and, hopefully, other more generalized additions to knowledge scope that can be utilized elsewhere in the group. Thus logical PMs should be coherent with existing and evolving MNE capabilities so as to provide positive group externalities beyond direct product development.[17] For host countries the PM mode of behavior provides benefits both through dynamism (since it is inherent to the motivation of such subsidiaries to pursue and support those upgraded local capacities that will emerge in economic development) and embeddedness (since it is the unique facets of local inputs that make them attractive to MNEs). The survey evidence showed a strong emerging presence of PM subsidiaries in the UK (Table 2.1).[18]

Sources of technology used in subsidiaries

The metamorphosis of TMR or RP subsidiaries into WPM/RPM operations can be seen as essentially defined by a fundamental repositioning of their technological status. This we have designated as a process of creative transition. In the case of TMRs and RPSs the existence and nature of the subsidiary is determined by other host-country characteristics (market size; trade restraints; costs of standardized inputs; etc.) with its capability to play the role entirely dependent on the import of those aspects of established group technology that are appropriate to the goods to be supplied. The subsidiary is *allocated* a role and also the group-originated competences to play it. In the case of PMs the causation is reversed. It now becomes the in-house technology and skill-related competences that are generated by the subsidiary itself that allow such units to *claim* an individualized PM-type status in the group. To investigate the technology content of subsidiary evolution and creative transition the survey asked respondents to evaluate the relevance of seven sources of technology in their operations.

The first of these sources of technology was defined as 'existing technology embodied in established products we produce' (ESTPRODTECH). This clearly represents the source of technology around which TMR and RP subsidiaries would be expected to most strongly assert their position, so that positive relationships are hypothesized for the regression tests. By contrast the PM subsidiaries seek product development processes that move away from existing embodied technology and towards mainly individualizing host-country sources, so a negative relationship is predicted. In fact 7.7% of respondents rated ESTPRODTECH as their only source, with 74.6% considering it a major one and 13.3% more a secondary one. Thus this technology is indeed as widely pervasive as would be expected, but rarely so totally dominant as to exclude room for other sources (which may be either supporting its effective use or seeking to supplant it in the process of subsidiary evolution).

The second MNE-group-originated source of technology available to subsidiaries was defined as 'technology of our MNE group from which we introduce new products for the UK/European market that differ from other variants introduced in other markets' (GROUPTECH). Here the subsidiary is perceived as having the potential to access significant elements of its group's core technologies (especially recently generated ones) in a disembodied form, and to provide one (of perhaps a number) of the ways in which it is applied commercially.[19] Access to GROUPTECH can provide an early possibility for subsidiaries to move from dependence on standardized group technology towards an interdependent association with how the scope of group knowledge capacity evolves and is applied. The most logical context for this is in product development so that there is a clear prediction of a positive relationship between GROUPTECH and PM. By contrast the aim of a pure RPS to utilize ESTPRODTECH as effectively as possible provides no room for the differentiating capacities of GROUPTECH, which is thus expected to be negatively related to these roles. Though TMRs may perform some locally-responsive adaptation this is unlikely to require essentially new technologies, so that (though a little less decisively than for RPS) GROUPTECH is again expected to be negatively related to this role. GROUPTECH was reported as the only technology source for 4.4% of respondents, a major one for 44.2% and secondary one for 28.8%. Though, overall, this makes it less powerfully influential in subsidiaries' current operations than ESTPRODTECH, the fact that only 22.6% of

Table 2.2 Relative importance of sources of technology in MNE subsidiaries in the UK

	Technology sources (average response)[1]						
	EST PROD TECH	GROUP TECH	OWN LAB	GROUP LAB	OTHER FIRM	LOCAL INST	ENG UNIT
By industry							
Food	2.89	2.22	2.50	1.78	1.56	1.67	2.00
Automobiles	2.72	2.18	1.83	2.65	1.71	1.39	2.00
Aerospace	2.60	2.50	1.50	1.83	1.17	1.33	2.17
Electronics	2.79	2.35	1.98	2.33	1.43	1.32	2.13
Mechanical engineering	2.85	2.46	1.85	2.00	1.42	1.62	2.19
Instruments	2.82	2.00	2.27	2.18	1.45	1.73	2.50
Industrial chemicals	3.24	2.21	2.31	2.31	1.62	1.52	1.79
Pharmaceuticals	3.00	2.40	2.30	2.40	1.70	1.60	1.70
Metals	2.91	2.09	1.91	1.82	1.27	1.36	2.09
Other manufacturing	3.13	2.47	1.71	2.14	1.29	1.50	1.64
Total	2.86	2.30	2.02	2.22	1.48	1.48	2.02
By home country							
USA	2.78	2.25	2.15	2.18	1.57	1.62	2.06
Japan	2.88	2.35	1.78	2.23	1.31	1.27	2.02
Europe	2.91	2.30	2.12	2.25	1.57	1.55	1.88
Total[2]	2.86	2.30	2.02	2.22	1.48	1.48	2.02

Sources of technology:
ESTPRODTECH – existing technology embodied in established products we produce.
GROUPTECH – technology of our MNE group from which we introduce new products for the UK/European market, that differ from other variants introduced in other markets.
OWNLAB – R&D carried out by our own laboratory.
GROUPLAB – R&D carried out for us by another R&D laboratory of our MNE group.
OTHERFIRM – R&D carried out in collaboration with another firm.
LOCALINST – R&D carried out for us by local scientific institutions (e.g. universities; independent labs; industry labs).
ENGUNIT – development and adaptation carried out less formally by members of our engineering unit and production personnel.

Notes:
1. Respondents were asked to grade each source of technology for their operations as (i) our only source, (ii) a major source, (iii) a secondary source, (iv) not a source. The average response was calculated by allocating 'only source' the value of 4, 'major source' the value of 3, 'secondary source' the value of 2, 'not a source' the value of 1.
2. Includes subsidiaries of MNEs from Australia and Canada.

respondents made no use of it also indicates a degree of presence that can often lessen the dependence on standardized technologies and provide an individualizing impetus towards a subsidiary-level creative transition.

A more complete and definitive creative transition should depend, however, on technological inputs that are accessed or generated within the host country. The first, and potentially most powerful, possibility investigated was defined as 'R&D carried out by our own laboratory' (OWNLAB). Such in-house R&D can support subsidiary-level product development directly by working in close collaboration with other creative functions (marketing; engineering; strategic planning), help to generate less immediate potentials through its own more speculative (basic or applied) research and articulate and coordinate access to other knowledge inputs (either intra-group [GROUPTECH; GROUPLAB] or through local collaborations [OTHERFIRM; LOCALINST]). This provides a strong positive hypothesis for the relationship between OWNLAB and WPM/RPM operations. Equally decisively the cost priorities of pure-RPS behavior and its lack of need for any technological individualization, generates a negative expectation for the relationship between OWNLAB and these roles. For TMRs we predict an insignificant relationship with OWNLAB. The absence in TMRs of a comparable degree of cost obsession removes the key basis for the negative relationship predicted for RPS, but the likely presence of some potential for adaptation nevertheless seems unlikely to systematically generate the positive need for in-house R&D predicted for PMs.

OWNLAB was rated as their only source of technology by 3.5% of respondents, as a major one by 35.8% and as a secondary one by 20.1%. This may provide some immediate indication of in-house R&D as a crucial element in determining the overall position of technology in a subsidiary (i.e. the status of its creative transition). Thus whilst 40.7% of subsidiaries found no role for the results of in-house R&D, this source of technology was then rated as a major (or only) source for 66.0% of those that did use it.

We have suggested that one possible function for in-house R&D may be to formulate and organize access to other sources of R&D through collaborative arrangements. One such source returns us to intra-group interdependency in the form of 'R&D carried out for us by another R&D laboratory of our MNE group' (GROUPLAB). Once again we can hypothesize that this type of R&D support is most likely to be positively related to PM responsibilities in subsidiaries and negatively related to their commitment to the RPS roles. Such support might also provide the needed technological inputs to localized adaptation in TMRs if an in-house R&D unit is not considered necessary, but (as with OWNLAB) this does not generate a systematic expectation of a positive relationship. GROUPLAB was rated the only source of technology by

5.0% of respondents, a major one by 38.1% and secondary one by 30.4%. Thus it is actually present in more cases than OWNLAB, though most of the extra occurrences are as only a secondary source. Nevertheless this does suggest that GROUPLAB can, on occasion, be acquired as a substitute for OWNLAB rather than as a supplement (we have indicated TMRs as one such context).

The first of two external sources of collaborative R&D was described as 'R&D carried out in collaboration with another firm' (OTHERFIRM). This is unlikely to be a source of technology that would be expected to systematically support product development in subsidiaries, but also is probably not naturally alienated by it (and indeed could provide supplementary problem solving capability on an *ad hoc* basis). Thus we have a neutral prediction for the relationship between PM and OTHERFIRM. Once again the dependent positioning of pure-RPS operations within mature MNE-networked supply provides no logic for either R&D or any overlapping interests with independent firms, so a negative relationship between OTHERFIRM and RPS is strongly asserted. TMRs might, however, provide a context for such R&D collaborations if host-country enterprises can use their experience to help solve problems relating to the improved application of MNEs' products and technologies to local-market needs and production conditions. In fact OTHERFIRM was a relatively rare source of technology, being absent from 58.9% of respondents' operations and only a secondary source in 35.0% more.[20]

The second source of collaborative R&D outside the firm was 'R&D carried out for us by local scientific institutions (e.g. universities; independent labs; industry labs)' (LOCALINST). The expectation here is that the aim will be to secure an involvement in those very distinctive lines of scientific investigation which reflect the most distinguished research traditions of the host country. To an operating subsidiary the results of such research are most likely to provide inputs to quite original lines of product development (positive relationship between LOCALINST and PM) and not to in any way target solutions to short-run problems with existing technology (negative relationships with not only RPSs but also TMRs). LOCALINST was not considered to be a source of technology by 56.5% of respondents and only a secondary one for 40.3%. This may, indeed, reflect the fact that the most likely content of MNE/local laboratory collaborations would involve speculative precompetitive research to help with the longer-term regeneration of the group's core technological capacity (i.e. the longer-term, rather than the medium-term, needs of strategic competitiveness).

Producing subsidiaries (who would not normally be expected to use such radical new technology in their more evolutionary product development) may not be the best vehicles to articulate such collaborations, which are likely to be the province of stand-alone MNE laboratories.

The last source of technology was defined as 'development and adaptation carried out less formally by members of our engineering unit and production personnel' (ENGUNIT). The essence of this source is the tacit knowledge embedded in a subsidiary's experienced engineering personnel. This is likely to reflect both an understanding of the mainstream characteristics of the group's mature technology and certain elements of the subsidiary's own more distinctive (locally-derived) knowledge scope and heritage. To the extent that a TMR wishes to deepen its local competitiveness through adaptation of ESTPRODTECH it is ENGUNIT that possesses the unique mix of capabilities to help facilitate this. Thus we hypothesize a positive relationship between TMR and ENGUNIT. Perhaps more crucially we can also suggest that such competences in engineering personnel are ideally positioned to support OWNLAB (amongst other sources) in securing successful product development.

The prediction of a positive relationship between ENGUNIT and PM may, in fact, be a key manifestation of creative transition in that competences generated within earlier roles are being leveraged as a crucial element onto which an upgraded and extended technological scope can be effectively and realistically built. It may also serve the purpose of providing an anchor which restrains subsidiary-level product development as a coherent and logical (rather than illogical and disruptive) evolution in the MNE group's commercial scope and technological capacity. Though RPSs need sufficient routine engineering competence to assimilate and apply ESTPRODTECH locally, this does not extend to the sorts of adaptive capabilities that define ENGUNIT as a separate source of technology. Once again the prediction for RPSs is a negative relationship. Perhaps in line with these expectations for the positioning of ENGUNIT it was reported as a secondary (supporting) source by 54.5% of respondents, but as more than that by only 23.5%.

Regression tests

Regression tests of the prevalence of sources of technology (reported in Table 2.4) were carried out, controlling for industry and home-country of the subsidiary through dummy variables and using the four subsidiary roles as independent variables. The relevant hypotheses

Table 2.3 Summary of hypotheses

Dependent variable[2]	Independent variable[1]			
	TMR	RPS1	RPS2	WPM/RPM
ESTPRODTECH	+	+	+	−
GROUPTECH	−	−	−	+
OWNLAB	"	−	−	+
GROUPLAB	"	−	−	+
OTHERFIRM	+	−	−	"
LOCALINST	−	−	−	+
ENGUNIT	+	−	−	+

Notation:
+ Hypothesis of positive relationship
− Hypothesis of negative relationship
" Neutral prediction

Notes:
1. For definitions see Table 2.1.
2. For definitions see Table 2.2.

were generated in the previous section and are summarized in Table 2.3.

Though several technology sources are correctly signed (GROUPTECH, LOCALINST, ENGUNIT, as well as the predicted insignificance of OWNLAB and GROUPLAB) the results for TMR are essentially weak and indecisive. This is most notably manifest for ESTPRODTECH which is not only insignificant but negatively signed. Generally this suggests that TMR status is now a strategically-archaic and incoherent residual role in which subsidiaries have moved some distance from an initial positioning around particular product technologies, without asserting a new status around other knowledge capabilities.

The results for RPS1 are rather more decisive, but in a manner that points to a somewhat different positioning than the pure form of this role. Here ESTPRODTECH is strongly positive as predicted, confirming the core imperative of the role as the supply of established products. But OWNLAB is also (against hypothesis) significantly positive, whilst other sources that point towards subsidiary-level technological differentiation (GROUPTECH, GROUPLAB, OTHERFIRM, ENGUNIT) are also positively (rather than negatively as predicted) signed.

As earlier discussion considered as a possibility, these sources of 'impurity' in a RPS's technological scope may be speculatively allowed as the potential bases of a creative transition to product development capacity. In line with this it can be observed that elsewhere in the

Table 2.4 Regressions with subsidiaries' sources of technology as dependent variable

	ESTPROD TECH	GROUP TECH	OWN LAB	GROUP LAB	OTHER FIRM	LOCAL INST	ENGUNIT
Intercept	2.8738‡ (10.85)	2.1902‡ (5.68)	0.9336‡ (2.61)	2.4279‡ (6.27)	1.3004‡ (4.81)	1.8209‡ (7.30)	1.1469‡ (3.94)
Food	-0.0560 (-1.02)	-0.0569 (-0.72)	0.0313 (0.41)	-0.0669 (-0.83)	0.0209 (0.37)	-0.0008 (-0.01)	0.0407 (0.65)
Automobiles	-0.4316* (-1.89)	-0.4362 (-1.34)	-0.2593 (0.85)	0.6105* (1.82)	0.2532 (1.09)	-0.2065 (-0.96)	0.1946 (0.78)
Aerospace	-0.2087 (-1.28)	0.0181 (0.08)	-0.2760 (-1.34)	-0.1330 (-0.59)	-0.1484 (-0.95)	-0.1849 (-1.28)	0.2157 (1.29)
Electronics	-0.0960† (-2.00)	-0.0602 (-0.89)	0.0246 (0.36)	0.0609 (0.86)	0.0133 (0.27)	-0.0410 (-0.91)	0.0938* (1.79)
Mechanical engineering	-0.0466 (-1.52)	-0.0275 (-0.65)	-0.0246 (-0.61)	-0.0033 (-0.07)	-0.0001 (-0.00)	0.0081 (0.29)	0.0588* (1.80)
Instruments	-0.0514 (-1.17)	-0.0657 (-1.03)	0.0276 (0.47)	0.0041 (0.06)	0.0087 (0.19)	0.0129 (0.31)	0.1201† (2.50)
Chemicals	-0.662 (-0.96)	-0.1134 (-1.16)	0.0861 (0.93)	0.0722 (0.72)	0.0436 (0.62)	-0.0519 (-0.65)	0.0046 (0.06)
Pharmaceuticals	-0.0190 (-0.65)	-0.0314 (-0.75)	0.0359 (0.91)	0.0167 (0.39)	0.0108 (0.36)	0.0090 (0.33)	-0.0121 (-0.38)
Metals	-0.0402 (-0.34)	-0.0649 (-1.41)	-0.0236 (-0.55)	-0.0230 (-0.49)	-0.0088 (-0.27)	-0.0246 (-0.82)	0.0634* (1.82)
USA	-0.0067 (-0.56)	-0.0031 (-0.18)	-0.0025 (-0.15)	-0.0085 (-0.47)	-0.0034 (-0.28)	0.0073 (0.63)	-0.0086 (-0.64)

Table 2.4 Regressions with subsidiaries' sources of technology as dependent variable – continued

	ESTPROD TECH	GROUP TECH	OWN LAB	GROUP LAB	OTHER FIRM	LOCAL INST	ENGUNIT
Japan	0.0012	0.0050	−0.0311†	−0.0130	−0.0232†	−0.0244†	−0.0098
	(0.10)	(0.30)	(−2.02)	(−0.77)	(−1.99)	(−2.27)	(−0.78)
TMR	−0.0444	−0.0991	−0.0509	0.0465	−0.0724	−0.0685	0.0195
	(−0.81)	(−1.25)	(−0.69)	(0.58)	(−1.30)	(−1.34)	(0.32)
RPS1	0.1398†	0.1087	0.1626†	0.0282	0.0354	−0.0185	0.0510
	(2.44)	(1.32)	(2.12)	(0.34)	(0.61)	(−0.35)	(0.82)
RPS2	−0.0557	0.1405	−0.0596	−0.1163	0.1732†	−0.0159	0.1560*
	(−0.75)	(1.32)	(−0.59)	(−1.07)	(2.28)	(−0.23)	(1.90)
WPM/RPM	0.0681	0.0666	0.4799‡	−0.1213	0.0298	0.0170	0.1444†
	(1.27)	(0.86)	(6.70)	(−1.56)	(0.55)	(0.34)	(2.45)
R	0.0802	0.0604	0.3279	0.0946	0.1253	0.1322	0.1564
F	0.92	0.69	5.14‡	1.12	1.53	1.62*	1.95†
n	175	178	174	177	176	174	174

‡ significant at 1%   † significant at 5%   *significant at 10%   n number of observations

survey (Papanastassiou and Pearce, 1999, p. 132) it was RPS1 subsidiaries that indicated the greatest fear of decline in their in-house R&D capacity. This is in line with a speculative and time-limited status for such an overhead expenditure that is targeting the capacity for evolution to a role that can then encompass such creative expenditures more naturally. Overall, then, it appears that in an industrially-mature and technologically-advanced economy such as the UK there are often calculated attempts to avoid the innate footloose propensity of the pure efficiency-seeking behavior of RPSs by coopting the evolutionary potentials of knowledge-seeking.

RPS2 also produces unexpected results, with ESTPRODTECH here insignificant (indeed negatively signed) and OTHERFIRM and ENGUNIT significantly positive (with GROUPTECH also clearly positively signed). Particular aspects of creative positioning are again indicated by these results. It thus seems plausible that, in the UK at least, component supply subsidiaries are by no means always technologically-dependent suppliers of standardized inputs to mature products. Instead they may have responsibility for creation of new components as part of networked development of final products. Within the MNE access to GROUPTECH supports this process. In addition the strong relevance of OTHERFIRM indicates collaborative R&D to help RPS2 subsidiaries to extend their customer base outside their parent MNE's networks. In such close collaborative creative contexts it is then logical that a strong influence emerges for the types of tacit knowledge and distinctive skills of ENGUNIT in securing coordination and effective technology exchange.

For WPM/RPM operations the key results confirm the positive significance of OWNLAB and ENGUNIT, demonstrating the decisive impulsion deriving from in-house capabilities in subsidiary-level product development. Mirroring this the negative sign on GROUPLAB (near to significance) and insignificance of GROUPTECH emphasize the complementary independence of PM operations from new technological inputs from other sources in the group. The danger that this might then be resulting in anarchic lines of subsidiary development that ultimately cannot be sustained in isolation, or that disrupt more orderly progress for the group, would seem to be mitigated by the influence of ENGUNIT (as explained in the previous section) and the unexpected positive sign for ESTPRODTECH. The presence of ESTPRODTECH indicates that the product development of PMs is substantially influenced by a core of mature and well-understood technology that has asserted itself as a defining competence of these subsidiaries during their earlier incarnation as TMRs or RPSs. Once again, in the technological scope of these PM operations, we can trace evidence of the creative transition process that secures subsidiary survival through a logical and evolutionary enhancement of technological scope.

Conclusions

The chapter has used evidence from a wider analysis of foreign MNEs' operations in the UK to document aspects of these companies as dynamic differentiated networks, and to point towards a generalized understanding of the implications for host-country industrialization and development. The dynamic and variegated positioning of particular operating subsidiaries can be seen as conditioned by two broad strategic imperatives of the contemporary MNE. The first of these is efficiency-seeking (activated through RPSs), in which individual subsidiaries play specialized roles in cost-effective supply networks for mature and standardized goods (that are expected to compete on a predominantly price basis). The second (the responsibility of WPM/RPMs) is knowledge-seeking, in which a subsidiary detects and activates distinctive host-country technology and marketing insights into localized product-development operations, which can also have positive externalities for the MNE group (by providing synergistic spillovers that reinforce its wider, and longer-term, creative competences). The ability of subsidiaries to secure the metamorphosis from efficiency-seeking RPS status to the more creative and individualistic knowledge-seeking of WPM/RPMs is seen as the key dynamic potential in the modern MNE. The core of this evolution we discern as being defined by a process of creative transition. A crucial aim of the chapter has thus been to secure an understanding of the technological content of this knowledge-driven process of subsidiary development.

Two vital dimensions of the creative transition process emerge from the analysis. The first of these is the sustained importance of those mature standardized technologies of the MNE group (designated as ESTPRODTECH) that are already embodied in successful products. These technologies not only play their anticipated role as the key group-supplied capacities around which RPSs assert a position in their MNEs' networks, but also prolong their relevance as one of the knowledge inputs into the operations of WPM/RPMs. The latter positioning indicates a strongly evolutionary content to the process of subsidiary development, in which ESTPRODTECH plays the valuable role of anchoring such upgrading, in a coherent and logical fashion, within the wider parameters of the MNE group's technological trajectory.[21]

The second key element in creative transition is the role of subsidiaries' in-house R&D labs (OWNLAB). The unexpected presence of these in RPSs can be interpreted as being at the core of the attempt to build up the restructured knowledge-scope perceived to be needed for the transition to the PM role. The decisive presence of in-house R&D in WPM/RPMs then confirms its crucial status in these operations, where it acts as a coordinating fulcrum from which such subsidiaries articulate beneficial interdependence within both the MNE group and the host country.

This characterization of dynamic processes within the contemporary MNE indicates that host-country obsession with their footloose potentials can lead to a myopic policy perspective which fails to address the more sustained and regenerative possibilities. In effect we can argue that MNE operations in a particular country are entirely compatible with intensive development processes that encompass the precepts of modern growth theory (knowledge progress and enrichment of human capital) and are not constrained to use of traditional extensive sources of comparative advantage (standardized cost-effective inputs).[22] In our terms policy dimensions that target only RPS behavior are inimical to true and sustainable development, but comprehension of creative transition and the dynamic scope of PMs can set up a symbiotic context of mutually-supportive knowledge enrichment for MNE/host-country cooperation.[23]

Notes

1. Kojima (1978) extols the virtues of such foreign direct investments as trade-creating and welfare-enhancing, since they relocate production from a newly comparatively disadvantaged sector in the MNE's home country to a *potentially* comparative advantaged sector in a host country. The 'footloose' characterization of MNE motivation assumes that inevitably the newly activated sector in the host country will eventually itself become disadvantaged, so that Kojima's optimizing trade-creation behavior provokes a move to a third country which replicates the state of *potential* comparative advantage.
2. In pure efficiency-seeking the relevant firm-level assets are assumed to operate, within the companies, as a public good. Thus they can be reapplied with equal facility in a new location as soon as local cost rises alienate their competitiveness at the first site. Crucially for our exposition a pure efficiency-seeking subsidiary is assumed not to generate any forms of individuality (i.e. its own unique capabilities derived from more distinctive local inputs) that can embed it (in a non-replicable fashion) in the host-country economy.
3. Other influential characterizations of the contemporary MNE, essentially compatible with that used here, include the heterarchy (Hedlund, 1986, 1993; Hedlund and Rolander, 1990; Birkinshaw, 1994), the horizontal organization (White and Poynter, 1990), and the transnational (Bartlett and Ghoshal, 1989, 1990).

4 Though this more scientifically-speculative and, at this stage, non-commercially-driven, research may be done in laboratories within subsidiaries a frequently observed alternative are stand-alone labs with close association with local universities' research units. The decentralization of R&D in MNEs is, of course, a key component in the strategic evolution of MNEs that is central to this chapter. Niosi (1999) provides a collection of recent papers on this.

5 The initial mailout of the questionnaire was in late 1993 with a follow up in the early Spring of 1994. It was addressed, in the first instance, to the Managing Director, though there is evidence that in some cases the responsibility for reply was delegated to senior subordinates. The composition, by industry and home country, of respondents is given in Papanastassiou and Pearce (1999, p. 15).

6 Other studies that have used this approach to analyses of MNEs' operations in the UK include Papanastassiou (1995, 1999), Hood and Young (1988), Hood et al. (1994), Young et al. (1988), Taggart (1996, 1999a).

7 See Papanastassiou and Pearce (1999, pp. 63–5) for evidence on the changing relative status of these subsidiary roles in the UK. Comparable evidence of role change, within the scope typology approach, can be found in Taggart (1996, 1999a) and Hood, et al., (1994). Studies detecting role change in terms of alternative subsidiary typologies include Taggart (1997a, 1998) and Jarillo and Martinez (1990).

8 TMR behavior was defined for respondents as 'to produce for the UK market products that are already established in our MNE group's product range'. Of the respondents 8.1% considered this was their 'only' role, 37.3% felt it took a 'predominant' position, 27.0% rated it as a 'secondary' role and 27.6% did not include it.

9 Indeed RPSs are likely to be even more comprehensively truncated than TMRs, since the latter might have some limited R&D and market-research capacity to secure the adaptation of existing goods to local market conditions. This would not be applicable to the RPS, supplying goods to a wider market area for which their characteristics have already been fully formalized.

10 Though it may be unavoidably necessary to train local labor in process-specific practices (as would be the case in whatever location the technologies were utilized) the need to train these workers in more routine and generalized industrial skills would be considered to be compromising to an RPS's cost effectiveness.

11 RPS1 behavior was defined for respondents as 'to play a role in the MNE group's European supply network by specializing in the production and export of part of the established product range'. Only 3.2% of respondents said this was their only role, but 46.5% rated it as a predominant one and 21.6% more felt it took a secondary position.

12 RPS2 behavior was defined for respondents as 'to play a role in the MNE group's European supply network by producing and exporting component parts for assembly elsewhere'. Only 1.1% of respondents said this was their only role and only 6.1% considered it was a major part of their operations, whilst 70.2% did not include it in their activity.

13 Whose production in another site may have lost competitiveness in a similar fashion.

42 *Creative Transition in MNE Subsidiaries*

14 Birkinshaw and Hood (1997, 1998) document subsidiary development as responding to parent-company, subsidiary and host-country driven processes of resource accumulation.
15 Theoretically a MNE would allow a PM subsidiary to proceed with all lines of development where it can convincingly indicate the possession of potentials that are unmatched elsewhere in the group's network.
16 The actual international distribution of a PM's goods may, as with a RPS, make use of the existing networks of the MNE group. However, by contrast with the RPS (which is totally dependent on orders initiated by the network) the PM retains *responsibility* for distribution, using the established group network (to their mutual benefit) on a collaborative contractual (rather than imposed) basis (Papanastassiou and Pearce, 1999, p. 29; Pearce, 1992).
17 Poor central decision making could, however, allow too much scope to PMs whose initiatives lack coherence and cohesion with the mainstream of the MNE and may generate negative externalities by absorbing excessive resources from elsewhere in the group and thereby distort the more logical lines of progress (Pearce, 1999b).
18 The PM roles were defined for respondents as 'to develop, produce and market for the UK and/or European (or wider) markets, new products additional to the MNE group's existing range.' This was the only role of 8.7% of respondents, the predominant one of 27.2% and a secondary one for 34.2%.
19 This can be articulated most formally as part of a global innovation strategy (Papanastassiou and Pearce, 1999, pp. 93–5, p. 101).
20 This does not contradict the view of a strong growth in international strategic technology alliances (Dunning, 1993b; Chesnais, 1988; Hagedoorn, 1993), but does suggest that the very strategic nature of these leads to their being implemented at the parent-company, rather than subsidiary, level.
21 The importance in WPM/RPM operations of the creative capacities within the tacit knowledge of engineers and production personnel (ENGUNIT) can also be interpreted as playing this role.
22 Dunning (1994a) suggests that a crucial contribution that governments should expect from MNEs' operations is a 'wider impact on the upgrading of the competitiveness of host countries' indigenous capabilities and the promotion of their dynamic comparative advantages.'
23 In a detailed review of the operations of investment agencies in the EU Young and Hood (1994) note that these should be 'designed to facilitate both the successful start-up and the continuing development of a foreign affiliate in a host-country or region, with a view towards maximising the local economic development contribution of that affiliate'. Thus 'after-care programmes are designed to exploit the opportunities and minimise the threats of highly dynamic [MNE] networks....[so that] services of a strategic nature are designed to support an affiliate within its [multinational] corporate framework'.

3
Strategic Internalization and the Growth of the Multinational Firm

Marina Papanastassiou, Robert Pearce and Fragkiskos Filippaios

Introduction

The most readily available scenario for the early analysis of the Multinational Enterprise (MNE), rather than foreign direct investment (Hymer, 1960/1976), was the horizontally-integrated international firm. This involved the use of existing sources of firm-level competitive advantage (usually presumed to have been centrally generated) in the production of a fairly similar range of goods in a number of countries, in response to negative location characteristics (mainly restraints on trade). The invocation of internalization theory, in this case, then addressed the issue of why these existing sources of competitiveness were retained within the firm (in the process initiating or increasing its status as a multinational) when used in foreign countries. Thus the theory indicates failures in the markets for competitive advantages as intermediate goods as often preventing their marketing (through licensing, etc.) to local firms. Proprietary firm-level knowledge proved an ideal and relevant case for exposition of internalization, and was addressed systematically by Buckley and Casson (1976) in, for example, their invocation of buyer uncertainty. Throughout the book, though, their concern is with the MNE as both a 'developer and transferor of various kinds of knowledge and skill' (1976, p. 109). This chapter suggests that one of the crucial ways in which the MNE has developed away from a horizontally-integrated hierarchy, is in the form of increased use of decentralized learning processes that become key forces in driving their competitive development. Thus we adopt the concept (Papanastassiou and Anastassopoulos, 1997, p. 368) of strategic internalization, which 'involves the absorption and development by the subsidiary of competitive advantages existing in the host environments.'

A number of literatures have addressed aspects of the types of strategic evolution defined by strategic internalization. The one that mainly underpins the mode of analysis developed here is that of the different roles now available to subsidiaries in MNEs. The most relevant approach is the 'scope typology' of roles (White and Poynter, 1984; D'Cruz, 1986). This delineates subsidiaries according to their geographical market scope, product (range) scope and, most crucial for our purposes, functional (or value-added) scope.[1] Mainly independent of this literature, but in effect paralleling and complementing it, has been the interjection of technological capabilities as relevant host-country factors in investigation of foreign direct investment flows (Kogut and Chang, 1991; Neven and Siotis, 1996; Barrell and Pain, 1997, 1999a; Filippaios and Papanastassiou, 2001).

The perception of absorption and development of host-country sources of competitive advantage has also been central to the burgeoning literature on decentralized R&D in MNEs (Håkanson and Nobel, 1993a, b; Howells, 1990, a, b; Kuemmerle, 1997, 1999a, b; Casson, 1991; Casson *et al.*, 1991; Pearce, 1989, 1999a; Papanastassiou and Pearce, 1999; Pearce and Papanastassiou, 1999). Buckley and Casson (1976, p. 35) anticipate this development in MNE strategy very precisely. Having underlined the view that, as proprietary knowledge is a 'public good within the firm' with low transmission costs, its 'exploitation...is logically an international operation. For similar reasons the search for relevant knowledge in a particular field is also an international operation.' This would lead to MNEs operating 'an international intelligence system for the acquisition and collation of basic knowledge relevant to R&D, and for the exploitation of the commercially applicable knowledge generated by R&D.'[2] That knowledge can now be generated and/or applied at any location in the contemporary MNE is also invoked in the literature on "reverse technology transfer" (Håkanson and Nobel, 2000, 2001; Yamin, 1995, 1999).

In fact the types of localized learning processes encompassed by strategic internalization cover very much the aspects of the broad conceptualization of R&D adopted by Buckley and Casson (1976, pp. 51–3). Thus it includes "not only technical R&D but also marketing-oriented R&D" and perceives the inputs to R&D as "highly skilled labor, sophisticated durable equipment and information obtained from the scientific and business environment". The application of such R&D within creative subsidiaries (Pearce, 1999b) is also prefigured in Buckley and Casson's (1976, p. 76) view of the refocusing of the innovation process in MNEs. An increasingly highly organized approach to product development and innovation meant that "products are no longer planned for one market and then transferred to another, but planned and differentiated at the outset to suit different tastes in different markets".

Though implicitly or explicitly (Pearce, 1989, 1992, 1999b, 2001; Papanastassiou and Pearce, 1994, 1999; Tavares, 2001) positioned within the scope typology of subsidiaries noted earlier, the world product mandate (WPM) has subsequently generated a distinctive literature of its own (Bonin and Perron, 1986; Etemad, 1986; Roth and Morrison, 1992; Birkinshaw and Morrison, 1995; Birkinshaw, 1996; Cantwell and Mudambi, 2005) and is central to the application of strategic internalization processes in MNEs. Thus this type of role "confers on a national subsidiary of an MNE an overall responsibility for seeing an innovative project through from formulation to implementation" (Buckley and Casson, 1992, p. 227). This role is then "inherently location-specific" (1992, p. 228) since the ability of a WPM to gain and maintain this status depends on its ability to internalize strategic capabilities derived from its host-country's economy and science-base.

Aspects of strategic internalization are investigated here using material from a survey (carried out in 1993/4) of foreign MNEs' subsidiaries operating in the UK. A questionnaire was sent to 812 such subsidiaries and satisfactory replies received from 190 of them.[3] The next section describes four sources of knowledge, whose use by these subsidiaries is seen to represent aspects of strategic internalization. The subsequent section introduces four roles played by these subsidiaries and generates hypotheses relating the four types of knowledge input to these roles. The penultimate section reports the results of regression tests and assesses them in the light of perceptions of strategic internalization and evolutionary forces in MNEs.[4] The final section draws overall conclusions.

Sources of creative knowledge

The survey asked MNE subsidiaries in the UK to evaluate the importance in their operations of seven potential sources of technology (see Chapter 2). The most pervasive of these was, in practice, existing standardized technology of the MNE group as embodied in those already successful products that the subsidiary produces. In terms of the subsidiary roles described in the next section three (ESTPROD/UK; ESTPROD/EUR; COMPART) would indeed be expected to be based around application of extant technology. These subsidiaries are expected to gain their position in reflection of non-technological characteristics of the host-country (market size and income levels; degree of protection; cost of labor and material inputs; etc.) and then be allocated existing technology that is already formulated to play this role. The emergence of product mandate subsidiaries (DEVELPROD in the next section) represents a process of creative transition (see Chapter 2) since now, we suggest, the subsidiary claims its role on the basis of its distinctive dynamic competences resulting from strategic internalization of local knowledge capabilities. The four sources of technology discussed here will not yet be fully defined in commercial applications and it is expected to be the subsidiary's responsibility to do this. Though this is the inherent role of DEVELPROD (product mandate) operations, the possibility of the activation of any of these knowledge sources by other types of subsidiary is also acknowledged. The reason for this is the process of subsidiary evolution (Birkinshaw, 1996, 1997, 2000; Birkinshaw and Hood, 1997; Pearce, 2001), in which currently cost-based or local-market-oriented subsidiaries perceive an intra-group vulnerability and pursue scope enrichment as a possible escape route.

The first of these four knowledge sources accessed by subsidiaries was 'R&D carried out by our own laboratory' (OWNLAB). An in-house R&D unit may support a subsidiary's ability to assimilate and apply existing technologies. Where its aims are more decisively strategic, however, it will be internalizing and leveraging local scientific capabilities for the technological and competitive expansion of the wider MNE group. In doing this it will be tapping into those scientific disciplines that represent the most notable path dependent technological specialisms of the host country. The laboratory may achieve this role for its MNE in two ways. Firstly, by recruiting, and building research programs around, outstanding host-country scientists whose capabilities reflect aspects of the distinctive local specialisms (learnt in PhD and, probably, postdoctoral work in the Universities whose personnel embody and progress the unique aspects of the country's technological heritage). Secondly, the MNE lab may articulate, participate in and leverage the results of, collaborative R&D projects with local Universities (HOSTINST below).

The second knowledge source was 'R&D carried out for us by another R&D laboratory of our own MNE group' (GROUPLAB).[5] Though this type of R&D support is likely to be very relevant to subsidiaries aiming to apply existing MNE technology locally it can also be relevant to those aiming at product development. Thus a very powerful in-house laboratory may find it necessary to complement its indigenous sources of creativity from the existing knowledge and research capabilities of its parent company. Indeed involvement of GROUPLAB may serve the function of anchoring the subsidiary's developmental activity within the technological trajectory of the MNE group. This may mitigate the danger that excessively radical initiatives at the subsidiary level might disrupt and unbalance the progress of the wider group (Pearce, 1999b).

As already observed 'R&D carried out for us by local scientific institutions (e.g. Universities; independent laboratories; industry laboratories)' (HOSTINST) may provide a means through which an MNE subsidiary can access directly those sources of research which represent the most distinctive scientific capabilities of a country. Finally 'development and adaptation carried out less formally by members of our engineering unit and production personnel' (ENGUNIT) was included as a source of tacit competence and knowledge that can support a subsidiary's competitive progress. Thus talented engineers and shop-floor personnel may often bring distinctive capabilities and expertise (reflecting experience elsewhere in the MNE and/or local industry) that make a significant contribution to either applying existing MNE technology to local conditions or to getting new technologies operationalized effectively. In the latter case this type of expertise, embedded in the mature knowledge of the group and/or of local industry, may again serve to mitigate the danger of more unrealistic proposals which lack synergies with the competitive contexts to which they are expected to be applied.

Subsidiary roles and hypotheses

The first role (ESTPROD/UK) is defined as 'to produce for the UK market products that are already established in our MNE group's product range'. This represents the traditional behavior of a horizontally-integrated MNE, based around the intra-group transfer (and therefore internalization) of mature standardized technology. In a contemporary strategic context it can be suggested that retention of this mode of behavior is more likely to reflect a proactive desire to respond to local market conditions than to trade-restraint at the national level. Where this involves adaptation of the products and/or production processes, and therefore of imported technology, R&D support may be needed to implement this. If interaction with local conditions is crucial a local laboratory (i.e. OWNLAB) can secure this. If the comprehension and interpretation of the group technology is more the key problem then assistance from another lab (i.e. GROUPLAB), where the knowledge is fully understood may be more effective. This provides positive predictions for the relationships between OWNLAB and GROUPLAB and ESTPROD/UK. More decisively positive, perhaps, would be the relationship of ESTPROD/UK with ENGUNIT, suggesting that such tacit shop-floor competences would relate more effectively to assimilation of extant operational technologies to a precise new context. The more scientific- and/or creativity-oriented inputs of HOSTINST are likely to be alien to the ESTPROD/UK role, providing a clear negative prediction.

The first of the positions for subsidiaries that may represent MNEs' moves towards more globalized aspects of competitiveness was defined as 'to play a role in the MNE group's European supply network by specializing in the production and export of part of the established product range' (ESTPROD/EUR). Whilst still based around existing goods and technologies this role moves the subsidiary into a network-supply context. This may invoke two contradictory pressures on subsidiary management, which will condition their attitude to the knowledge individualization processes of strategic internalization. Firstly, the degree of local-market-motivated autonomy that was allowed to ESTPROD/UK operations will be lost as subsidiaries move into more decisively hierarchically-networked positions. Secondly, ESTPROD/EUR managers will perceive (more than those in ESTPROD/UK may have done) the vulnerability of the purely cost-based role and the presence elsewhere in the network of higher-value-added subsidiaries with creative scope. These contradictory forces on ESTPROD/EUR subsidiary management can provide differing attitudes to the knowledge sources analyzed here.

Total submission to the pure form of ESTPROD/EUR means the subsidiary contributes only to the short-term cost-minimizing objectives of the MNE, through the optimally-efficient supply of goods whose creation or evolution occurs elsewhere in the network. National sources of static comparative advantage may attract such operations, with the subsidiary-level priority reflecting the pressure to sustain a cost-edge in intra-group competitive processes. Unequivocal positioning of ESTPROD/EUR subsidiaries in this optimizing scenario would point to the scrupulous avoidance of any overhead expenditures that do not directly support cost-efficiency in supply of current standardized goods. This would rule out pre-emptive 'tinkering' with goods or production processes, and decisively prohibit the more speculative work that would be pursued through the strategic internalization of sources of local knowledge. This provides clear predictions of negative relationships between ESTPROD/EUR and OWNLAB and HOSTINST. With the ESTPROD/EUR operations inheriting goods from elsewhere and (in the purely-motivated response to the role) under greater pressure than ESTPROD/UK to supply them optimally effectively to an externally-monitored group network, problems in assimilating the associated technology would need to be competently addressed.

This may be secured through advice from a laboratory elsewhere in the group, that is familiar with the technology, or by exercise of the capabilities of skilled shop-floor personnel. Thus GROUPLAB and ENGUNIT may be positively related to ESTPROD/EUR in this optimizing scenario.

However, behavior may differ where managers in ESTPROD/EUR operations perceive, and attempt to respond to, the vulnerabilities in an immutably static-efficiency optimizing positioning. This status may be seen as not only short-run but also short-sighted, in terms of the wider needs of both the MNE and the host country. Both of these contexts for a subsidiary's activity inevitably encompass dynamic, developmental, needs and the compartmentalizing of its role outside of these processes will be seen by more ambitious ESTPROD/EUR managers as economically and organizationally wasteful and unsustainable. Changes in host-country input costs and quality will occur as part of the process of development, and will require some revision of a subsidiary's role. The negative extreme is 'footloose' closure, the positive alternative the ultimate activation of creative functions and product-development scope. The ESTPROD/EUR managers may deny the extreme pressures of the pure optimizing form of the role and, with or without the comprehension or approval of network HQ, inculcate knowledge-sourcing behavior. This would provide a positive relationship between OWNLAB, HOSTINST, ENGUNIT and ESTPROD/EUR. We can suggest a negative relationship for GROUPLAB, however. Certainly, if the scope enhancement is being pursued pre-emptively (or subversively) by the ESTPROD/EUR operations, association with GROUPLAB would reveal these moves. Even with external approval the aim of acquiring a higher positioning may be expected to derive from distinctive individualized capacities, again indicating a creative autonomy that might be compromised by GROUPLAB.

The third subsidiary role, COMPART, is defined as 'to play a role in the MNE group's European supply network by producing and exporting component parts for assembly elsewhere'. The intuitive preoccupation of COMPART subsidiaries would, therefore, be expected to be cost-effective supply of intermediates. However, there is again a plausible creative variant, in which a COMPART subsidiary works in association with subsidiaries that are developing final products and, therefore, take responsibility for generating new components. The relationship of OWNLAB with COMPART could then be positive (if networked with creative subsidiaries) or negative (if targeting pure cost efficiency). Both GROUPLAB and ENGUNIT can be expected to be positively associated with COMPART, since either assimilation of existing group technology and/or networked generation of new components can benefit from these knowledge sources. Finally, we hypothesize a negative relationship between COMPART and HOSTINST since, even where such a subsidiary is involved in creative activity, its position is likely to be most strongly conditioned by needs that are mainly defined elsewhere in the group.

The role that is most clearly defined around the activation of knowledge sourced at the subsidiary level is 'to develop, produce and market for the UK and/or European (or wider) markets, new products additional to the MNE group's existing range' (DEVELPROD). As already indicated this product mandate role is likely to be driven by the ability of entrepreneurial subsidiary management (Birkinshaw, 2000) to internalize and synthesize a number of knowledge sources in a manner that impels the strategic competitiveness (Pearce, 1999a) of the MNE group. A core aspect of this is expected to be the recruitment of talented local scientists, whose scope and capabilities to some degree reflects aspects of host-country technological comparative advantage, to staff the DEVLEPROD subsidiaries own laboratory. This invokes a decisive prediction for a positive relationship between OWNLAB and DEVELPROD. Complementary access to distinctive elements in local research specialisms may also be accessed through collaborative research with host-country university and other independent laboratories, providing a positive prediction for HOSTINST. Generating a desirable interdependence between the individualized knowledge dimensions that are internalized by a DEVELPROD subsidiary and the capabilities of the rest of the MNE group may be expected to be also reflected in positive relationships with GROUPLAB and ENGUNIT. The hypotheses are summarized in Table 3.1.

Table 3.1 Summary of hypotheses

Subsidiary role	Dependent variable (predicted sign)			
	OWNLAB	GROUPLAB	HOSTINST	ENGUNIT
ESTPROD/UK	+	+	–	+
ESTPROD/EUR[1]	+	+/–	–/+	+
COMPART	–/+	+	–	+
DEVELPROD	+	+	+	+

1. First prediction derives from assumption of total commitment to short-run cost minimising behaviour. Second prediction indicates direction of any influence from building of forward-looking creative competences.

Results

In the regression tests (Table 3.2) for ESTPROD/UK OWNLAB is very weak in the US and Japanese samples and the predicted positive sign is short of significance for the European sample. GROUPLAB here is positively signed, as predicted, for US and Japanese samples, but approaches negative significance for European subsidiaries. For Europe these results are compatible with a generally greater pursuit of autonomy in UK-based subsidiaries (localized, rather than group-derived, inputs into product individualization processes). As predicted HOSTINST is negatively signed in all the samples, approaches significance for the Japanese and achieves it for the European. ENGUNIT is only significantly positively related to ESTPROD/UK in the Japanese sample, suggesting there is a concern to base any local-market-oriented responsiveness around use of internalized tacit capabilities to apply effectively well-established competitive technology on the shop-floor, rather than potentially more risky adjustments emanating from laboratory work.

For ESTPROD/EUR the relationship with OWNLAB is very weakly positive for US and Japanese samples, which may reflect the presence of the two offsetting influences hypothesized for subsidiaries taking this role. For European ESTPROD/EUR subsidiaries, however, the positive sign on OWNLAB does become significant. This, our hypotheses suggest, would indicate the presence of subsidiary-level strategic internalization, as these subsidiaries proactively pursue the knowledge to move to more creative scopes. GROUPLAB is quite strongly positively signed (though short of significance) for Japanese subsidiaries. This indicates support of other group labs for technology assimilation in Japanese MNEs' UK subsidiaries, as they initiate new European-market supply units. However, GROUPLAB is significantly negative for European subsidiaries. This notably complements the positive result for OWNLAB in suggesting that knowledge-internalization aims in those subsidiaries are systematically pursued away from the influence or intervention of home-country laboratories. ENGUNIT is weak in all regressions, despite clear expectations of positive signs. Surprisingly, therefore, neither assimilation of extant technology, nor generation of new subsidiary-level capabilities, seems to require a particular commitment from skilled shop-floor personnel.

The results for COMPART are, in the main, indecisive, and suggest (especially for European subsidiaries) either incoherent or currently evolving strategic positioning. The suggestion of involvement in creative networks is strongest for US, where OWNLAB is clearly positively

Table 3.2 Regression tests of knowledge sources accessed by MNE subsidiaries in UK: home-country samples

Dependent variable – sources of knowledge

	Subsidiaries of US MNEs				Subsidiaries of Japanese MNEs				Subsidiaries of European MNEs			
	OWN LAB	GROUP LAB	HOST INST	ENG UNIT	OWN LAB	GROUP LAB	HOST INST	ENG UNIT	OWN LAB	GROUP LAB	HOST INST	ENG UNIT
Constant	2.261** (2.67)	0.728 (0.89)	1.914*** (3.28)	1.704*** (3.12)	0.788 (1.14)	2.277** (3.27)	1.029** (2.86)	0.496 (1.02)	−0.196 (−0.34)	3.359*** (4.66)	2.804*** (5.11)	1.323* (1.81)
Food	−0.273 (−1.41)	0.144 (0.77)	−0.107 (−0.80)	0.001 (0.01)					−0.130 (−0.87)	0.004 (0.03)	−0.051 (−0.47)	−0.167 (−0.09)
Automobiles	−1.879** (−2.08)	1.205 (1.39)	−0.608 (−0.98)	0.062 (0.11)	−0.168 (−0.34)	0.456 (0.92)	−0.079 (−0.31)	−0.070 (−0.21)	−0.634 (−0.95)	1.894** (2.31)	−0.947 (−1.52)	0.089 (0.11)
Aerospace	−0.964** (−2.12)	0.329 (0.75)	−0.336 (−1.08)	−0.064 (−0.22)								
Electronics	−0.365 (−1.65)	0.295 (1.40)	−0.132 (−0.88)	−0.071 (−0.50)	0.036 (0.36)	−0.014 (−0.14)	−0.064 (−1.23)	0.188*** (2.76)	0.061 (0.58)	0.242* (1.86)	−0.029 (−0.29)	−0.012 (−0.09)
Mechanical engineering	−0.288* (−2.20)	0.026 (0.21)	−0.107 (−1.19)	0.020 (0.24)	−0.036 (−0.55)	0.005 (0.07)	0.032 (0.95)	0.082* (1.84)	0.047 (0.78)	0.114 (1.54)	0.011 (0.19)	0.015 (0.20)
Instruments	−0.257* (−1.68)	0.166 (1.13)	−0.045 (−0.43)	0.112 (1.13)	0.061 (0.57)	−0.020 (−0.19)	0.069 (−1.24)	0.075 (1.03)	0.152 (1.23)	0.027 (0.17)	0.233* (2.03)	0.017 (0.11)
Chemicals	−0.499 (−1.67)	0.408 (1.42)	−0.146 (−0.71)	−0.230 (−1.19)	0.008 (0.04)	−0.280 (−1.44)	0.059 (0.59)	0.107 (0.82)	0.243* (1.86)	0.265 (1.66)	−0.197 (−1.62)	0.027 (0.17)
Pharmaceuticals	−0.174 (−1.62)	0.153 (1.47)	−0.011 (−0.15)	−0.058 (−0.83)	0.093 (0.84)	−0.145 (−1.29)	0.065 (1.12)	−0.075 (−0.99)	0.079 (1.42)	0.105 (1.54)	−0.065 (−1.25)	−0.009 (−0.14)
Metals	−0.212* (−1.79)	0.033 (0.28)	−0.043 (−0.53)	−0.053 (−0.069)	0.006 (0.08)	−0.033 (−0.44)	−0.052 (−1.35)	0.121** (2.36)				

Table 3.2 Regression tests of knowledge sources accessed by MNE subsidiaries in UK: home-country samples – continued

Dependent variable – sources of knowledge

	Subsidiaries of US MNEs				Subsidiaries of Japanese MNEs				Subsidiaries of European MNEs			
	OWN LAB	GROUP LAB	HOST INST	ENG UNIT	OWN LAB	GROUP LAB	HOST INST	ENG UNIT	OWN LAB	GROUP LAB	HOST INST	ENG UNIT
ESTPRODUK	−0.086 (−0.64)	0.059 (0.54)	−0.013 (−0.14)	−0.040 (−0.47)	0.032 (0.21)	0.098 (0.63)	−0.130 (−1.59)	0.199* (1.77)	0.174 (1.29)	−0.225 (−1.38)	−0.225* (−1.82)	0.058 (0.35)
ESTPRODEUR	0.080 (0.56)	0.123 (0.91)	0.006 (0.06)	0.027 (0.30)	0.107 (0.67)	0.208 (1.27)	0.110 (1.31)	−0.024 (−0.21)	0.272** (2.09)	−0.452*** (−2.87)	0.040 (0.33)	0.079 (0.49)
COMPART	0.201 (1.29)	0.118 (0.78)	0.011 (0.10)	0.187* (1.85)	−0.212 (−1.07)	−0.481** (−2.42)	0.144 (1.40)	0.093 (0.69)	−0.169 (−0.70)	−0.017 (−0.06)	−0.007 (−0.003)	0.010 (0.03)
DEVELPROD	0.543*** (4.27)	−0.038 (−0.31)	0.082 (0.94)	0.123 (1.150)	0.456*** (2.95)	−0.035 (−0.24)	0.095 (1.24)	0.245** (2.36)	0.611*** (5.18)	−0.200 (−1.37)	−0.266** (−2.40)	0.123 (0.82)
R^2	0.399	0.326	0.131	0.451	0.210	0.233	0.264	0.325	0.649	0.367	0.406	0.085
F	2.45**	1.83*	0.57	3.09***	1.26	1.46	1.70	2.28**	4.89***	1.59	1.86*	0.24
n	62	63	63	63	64	65	64	64	41	42	42	40

n = Number of observations   *** significant at 1%   ** significant at 5%   * significant at 10%.

signed and ENGUNIT significantly so. By contrast for Japanese units OWNLAB is negatively signed and, against hypothesis, GROUPLAB is significantly negative. This may indicate that Japanese COMPART subsidiaries have settled into routine cost-driven positions in their MNEs' European operations.

The core prediction for DEVELPROD, of a positive relationship with OWNLAB, is strongly verified through significant results in all three subsamples. Support for the proactive activation of knowledge generated by in-house R&D through the work of creative engineering personnel also tends to be confirmed, with ENGUNIT always positively signed, significantly so in the Japanese regression and approaching this level for US subsidiaries. The role of contractual relationships with other host-country scientific institutions is less clear, with positive signs for HOSTINST in US and Japanese samples not achieving significance. Contrary to hypothesis HOSTINST is significantly negative in the sample of European subsidiaries. Also counter hypothesis GROUPLAB is always negatively signed, and quite close to significance in the European sample. There may then be a common explanation for the negative signs on GROUPLAB and HOSTINST for the European subsidiaries. This is that the main source of product development in Europe for these MNEs will be in their continental home country. Unlike in US or Japanese subsidiaries a strong mandate for development-oriented activity is unlikely to be forthcoming for European MNEs' affiliates in UK. Where DEVELPROD does emerge it will lack systemic interdependence with other operations (notably being alienated from GROUPLAB knowledge) and be denied (or feel reluctant to request) funding for relationships with scientific institutions outside the subsidiary.

Conclusions

In the first two pages of *The Future of the Multinational Enterprise* Buckley and Casson argue for the need to refine an economic theory of the MNE as a means of securing an effective basis for public policy towards these firms.[6] A crucial subtext of the ideas developed here is that an informed understanding of how MNEs operationalize various levels of their global strategies increasingly acts as a glue that brings together the normative concerns of economic theory and the prescriptions of public policy.

Thus the two routes through which MNE subsidiaries have moved away from their local-market focus in the horizontally-integrated organizational structure provide very different benefits and implications for host countries. When entering group supply networks for well-established goods a subsidiary applies mature MNE technology to sources of host-country static comparative advantage (standardized low-cost inputs) in ways that provide the benefits of improved allocative efficiency. However, the process does not embed the subsidiary in distinctive local inputs or generate any dynamic impetus (Pearce, 2001). Thus Buckley and Casson (1976, p. 13) observed the 'threat to national interests' of the potentially footloose behavior available to MNEs once they understand the flexibility available from internationalization *per se*. In line with their concern with public policy Buckley and Casson (1976, p. 1) emphasized the dangers of restrictive national policies 'in driving out foreign investors to a more favourable climate'. Contemporary government policies that emphasize low input costs and avoidance of 'undesirable' overheads as attractive, or supportive, factors for inward investment view MNE operations from this perspective.

The second emerging role for subsidiaries, the product mandate, avoids these risks and embeds activity in the host-country's dynamic capabilities (i.e. becomes involved interactively with the local economy's pursuit of created comparative advantage). Our results show the presence in product creating subsidiaries of the processes of internalizing strategic, development-oriented, local creative scopes, particularly in the form of the work of in-house R&D units[7] and the application of tacit knowledge of engineering personnel. Thus this suggests that rather than fearing one aspect of MNE flexibility (footloose migration of cost-driven units) national policy makers should embrace the more embedded and path-dependent potentials of these companies' other, more dynamic, competitive concern, in the form of the constant pursuit of new knowledge and scope enhancement leveraged into the process of product development.

Notes

1 This approach has been applied in a number of investigations of MNEs' operations in the UK (Hood and Young 1988; Hood *et al.*, 1994; Young *et al.*, 1988; Taggart, 1996, 1999a; Tavares, 2001).
2 Acknowledging the work of Cantwell (1989), Buckley and Casson (1992, p. 215) revisited these perceptions in the light of changes in MNEs' competitive environment, notably that 'firms now have more sources of potential competition to monitor'. Therefore 'to match foreign competitors they need to tap foreign as well as domestic sources of technical expertise, so that the synthesis of information becomes a globalized activity.'
3 Details of the wider coverage of the survey and composition of the responding sample by industry and home-region can be found in Papanastassiou and Pearce (1999, pp. 14–15).
4 Respondents to the questionnaire were asked to evaluate each role as their only role, predominant role, secondary role or not a part of their role. In formulating

the independent variables (Table 3.2) 'only' was given the value of 4, 'predominant' the value of 3, 'secondary' the value of 2 and 'not' the value of 1. Similarly each of the four knowledge sources was graded as their only source, a major source, a secondary source or not a source. In operationalizing these as dependent variables (Table 3.2) 'only' was given the value of 4, 'major' the value of 3, 'secondary' the value of 2, and 'not' the value of 1.

5 Citing the work of Casson, Pearce and Singh (1991) Buckley and Casson (1998, p. 28) note the repositioning of previously 'powerful central research laboratories of high technology MNEs'. When not actually closed down these were 'shifted to the divisions, or forced to operate as suppliers to "internal customers" in competition with outside bodies such as Universities'. GROUPLAB is then very much in line with such an internal market for R&D work and results (Buckley and Casson, 1998, p. 30).

6 Interestingly, and in a manner that prefigures contemporary debates on globalization, Buckley and Casson (1976, p. 1) suggest the need for such policy, in practice, to operate at a supranational level. This has provocative resonances with their more recent (Buckley and Casson, 1998, p. 21) emphasis on flexibility as a major attribute of MNE behavior, including an enthusiasm for 'locations with flexible host governments'.

7 The context specificity of these processes also emerges in the results. Notably European MNEs' subsidiaries in the UK seem to adopt a definite strategic internalization approach, but in a way that appears to be pursuing separate lines of development from those driven by parent (home-country) technology and interests (e.g. their ESTPROD/EUR operations seem to be inculcating independent evolutionary creative scopes).

4
Technology Sourcing in Multinational Enterprises and the Roles of Subsidiaries: An Empirical Investigation

Dimitris Manolopoulos, Marina Papanastassiou and Robert Pearce

Introduction

This chapter views the Multinational Enterprise (MNE) as a differentiated learning network with subsidiaries playing a critical role in managing knowledge (Gupta and Govindarajan, 2000; Birkinshaw et al., 1998). Today, rather than accepting predetermined roles, subsidiaries are asked to actively engage in developing their operations and explore procedures that would increase the efficacy of the whole MNE network (Birkinshaw, 1996; Crookell and Morrison, 1990). Building on recent advances regarding the strategic evolution of subsidiary roles, we argue that the MNE is a vehicle for integrating knowledge generated internally and externally from its global operations (Bartlett and Ghoshal, 1989). There are many cases of subsidiaries that perform specific value-added activities, which are fundamentally 'embedded' in their respective host-countries' knowledge systems (evidence is provided by Kuemmerle, 1999a; Dunning, 1996; Jarillo and Martinez, 1990).

Technological competencies have been theoretically and empirically verified (Asakawa, 2001; Pearce, 1994) as likely to be central to creation of ownership advantages for many MNEs. Technology acquisition decisions have traditionally addressed the firm's choice either to use internal technology-related capabilities or to acquire technology from outside sources (Murray *et al.*, 1995). As globalization of markets and the consequent changes in competitive and technological environments, R&D internationalization (Peng and Wang, 2000) and the new perspectives of international technology management (Chatterji, 1996) have moved up the technology research agenda (Chiesa, 2000; Gassman and Von Zedtwitz, 1998), there is scope for further exploration through current quantitative and qualitative research. Most firm-level empirical findings and theoretical contexts examined technology transfer (Conner and Prahalad, 1996; Kogut and Zander, 1993), the 'absorptive capacity' of firms (Cohen and Levinthal, 1990), the spillover effects of technology, and survey the impact of technology on productivity and firm performance (Kotabe *et al.*, 2002). Moreover, the larger part of research undertaken in related issues has been carried out at the level of the parent firm (Cantwell, 2001). Technology sourcing and the strategic role of subsidiaries as organizational units that could comprise an influential factor in technology acquisition and development has received relatively little attention.

This chapter departs from the literature in supporting the view that knowledge generation, deployment, acquisition and diffusion may derive from both MNEs' external and internal environments (Minbaeva *et al.*, 2003; Gupta and Govindarajan, 2000). Drawing on a sample of 92 subsidiaries operating in Greece, the research is centered on MNEs' technology inputs and empirically tests the relationship between sources of technology acquired and/or generated (internally or externally) and relates them to differently strategically-motivated subsidiaries. Greece was selected as the focal country since the opening up of new markets (mainly Eastern European) accelerated the process of restructuring on behalf of Greece-based MNE subsidiaries. Recent developments have turned the attention of foreign investors to Greece's competitive advantages, including the existence and potential of knowledge generating assets. There are two distinctive contributions deriving from this analysis. First, we show strong evidence that the operations of MNE subunits in an otherwise peripheral economy of the EU in fact rely on a multifaceted knowledge creation network that goes beyond mere technology transfer. Second, we present for the first time a detailed subsidiary-level analysis regarding foreign operations in Greece. The rest of the paper is organized as follows: section 2 sets the theoretical background, section 3 analyses the proposed research questions and presents the sample characteristics, section 4 evaluates subsidiaries' sources of technology, section 5 lays down the methodology of the study, presents and discusses the empirical findings, and in section 6 we conclude by putting the findings into a working strategic and managerial perspective.

Theoretical background and literature review

According to Dunning (1993a) technology embraces all forms of a corporation's physical assets, human learning and capabilities, that lead to efficient production of goods and services. Thus the effective application of technological resources and advancements worldwide may lead a corporation to an upgrading involvement in global innovative activities which, in turn, may generate distinctive capabilities for the whole MNE environment (Birkinshaw et al., 2002). Technology-sourcing research stresses the role of technology in the acquisition of firms' competitive advantage. Superior, firm-specific technology, may lead the contemporary MNE to develop unique capabilities, which may induce and facilitate the penetration of foreign markets through exports and local production (Håkanson, 1981; Johanson and Vahlne, 1977; Buckley and Casson, 1976), by capturing the distinctive needs of host customers and adapting subsidiaries into new environments. Nevertheless, the literature provides ambiguous evidence concerning the relative mix and scope of internal diffusion and technology outsourcing. Earlier thinking associated the generation of technology in MNEs with home-country innovation procedures, justifying the notion of a competitive advantage reflecting the resource competencies and market conditions of their home countries (Hymer 1960/1976; Caves, 1971; Vernon, 1966). In the tradition of transactions cost economics (Williamson, 1985) the organization of economic activity is driven by the minimization of production costs and information monitoring. The ability of MNEs to engage in internal knowledge sources '...does not imply that such knowledge transfers are necessarily easy, successful, or routine' (Allred and Swan, 2003, p. 3). However, firms exploit technological assets' interdependencies internally (rather than outsourcing) in developing unique organizational competencies through such means as the accumulation of proprietary knowledge (Pavitt, 1990).

The above perceptions are consistent with traditional roles played by MNEs' overseas subsidiaries. The role of these dispersed subunits has been determined by factors that are predominantly related to market orientation and the availability and cost of physical inputs into the production process. Once such influences have determined the role that is to be allocated to a subsidiary within the MNE's overall operations, its basic technological needs will follow, and can then be supplied from the group's established knowledge capacity (Papanastassiou and Pearce, 1997a). This approach is motivated by demand-side factors, such as the importance of proximity to final markets, a need for local responsiveness and support of local production and marketing operations (Ivarsson and Jonsson, 2003).

In the contemporary perspective, however, subsidiaries are facing the challenge of their creative transition into a globalized market (Tallman and Fladmoe-Lindquist, 2002). Apart from demand-side factors, subsidiaries should also take into consideration supply-side and environmental factors (Granstrand et al., 1993). This process of creative transition is determined by the degree of subsidiaries' local embeddedness. Assessing the volume of innovative activities that subsidiaries undertake in close relation with host-countries' environments is empirically tested and well justified (Phene and Almeida, 2003). External technology reliance, as a source of competitive advantage, was mentioned by Porter (1985), expanded in international business by Kotabe and Murray (1990) and further justified by Birkinshaw (1996), who argued that effective local embeddedness should build upon subsidiaries' distinctive capabilities; where technology has a central role (Asakawa, 2001). At the same time, the benefits of a more decentralized technological approach have been gaining growing recognition (Hedlund and Rolander, 1990). In a global environment that is increasingly characterized by technological and market heterogeneity, creative subsidiaries with specific product mandates may provide the optimal way of effectively monitoring knowledge flows on an MNE-group's behalf. Therefore, a headquarter's technology planning should screen not only the diffusion of technology generated in the home country, but also the technological inputs derived from overseas subunits, stemming from either their in-house R&D departments or established localized knowledge (Ivarsson and Jonsson, 2003; Håkanson and Nobel, 2001; Andersson and Forsgren, 2000; Dunning, 2000; Kuemmerle, 1999a; Patel and Vega, 1999).

Research questions and sample characteristics

The mounting evidence that MNEs have increased the extent of R&D activities performed outside their home countries (Almeida et al., 2002; Cantwell and Janne, 1999; Granstrand, et al., 1993; Pearce and Singh, 1992a; Hedlund, 1986) lead us to investigate the sources of knowledge inputs that MNEs intend to use in this procedure of technology decentralization. There are two basic research questions this study aims to answer:

Research Question 1 (RQ1): To what extent do subsidiaries operating in a peripheral economy utilize internal and external channels of knowledge transmission?

Research Question 2 (RQ2): Is the subsidiary role a decisive factor in determining which of the technological sources will be accessed?

Information regarding the sample was collected via a nationwide postal survey through questionnaires between 2000 and 2003. The study uses data, issued by the International Capital (ICAP) database, for the subsidiaries of foreign firms established in Greece in 2000. The ICAP database included 317 foreign firms. The industries involved include pharmaceuticals, chemicals, electronics and IT, machinery, food and beverages, textiles, miscellaneous services and other manufacturing. Major sources of inward investment include the US, Japan, EU and other European countries. The response rate is approximately 29% (92 responses out of 317 corporations comprising the whole population of the database provided), higher than the minimum recommended level of 20%. It is considered to be perfectly acceptable in comparison to similar mail surveys (Harzing, 1997). Appendix 4.1 summarizes the response rates and the number of respondents by industry and country of HQs' location.

The questionnaire sent to subsidiaries was developed through a three-stage process. Firstly, two academicians and a professional consultant, who suggested improvements in wording and advice on layout, reviewed the draft questionnaire. Secondly, following a major revision of the questionnaire, it was sent out to five chief executive officers (CEO) of subsidiaries operating in different industrial sectors. In most cases corrections were similar. After the second revision, the questionnaire was sent to selected firms, chosen by their country of HQ origin, for the final pre-testing. Wording and structure were not improved, though two more questions were added.

To ensure validity, inter-rater reliability by a follow-up telephone conversation with managers from 12 randomly selected subsidiaries was carried out. The reported results demonstrated a high consistency with original answers (Test – retest 0.88). To examine potential non-response bias we compared respondents and the population on three variables: number of employees, sales and the age of the subsidiary. None of these t-tests for differences between the sample and the population means was statistically significant at the level of 0.10 (t-test in order to evaluate the potential non-response bias was used by many authors, see for example Luo, 2001). To further test the non-response bias, personal interviews with managers of selected non-respondent firms (according to the classification of country of origin) was arranged. Results were quite similar with those of the sample.

Sources of technology in foreign subsidiaries in Greece

Against this background, and in order to evaluate the technological scope of foreign MNEs' operations in Greece, seven possible sources are investigated so as to understand the impact of technology transfer and creation on specific subsidiary roles. The sources of technology are classified as (i) internal, referring to the technological knowledge that is produced mainly through investing in the internal environment of the MNE and (ii) external, including the technological knowledge inputs derived from relations to external partners.

There is a wide literature concerning the different roles a subsidiary can assume (Taggart, 1997; Jarillo and Martinez, 1990; Bartlett and Ghoshal, 1986; White and Poynter, 1984). In this chapter we adopt a typology emerging from White and Poynter (1984) and we distinguish four major subsidiary roles, i.e. Truncated Miniature Replicas (TMRs), Specialized Miniature Replicas (SMRs), Rationalized Product Subsidiaries (RPSs) and World Product Mandates (WPMs). This represents a revised version of the role categorization, originally initiated by Canadian scholars and their research into centers of excellence. According to this classification, a TMR produces mainly well-established products. An additional form of TMR – being a more specialized-narrow product mandate, i.e. a SMR – is also investigated. An RPS is specialized in the production of component parts of the final product. WPM is ascribed with the task of creating and producing differentiated products (for an extended analysis of product mandates, see Birkinshaw and Hood, 2000; Crookell and Morrison, 1990; Rugman and Bennett, 1982; Poynter and Rugman, 1982). The specific typology was selected, because '...it emphasizes potentials for various evolutionary paths and restructuring processes, which are seen as interdependent with key changes in the global competitive environment' (Tavares and Pearce, 1999, p. 7). Moreover, 'scope' typologies can provide us with useful insights on the contribution of the subsidiary to the development of the focal market, since it is well founded that subsidiaries' operations eventually generate externalities in the host economy (Granovetter, 1985).

In the survey, respondents were asked:

Survey Question: Please grade the following sources of technology for your operation as being: (4) our only source of technology; (3) a major source of technology; (2) a secondary source of technology; and (1) not a source of technology

(a) *Existing technology embodied in established products we produce*
(b) *Technology of our MNE group from which we introduce new products for the European market, which differ from other variants introduced in other markets*
(c) *R&D carried out by our own laboratory*
(d) *R&D carried out for us by another R&D laboratory of our MNE group*

(e) R&D carried out in collaboration with another local firm
(f) R&D carried out for us by local scientific institutions (e.g. universities, independent laboratories, industry laboratories)
(g) Development and adaptation carried out less formally by members of our engineering unit and production personnel

The first source of technology subsidiaries were asked to evaluate, was 'existing technology embodied in established products we produce' (EST-PRODTECH). This type of technology provides the basis of an MNE network's current commercial success through embodiment in its most competitive commercial goods. In playing this role, ESTPRODTECH is an essential part of the 'inward investment' package that also contributes to the development of a host country. This source of technology is dominant in all industries, since 65.6% of the respondents characterized it either as 'only source of technology' or as 'main source'. Overall, this source of technology emerges as the most prevalent for all home countries with a quite high average response (AR) of 3.28. ESTPRODTECH also appears as the strongest source of technology in all four subsidiaries types.

The second source of technology was described as 'technology of our MNE group from which we introduce new products for the European market, which differ from other variants introduced in other markets' (GROUPTECH). Access to this source of technology allows for a more active participation in the innovation generation procedure. Here group-originated technologies have not yet been definitively embodied in products, but are available in sufficiently precisely defined forms as to be accessible to different subsidiaries for possible operationalization. 1.4% of respondents evaluated GROUPTECH as their only source, 4.8% as a major source, and 47% as a secondary source. The fact that over 50% of subsidiaries rated this source as a technological input for their operations provides evidence of a notable relevance of GROUPTECH. Nevertheless the ARs do indicate that its use is far behind the importance ascribed to ESTPRODTECH. Overall, we observe that GROUPTECH does not count as a dominant source of technology for subsidiaries' operations. Evidence so far, therefore, clearly indicates that overseas subsidiaries in Greece still operate mainly within the confines of well-defined group level technology.

Respondents were also asked to evaluate the importance of technology provided by an R&D laboratory of the subsidiary (OWNLAB). Of the 92 respondents which evaluated this source, 41.1% said it did not play any role in their technology, 23.4% rated it as a secondary source, 31.8% believed it to be a major source of their technology and 3.7%

the only one. Concerning the role of subsidiaries, ARs indicate that in-house R&D is more important to subsidiaries that produce well-established products and is almost irrelevant to subsidiaries that differentiate their production (WPMs). There is an extensive literature on the roles of overseas R&D units (Pearce, 1999b; Håkanson and Nobel, 1993b). Apparently, the weak support of OWNLAB to WPMs, in contrast to the rest of the subsidiary types, suggests the dominance of Support Laboratories (SLs), which are mainly involved in the technological adaptation of existing goods rather than the development of new products or processes (Papanastassiou and Pearce, 1994).

Another source of technology accessed by subsidiaries, 'R&D carried out for us by another R&D laboratory of our MNE group' (GROUPLAB), was rated the only source by 1.4%, a major one by 18.4% and a secondary one by 35.4% of the respondents. This indicates that 44.8% of subsidiaries do not rely upon this source. In terms of ARs, GROUPLAB is a weak internal technological source, with TMRs using it relatively more extensively.

A potential in-house source of technology, which nevertheless falls short of a formal R&D laboratory, was defined as 'development and adaptation carried out less formally by members of our engineering unit and production personnel' (ENGUNIT). The essence of this source is the exploitation of tacit knowledge embodied in such personnel, which is likely to reflect a variable mix of the mainstream characteristics of a subsidiary's own knowledge heritage (Almeida and Kogut, 1999). Table 4.1 provides evidence that this is the least important source concerning intra-firm knowledge sharing, as 69.8% of respondents evaluated it as 'not a source' of technology for their operations. In summarizing our results so far, it is evident that Greek subsidiaries are getting support for their operations from various intra-MNE sources of technology, including a local R&D unit.

Two more sources of technology were also examined which evaluate the existence of external linkages with the local economy or, to put it otherwise, test for the intensity of the subsidiaries' embeddedness. External technological linkages are considered critical for the sustained competitiveness of the MNE, since, according to Håkanson and Nobel (2001, p. 398) '...subsidiaries that are strongly embedded in the local environment...are believed to be in an advantageous position to absorb and combine new technical and market knowledge in innovative ways'.

The first external source of technology derives from a collaborative arrangement outside the group ('R&D carried out in collaboration with another firm' – OTHERFIRM). As mentioned above, there is evidence that collaboration between firms has emerged as a substantial source of technological inputs for subsidiaries (Hagedoorn, 1993). Nevertheless for foreign operations in Greece, 62.4% replied that it made no contribution to their technological scope and 24.7% rated it as only a secondary source for their operations. This could be a point for further discussion concerning subsidiaries, since such arrangements are likely to be relatively inexpensive means of attempting to secure subsidiary-level access to new technological perspectives. Moreover, there is significant empirical evidence to support the view that subsidiaries are involved in regional and/or global networks of knowledge (Almeida, 1996). According to the results provided by the ARs these inter-firm collaborations by Greece-based foreign operations are somewhat stronger for RPSs.

The interaction with local Greek scientific institutions as a second possible source of collaborative R&D accessed outside the firm was also reported as limited. Thus 'R&D carried out for us by local scientific institutions (e.g. universities, independent laboratories, industry laboratories)' (LOCALINST) was not perceived as a relevant technological source by 72.6% of responding subsidiaries and was rated as no more than a secondary source by 24.6% more. Consequently, LOCALINST seems more likely to be called into play to supplement efforts that are already established within subsidiaries than as a source of direct technological inputs (Papanastassiou and Pearce, 1994).

The findings of this section support other studies (Saez *et al.*, 2002) stressing the importance of internal sources as technology providers for foreign operations. The systematic use of varied MNE technology sources implies that firms appear to combine any available inputs offered by the MNE network, and this could be an indicator of high absorptive capacity, adjusted to the needs of the host environment.

Econometric analysis and results

Regression tests were run with each of the seven sources of technology (see Table 4.1 for definitions) as the dependent variable against the different subsidiary roles mentioned earlier and controlled by firm characteristics. The general model to examine the relationship between the different dependent variables (the importance ascribed to technology sources) and the various explanatory and control variables is provided by the following equation.

$$\text{Logit (p)} = a_0 + a_1X_1 + a_2X_2 + a_3X_3 + \ldots + a_vX_v \qquad (1)$$

where: X denotes the independent/explanatory and control variables.

The set of independent variables includes industry and country dummies, the age of subsidiaries, the number of personnel, sales (expressed in

Table 4.1 Relative importance of sources of technology in MNE subsidiaries in Greece

	Relative Importance of Sources of Technology[1] (Average Responses[2]), N=92						
	A	B	C	D	E	F	G
By Location of HQ							
EU Countries	3.21	2.03	2.25	1.59	1.65	1.68	1.53
Other European Countries[3]	3.14	1.92	2.50	1.78	1.50	1.42	1.35
US	2.78	1.85	2.35	2.28	1.55	1.35	1.42
Japan	3.62	1.66	2.00	2.62	1.33	2.00	1.33
Rest of the World[4]	3.66	1.33	1.66	1.33	1.33	1.72	1.45
Total	3.28	1.75	2.15	1.92	1.47	1.63	1.41
χ^2=2.99***							
By Sector[5]							
Manufacturing	3.41	1.83	2.43	2.12	1.55	1.76	1.44
Services	2.95	1.67	1.87	1.72	1.39	1.50	1.37
Total	3.28	1.75	2.15	1.92	1.47	1.63	1.41
χ^2=27.12							
By Type of Subsidiary[6]							
Production of well established products (TMR)	3.06	1.81	2.34	2.12	1.43	1.53	1.37
Specialization in supply to MNE network of part of the established product range (SMR)	2.50	1.96	2.33	1.86	1.43	1.68	1.16
Production of component parts for assembly elsewhere (RPS)	3.59	1.48	2.33	1.67	1.54	1.81	1.77
Production of differentiated products (WPM)	3.22	1.77	1.62	2.01	1.50	1.50	1.38
Total	3.28	1.75	2.15	1.92	1.47	1.63	1.41
χ^2=14.12*							

* significant at 10%   ** significant at 5%   *** significant at 1%

1. Sources of technology
A: Existing technology embodied in established products we produce – ESTPRODTECH.
B: Technology of our MNE group from which we introduce new products for the European market, which differ from other variants introduced in other markets – GROUPTECH.
C: R&D carried out by our own laboratory – OWNLAB.
D: R&D carried out for us by another R&D laboratory of our MNE group – GROUPLAB.
E: Development and adaptation carried out less formally by members of our engineering unit and production personnel – ENGUNIT.
F: R&D carried out in collaboration with another local firm – OTHERFIRM.
G: R&D carried out for us by local scientific institutions (e.g. universities, independent laboratories, industry laboratories) – LOCALINST.

Notes:
1. Respondents were asked to grade each source of technology for their operations as (i) our only source, (ii) a major source, (iii) a secondary source, (iv) not a source.
2. The average response was calculated by allocating the value of 4 to the only source of technology, the value of 3 to the main source, the value of 2 to a secondary source and the value of 1 to not a source.
3. Includes subsidiaries from Switzerland, Cyprus, Liechtenstein, and Russia.
4. Includes subsidiaries from South Korea, Panama and Canada.
5. Manufacturing sector includes Pharmaceuticals and Chemicals, Electronics and IT, Food and Beverages, Automobiles and Transport Equipment, General Manufacturing, Other Manufacturing, Miscellaneous and Textiles (For full description of Other Manufacturing and Miscellaneous see Appendix 4.1). Service sector includes Consulting Companies, Hotels, Banks and Publishing Corporations.
6. Covers subsidiaries that described themselves as only or predominately each type.

Source: Authors, Survey on Foreign Subsidiaries in Greece

million Euro) and the proportion of subsidiary's exports (i.e the ratio of exports to sales). The last three variables intend to capture the size of the subsidiary, and its market scope, respectively. Explanatory and control variables are defined in Table 4.2. The correlation matrix and descriptive statistics are presented in Appendix 4.2.

Ordered logit was applied as an econometric technique since the dependent variable is a qualitative one, ascribed with ascending degrees of importance. In this case y is not a quantity, but nevertheless a larger value of y means more, or better. So the dependent variable represents a ranking. The model is suited to discrete data, it is unhindered by large numbers of ties and it circumvents problems associated with heterogeneity (Han and Hausman, 1990). An ordered logit model is built around a latent regression, in the same manner as the binomial logit model, and it is of the following form:

$$y_i^* = \beta_i'x + u_i \qquad (2)$$

where:
β_i are the estimated coefficients,
x denotes the independent/explanatory and control variables.
u_i is a normally distributed error term,
y_i^* is unobserved and what we observe comes in the following form: When y^* takes on the values 0, 1, 2, ..., m, the ordered logit model estimates a set of coefficients (including one for the constant) for each of the m – 1 points at which the dependent variable can be dichotomized. We observe: P (Y < k) = F (–XB_k), k = 1,..., m (STATA 7.0, manual help guide under gologit).[1]

The relatively small sample made us relax the usual 0.05 criterion for statistical significance to the 0.1 level. (In various surveys, the criterion for statistical significance is relaxed to 0.2, with still effective significant prediction, e.g. Chang, 2003). The full logistic regression models used in the chapter have the following transformation: Regressions are run using dummies for the sector (services omitted) and the country of subsidiaries' origin (EU omitted). By doing so it helps to identify differences across markets and geographical locations with similar characteristics. Alternatively, binomial and ordered probit models were used by dividing sources of technology (important and not so important) and transforming the dependant variable into a binary dummy variable taking value one if the source is considered important by the subsidiary and zero otherwise, but they proved slightly inferior, providing at the

Table 4.2 Variable description

Variables	Type[a]	Operational definition
SUBSIDIARY RELATED VARIABLES		
SUBSIDIARY ROLE		In order to evaluate their role subsidiaries were asked to grade each of the following roles in terms of the importance in their operations as being : (i) not part of their role, (ii) secondary role, (iii) main role and (iv) only role (i) The production of standardized products (ii) The production of specific products of the whole range (iii) The production of component parts of the whole range (iv) The production of differentiated products
Truncated Miniature Replica (TMR)	L/D	Subsidiary that produces standardize products (4 = only role, 3 = main role, 2 = secondary role, 1 = not part of role)
Specialized Miniature Replica (SMR)	L/D	Subsidiary that specialized its production in specific products (4 = only role, 3 = main role, 2 = secondary role, 1 = not part of role)
Rationalized Product Subsidiary (RPS)	L/D	Subsidiary that specialized its production in component parts of the final product (4 = only role, 3 = main role, 2 = secondary role, 1 = not part of role)
World Product Mandate (WPM)	L/D	Subsidiary that produces differentiated products (4 = only role, 3 = main role, 2 = secondary role, 1 = not part of role)

Table 4.2 Variable description – *continued*

Variables	Type[a]	Operational definition
SUBSIDIARY CHARACTERISTICS		
Years of Operation	L/D	Age of Subsidiary (Number of years the subsidiary has been established in Greece). According to the years of operation subsidiaries were characterized as well established, recently established and new established. Well established are the subsidiaries that operate in Greece before 1970 and take the value of 3. Recently established are the subsidiaries that begun to operate between 1971 and 1990 and take the value of 2. Newly established are the subsidiaries that identified their presence after 1991 and take the value of 1
Sales	L/D	Volume of subsidiary's gross sales expressed in million Euros. Sales are grouped in three categories according to their volume. Less than 20 000 000 euros takes the value of 1, between 20 000 000–40 000 000 euros takes the value of 2 and more than 40 000 000 euros takes the value of 3
Personnel	C	Employment (Number of employees in the subsidiary)
Exports	B/D	1 = The subsidiary is exporting, 0 = otherwise
CONTROLS		
HOME COUNTRY		
EU	B/D	1 = parent from EU, 0 = otherwise
OtherEur	B/D	1 = parent from other European country, 0 = otherwise
Japan and Rest of World	B/D	1 = parent from Japan and rest of world, 0 = otherwise
US	B/D	1 = parent from USA, 0 = otherwise
Manufacturing	B/D	1 = Firms belong to manufacturing, 0 = otherwise

[a]Binary (B); / Likert – Type (L); / Continuous (C); / Discrete (D)

same time very similar results. Results on the regressions are presented in Table 4.3.

Tests on ordered logit models provide evidence that omitted uncorrelated explanatory variables and neglected heteroscedasticity may generate inconsistent parameter estimates in this type of model (Kiefer and Skoog, 1984). To test for these misspecifications, an artificial regression based on Lagrange multiplier (LM) tests was used (Murphy, 1996). In this case, no serious problem for the model was observed.

A positive relationship is observed between ESTPRODTECH and both SMRs and RPSs. This result confirms that established technology supports both more standardized horizontal (the case of SMRs) and vertical (the case of RPSs) production, aiming at wider intra-MNE markets. Moreover, ESTPRODTECH is positively related with newly established subsidiaries. This points towards the tendency of these new subsidiaries to dominate the Greek market through the local commercialization of well-established technology, taking advantage of the experience gained in operating in the market for the product elsewhere.

GROUPTECH is found to strongly support export-oriented subsidiaries, providing further support to our arguments regarding the restructuring of Greek-based foreign operations. This, however, cannot be achieved independently and requires technological support from the group. The strong positive sign for WPMs suggests that creative subsidiaries in Greece have not yet reached the level of emancipation to rely fully on their own forces through a locally-based laboratory. Instead, in order to cover the needs of their wider markets, they need to have access to updated technological information. This resembles a 'knowledge user' unit as defined by Randøy and Li (1999, p. 84). At the same time, the strong positive result of OWNLAB for TMRs, and its insignificance for WPMs supports the previously stated proposition. In line with existing literature (Håkanson and Nobel, 2001; Andersson and Forsgren, 2000), OWNLAB seems to favor large (in terms of sales) subunits. Large subsidiaries can in fact afford both to have their own R&D laboratory as well as to enjoy technological support from another MNE laboratory, whilst SMRs are less likely to have an interaction with such a laboratory. The specificity of their operations apparently does not imply any important trouble-shooting problems that they cannot resolve by applying other means, rather than needing to end up approaching another group laboratory, which could be a quite costly operation (Teece, 1981).

GROUPLAB is more widely used by subsidiaries coming from Japan and the rest of the world compared with their EU counterparts. (Results are consistent with the work of Collinson, 2001). This indicates that the HQs of these MNEs seek to involve them in a more creative process

Table 4.3 Regressions with sources of technology as the dependent variable

	Importance of sources of technology[1] in MNE subsidiaries in Greece N=92						
	A EST PROD TECH	B GROUP TECH	C OWN LAB	D GROUP LAB	E ENG UNIT	F OTHER FIRM	G LOCAL INST
By Profile of Subsidiary							
Years of Operation[2]	2.562++ (0.897)	0.378 (0.256)	−0.061 (4.350)	5.137+ (0.775)	0.012 (0.289)	−0.187 (0.081)	0.889 (2.201)
Personnel	−0.275 (3.760)	0.321 (0.288)	1.155 (3.677)	7.413 (2.166)	0.512 (1.113)	−0.451 (1.255)	0.020 (0.055)
Sales[3]	−0.062 (0.054)	−0.012 (0.206)	1.663 (2.280)	3.220 (2.280)	−0.799 (1.452)	−0.560 (0.390)	−2.990 (1.633)
Exports	0.644+ (1.670)	0.221+ (1.552)	2.133 (0.774)	−3.665++ (1.996)	0.644 (1.139)	1.174 (0.230)	−2.892 (1.740)
By Location of HQs							
Other European Countries[4]	−2.082 (1.472)	2.646 (1.566)	3.010 (1.964)	1.085 (0.088)	2.229 (0.189)	2.776 (1.773)	1.948 (1.818)
Japan and Rest of the World[5]	−2.217 (1.563)	3.822 (2.334)	2.081++ (1.487)	4.180++ (2.090)	1.448 (0.355)	2.820 (1.954)	1.663 (1.919)
US	−2.931++ (1.489)	2.324 (1.875)	3.533 (2.563)	2.804 (2.301)	1.961 (0.400)	2.985 (1.765)	2.446 (1.817)
By Sector[6]							
Manufacturing	−0.980 (3.345)	0.113 (0.470)	−0.414 (0.723)	5.137+ (0.775)	0.240 (0.168)	0.551++ (2.522)	0.045 (2.551)
By Type of Subsidiary[7]							
Production of well established products (TMR)	−0.025 (0.359)	0.375 (0.206)	0.043++ (0.453)	0.523 (0.227)	−0.658+ (0.292)	0.560 (0.390)	−0.634** (0.331)
Specialization and supply of MNE network part of the established product range (SMR)	0.513+ (0.931)	0.681 (0.392)	0.863 (0.403)	−0.372 (0.301)	0.454 (0.015)	1.174 (0.590)	0.132 (0.307)
Production of component parts for assembly elsewhere (RPS)	0.380 (0.433)	0.322 (0.261)	0.551 (0.088)	−0.326 (0.332)	0.175 (0.360)	0.588+ (0.386)	0.696* (0.575)
Production of differentiated products (WPM)	−0.280 (0.327)	0.430+ (0.399)	0.410 (0.037)	−0.015 (0.335)	0.030 (0.390)	0.791 (0.356)	0.307*** (0.353)
Statistics							
F	1.84+	1.18	2.24++	1.30+	1.41	1.14+	0.69
Cronbach a	0.81	0.71	0.84	0.82	0.69	0.75	0.72

Notes:
1. For full description of technology sources (dependant variables), see Table 4.1.
2. For the breakdown and classification of years of operation, see Table 4.3.
3. For the breakdown and classification of sales, see Table 4.3.
4. Includes subsidiaries from Switzerland, Cyprus, Liechtenstein, Luxembourg and Russia.
5. Includes subsidiaries from South Korea, Panama and Canada.
6. For analytical description of sector, see Table 4.1 and Appendix 4.1.
7. Covers subsidiaries that described themselves as only or predominantly each type.
Source: Authors, survey on Foreign Subsidiaries in Greece

concerning the Greek market by providing central-originated technological inputs that may, in the near future, generate decentralized innovative processes targeting specific market areas. In the case of European MNEs, because of the geographical proximity, it is possible that GROUPLAB is more likely to emerge in the continental home country operations of these companies, and the derivation of European market variations of the product to be carried out there. The positive relationship of GROUPLAB in manufacturing industry, compared with the service sector, was anticipated, since, by nature, industry requires more central-oriented technological inputs that will moderate the cost of production and/or ascribe an innovative nature to the outputs.

Regression results for ENGUNIT are very weak. This suggests that, so far, the types of tacit knowledge and engineering expertise possessed by these personnel are found to be useful in rather *ad hoc* circumstances that do not relate predominately to any specific motivation. There is though one survey in the literature that has stressed the positive statistical significance of the use of scientific personnel in R&D Departments of Greek manufacturing industry (Souitaris, 2002). Nevertheless, a statistical negative relationship is observed here between this technology source and TMRs, indicating the standardized technology procedures of this type of subsidiaries.

Regarding the last regressions with the two external sources of technology as dependent variables, we notice some interesting patterns: RPSs, which reflect efficiency-seeking motivations (Dunning, 1993a), are better integrated in the local productive and scientific community as they seek both the collaboration of local firms as well as local research institutions (Phene and Almeida, 2003). Moreover, the negative relation between LOCALINST and TMRs, and the positive relation between LOCALINST and WPMs, clearly indicates that product differentiation requires creative inputs that only research institutions such as universities can provide (Roth and Morrison, 1992). This last result provides, on the one hand, some encouraging signs regarding the capabilities of the local scientific community which apparently has gained the confidence and recognition of foreign investors and, on the other hand, the effectiveness of collaborative agreements at a pre-competitive stage (Porter, 1990).

Conclusions

In this chapter we argue that the contemporary MNE is a continuously evolving institution. Consequently, subsidiaries are not necessarily allocated *ad hoc* specific roles, and a more decentralized approach to technology generation and diffusion becomes central to the strategic evolution of the MNE.

Our findings reinforce the view that technology in MNEs is no longer simply the responsibility of the corporate center. The multinational seems to have been transformed from 'technology creator' to 'technology organizer' in its global operations (Cantwell, 2001). Foreign subsidiaries not only serve the traditional function of adapting the parent MNE's technology to local market needs and providing technical support to local factories and customers (Cantwell, 2001), but also have become significant sources of technology development (Cantwell, 1995).

Drawing on a data-set including 92 subsidiaries operating in a peripheral country in terms of FDI received, and by applying a typology of subsidiaries derived by White and Poynter (1984), we addressed two research questions regarding the extent and availability of various technological resources to MNE subsidiaries in Greece and the impact of specific subsidiary roles on the accessibility of technology. The selected typology enables us to extract useful insights concerning the contribution of subsidiaries in the technological development of the host country. Findings should not be restricted to the focal country only, but can be replicated to other peripheral countries that join the EU, since Greece has experienced similar economic characteristics.

Our results record the existence of a multifaceted network of technology generation and transmission, which is differentiated among the different types of subsidiaries. The results confirm the fact that larger and more innovative subsidiaries have been granted access to wider sources of internally-generated technology. Creative subunits (WPMs), as well as subsidiaries of a more efficiency-seeking nature (RPSs), are likely to collaborate more intensively with local firms and scientific institutions compared to TMRs. This clearly indicates that WPMs and RPSs are in a better position to scan the host environment for relevant external technology sources and deal more efficiently with local responsiveness pressures. Especially for WPMs, evidence provides ample support for the argument that the differentiated MNE is more favorably positioned than the non-differentiated MNE with respect to creation of knowledge as a medium for the development of competitive advantage, simply because of its access to more knowledge sources (Bartlett and Ghoshal, 1989; Hedlund, 1986). Nevertheless, all subsidiary types, regardless of their nationality or/and strategic roles are positively influenced by varied internal technology sources, which mainly result in reduction of transaction costs and the efficient exploitation of economies of scale and scope.

The recorded multifaceted technology sourcing has clear strategic and managerial implications since it may affect both the degree of subsidiaries' autonomy and the degree of integration with HQs. Subsidiaries are subunits under a hierarchical MNE organizational structure and simultaneously independent units competing in local markets. Their ability to act as 'technology vehicles' that absorb local knowledge and facilitate the MNEs' worldwide capabilities (Tallman and Fladmoe-Lindquist, 2002) can be hindered when they behave completely autonomously and strive for their own interests. However, the successful monitoring and exploitation of local technological resources lead MNEs to encourage localization of technology development. In that sense subsidiaries seek to create networks with host institutions of research generation for taking advantage of local ideas and products. Thus, the degree of integration, organizational architecture and the management control systems are of critical importance.

For management, evidence provided by this research assumes that subsidiaries are at least partly able to make independent decisions. Management should then seek to control the determinants of technology benefits and costs. This may be accomplished, among other things, through managerial choices relating to knowledge sources. In terms of our earlier discussion of the MNE knowledge-based structure, these managerial choices influence, and are influenced by, the complexity of the knowledge structure, the technology strategy of the network and the technological capabilities of the host environment. In line with existing evidence (Foss and Pedersen, 2001), we also assume that management will choose subsidiary knowledge sources and organizational mechanisms for transferring knowledge in such a way that the overall value of the network is maximized.

Apparently, our results support recent evidence which clearly demonstrates that current developments in the wider geographical region that Greece is part of, that is Balkans and Eastern Europe, has increased the level of value added activities of certain foreign subsidiaries which have been evolving into 'regional hubs' (Birkinshaw, 1998a). These subsidiaries seek for more sophisticated inputs which substantially support their 'new' upgraded mandates and thus become more embedded in the local environment. Given the advantages that innovative MNEs ascribe to host economies, and in order to attract foreign investments in technology, Greece should reconsider the structure and scope of its research policy aiming at the creation of continually upgrading innovation competencies. These competencies create competitive capabilities at the firm level and thus underwrite economic growth. Greece, having already adopted policies that have, over the past two decades, opened up and liberalized the economy, should emphasize investments in basic research so as to foster innovation and attract investments of worldwide technological excellence. As a final remark, the issue of embeddedness becomes central to policy making in terms of attracting FDI by encouraging the adoption of FDI promoting policies that place emphasis (among other things) on the quality of local scientific institutions and the creation of clusters. This will allow for a more substantial development of local channels of knowledge transmission, which is fundamental to the development of Greece's competitive advantages (Porter, 2003).

This research represents a static conceptualization of technology sourcing. A critical concern in technology management is to track the impact of various technological inputs over a greater period of time since, according to Pavitt (1990), technology reliance decisions have long-term impacts on a firm's profitability. No technological knowledge is entirely internally or externally oriented. Nevertheless, literature provides evidence mainly for internal sources (Kogut, 2000). Further research on the determinants of a subsidiary decision to make technology outsourcing (external sourcing) is required. Finally, by exploring different types of R&D professionals' motivation (Osterloh and Frey, 2000) future research could investigate which conditions constitute an impact factor in knowledge generation, deployment and the readiness of these high-valued employees to innovate.

Note

1 Data were run with STATA. The proportional odds property of stata's ologit command restricts the B_k coefficients to be the same for every dividing point $k = 1,..., m$.

Appendix 4.1 Response rates and the number of respondents by industry and country of origin

Sector	Total Sample	Number of Respondents	Response Rate
Automobiles and Transport Equipment	19	10	52,63%
Chemicals	18	5	27,78%
Electronics and IT	15	4	26,67%
Food and Beverages	47	27	57,45%
manufacturing	62	13	20,97%
Miscellaneous*	19	4	21,05%
Other Manufacturing**	34	7	20,59%
Pharmaceuticals	31	7	22,58%
Services	51	11	21,57%
Textiles	21	4	19,05%
Total	*317*	*92*	*29,02%*

HQs Country of Location	Total Sample	Number of Respondents	Response Rate
EU Countries	129	41	31,78%
Other European Countries	78	18	23,08%
Total European	**207**	**59**	**28,50%**
Japan	37	7	18,92%
US	52	22	42,31%
Rest of World	21	4	19,05%
Total non European	**110**	**33**	**30,00%**
Total	*317*	*92*	*29,02%*

* Miscellaneous includes Agribusiness, Home Equipment and Equipments for Bakeries
** Other Manufacturing includes Tobacco, Paper and Forest Products, Heating and Air Conditioning Equipment and Office Machinery

Appendix 4.2 Correlation matrix

Correlation among the Variables

Variables	Mean	s.d	min	max	Years of Operation	Personnel	Sales	Exports	EU Countries	Other European Countries	USA	Japan and Rest of World	Manufacturing	Services	TMR	SMR	RPS	WPM
Years of Operation	2,05	0,861	1	3	1													
Personnel	301	620,9	17	780	−0,347	1												
Sales	2,32	1,32	1	3	−0,103	−0,154	1											
Exports	15,1	21,88	0	67	0,097	0,215	−0,150	1										
EU countries	0,44	0,499	0	1	0,001	−0,122	−0,247	−0,248	1									
Other European	0,21	0,414	0	1	0,088	0,146	0,345	−0,006	−0,552	1								
USA	0,23	0,428	0	1	−0,096	−0,038	0,008	−0,263	−0,447	−0,247	1							
Japan and Rest of World	0,16	0,414	0	1	−0,086	0,165	−0,005	−0,011	−0,229	−0,127	−0,123	1						
Manufacturing	0,82	0,381	0	1	−0,067	−0,175	−0,225	−0,009	0,060	0,610	0,132	0,069	1					
Services	0,18	0,453	0	1	0,270	−0,064	0,988	0,142	0,344	0,270	−0,05	0,090	0,1	1				
TMR	3,22	0,441	2	4	0,214	0,017	−0,074	−0,329	−0,052	−0,253	0,101	0,084	−0,005	−0,123	1			
SMR	1,75	0,925	1	4	−0,039	0,190	−0,091	0,451	0,141	0,214	0,032	−0,065	0,003	0,146	−0,424	1		
RPS	1,35	0,643	1	4	0,056	0,107	−0,142	0,087	−0,101	0,796	0,073	0,092	0,182	−0,037	−0,226	0,202	1	
WPM	1,82	0,925	1	4	0,021	0,008	−0,007	0,011	−0,187	0,247	0,050	−0,034	−0,203	0,148	−0,454	0,241	0,418	1

5
Strategic Heterogeneity in MNEs and the Integrating European Economy

Dimitra Dimitropoulou, Robert Pearce and
Marina Papanastassiou

Introduction

In the world in which Multinational Enterprises (MNEs) increasingly operate as dynamic differentiated networks, their strategic response to processes of regional integration can be seen less in terms of the simple *quantitative* benefits of access to a bigger market space than in terms of a carefully-articulated ability to secure competitiveness there from the different *qualitative* capacities of different member economies. Thus our investigation here is of heterogeneity and differentiation in MNEs' operations in the EU. In fact three aspects of heterogeneity are invoked.

Firstly, the strategic heterogeneity of the contemporary MNE. Two broad aspects of competitiveness need to be pursued in MNE strategies. The first of these is to secure the greatest level of profitability available from use of the existing sources of competitiveness (technologies, products) of the firm. According to context this can be pursued through market-seeking or efficiency-seeking operations. Secondly, to continually reinforce and regenerate these sources of competitiveness through innovation and R&D. The increasing decentralization and networking of these knowledge-seeking activities is a major recent development in MNE strategy, and one that can plausibly be effectively operationalized in an integrating economic area such as the EU. These strategic options are discussed in detail in the next section of this chapter.

The range of locations available to MNE operations in the EU comprises the second aspect of heterogeneity in our analysis. The existing levels of development of member countries (and regions within them), and national policies in pursuit of further progress, help differentiate locations across dimensions that can attract varied mixes of MNE strategies. The ways in which aspects of these differences in location advantages can relate to MNE strategic motivations (and location decisions within the EU) are also elaborated in the next section. A familiar attempt to stratify EU members by development and economic status is to discern 'core' and 'periphery' groupings of countries. In operationalizing this for our analysis we ultimately discern the logic and value of placing an 'intermediate' grouping between the extremes. This process is elaborated in the third section.

Our investigation uses, as a third dimension of heterogeneity, three samples of FDI flows according to MNE origin. These then can contrast two sources from outside the EU (FDI of US and Japanese MNEs) with the intra-EU investment of Europe-based MNEs. The two external sources may themselves be contrasted if we suggest that US MNEs are often long-established in Europe and may, therefore, be undergoing processes of restructuring (as may also intra-EU investors) during the EU integration processes. By contrast Japanese FDI may be more recent and therefore can, from initiation, operationalize strategic networks responsive to locational differences.

In section four we introduce the data and methodology used to investigate the dimensions of strategic and locational heterogeneity. The results are presented and reviewed in section five and overall conclusions complete the chapter.

MNEs' competitive strategies and location factors

The dimensions of MNE competitive aims and motivations adopted here (Behrman, 1984; Dunning, 1993a, 2000; Dunning and Lundan, 2008; Manea and Pearce, 2004) suggest three different objectives that are likely to be pursued in these firms' European networks. These are market-seeking (MS), efficiency-seeking (ES) and knowledge-seeking (KS). The factors determining choice of locations for operationalizing these motivations are very different, and it is then the differentiated spread of such location determinants throughout the EU that provides our views of the dispersal of particular types of operations into selected economies. In terms of comprehending the implications of FDI for particular economies, at particular stages of development, and also for the wider processes of EU-wide integration and growth, it is thus seen as necessary to go beyond a location's ability to attract FDI and to evaluate the role the MNE will expect its operation to play. Here we elaborate on these three strategic motivations and generate hypotheses as to the types of host-country location characteristics likely to attract these operations. The independent variables used to test the presence of these motivations in the three groupings of EU members are also described.

Market-seeking (MS)

The traditional view of MS (Pearce, 2001) perceived this strategy as reflecting a need to invest in a particular economy to supply, very specifically, that country's market. This was viewed as being the response to high levels of trade restraint which prevented the MNE from supplying that market from a lower-cost (in effect ES) operation elsewhere. This type of MS behavior could then be argued to be inherently 'trade-destroying' (Kojima, 1978), with its aims limited to defending profitability rather than encompassing any ability to enhance it. But, of course, the very essence of the process of EU widening and deepening, through the period covered in this study, has been to lower trade restraints and generate the alternative ethos of a European 'single market'. But whilst this clearly removes the context for traditional 'tariff'jumping' MS operations it remains plausible that scope now exists for a more contemporary proactive variant of MS within MNEs' European networks. This reflects the value of responding to a 'presence effect' (Buckley and Artisien, 1988), which allows subsidiaries to respond to particular tastes and distinctive needs of their local markets.

This positively responsive explanation for persisting MS priorities in MNEs' strategies targets market expansion and the generation of new sources of profitability through the acknowledgment of significant persistence (or even enhancement) of different characteristics in different markets. Thus close collaboration between production and marketing in contemporary MS subsidiaries aims to tailor supply so as to meet the distinctive tastes of local customers in the most competitive manner available. A second, less competitively sensitive, context for persistence of MS-type influences on FDI location in Europe can also be suggested (Dimitropoulou *et al.*, 2008). Thus echoes of the earlier form of MS motivation could persist in a strategically myopic decision process by external (here US or Japanese) MNEs that are establishing production facilities in the EU for the first time. Here the initial decision to locate supply facilities in the EU for the first time may still be a negative and defensive response to the remaining (and perhaps potentially rising) *external* tariffs. Thus these pioneering investments may still reflect the (MS) fear of 'fortress Europe' rather than encompass a more contemporary, positive and optimizing, perspective on the (ES) potentials of Europe's internal free-trade. If this initial entry decision remains driven by a persisting MS mindset then the choice of location in Europe might also reflect market-oriented characteristics. So the pioneering facility might be located in one of Europe's more impressive 'core' market environments, rather than in a less obviously impressive 'peripheral' site that would in fact be more cost-competitive as a basis for possibly community-wide (ES) supply.

We include two independent variables that aim to directly reflect aspects of an MS motivation. Firstly, the GDP of each of the separate European economies for each year ($US million). This suggests simply that the sheer size of a national economy serves as an indicator of the potential profits available from supply of that market (Culem, 1988; Veugelers, 1991; Wheeler and Mody, 1992; Braunerhjelm and Svensson, 1996). Thus the more traditional formulation of MS suggests that MS-oriented MNE strategies would lead, at a point in time, to more investment in larger economies and also, over time, to the expansion of their investment in a particular economy in line with its market growth. This, we have suggested, mainly reflects a 'tariff jumping' context for MS, so that it is also dependent on the presence of quite extensive restraints on trade (Barrell and Pain, 1999a, 1999b; Neven and Siotis, 1996).

The second of these variables is GDP per capita (PERCAP) in $US. We see this as reflective of the more contemporary, market-differentiation, variant of the MS motivation (Filippaios *et al.*, 2004; Chakrabarti, 2001). As already noted, the extensive geographical space and physical variation of the EU, and the notable variation of average income levels between member economies, indicate clear competitive benefits to be gained from acknowledging differences in tastes and demand patterns. PERCAP can then serve as 'an indicator of both the extent of these taste differences (increasing prosperity may give consumers the ability to manifest previously suppressed sources of demand individualization) and the willingness of MNEs to respond to them through subtle locally responsive product differentiation' (Dimitropoulou and Pearce, 2006, p. 186). It can also be acknowledged here that PERCAP may also serve to proxy supply-side elements of the KS motivation. Thus it may indicate the degree of potential for accessing in a particular economy some of the aspects of human capital (for example, market researchers, design engineers, scientists and technologists) that can provide key inputs into desirable processes of locally-responsive adaptation and development.

These perspectives on the potential persistence of the MS motivation as an influence on MNE location decisions in the EU suggest that it would be at its strongest, and provoke the most carefully considered implementation, in large high-income economies. Thus our two most direct indicators of MS (GDP; PERCAP) would be most likely to provide significant results in core and, perhaps, intermediate country sub-samples.

Our emphasis on a potential persistence of MS in a context that is basically driven by an increasing intra-European openness to trade is encompassed within a third variable (OPEN). This is constructed to trace changes in EU-member economies' openness over time, and show the differences in levels between them. Thus OPEN is calculated as 'exports plus imports divided by GDP for each host country in each year'. A very low value of OPEN would indicate an economy that is isolated from international trade, probably due to trade and other policy factors. This would be reflective of a situation conducive to traditional MS supply behavior, so that a negative relationship between OPEN and FDI flows would reflect MNEs' continued pursuit of 'tariff jumping' local market supply.

But as OPEN takes higher values it becomes easier to supply a market through imports and concurrently less viable to sustain competitive local production of many of MNEs' goods. This follows from the presumption (Pearce, 2001, 2006) that most MS subsidiaries suffer from innate inefficiencies that reflect participation in an import-substitution (i.e. trade protected) environment. But at the same time rising OPEN is likely to be symptomatic of the wider free-trade situation of EU integration, so that internal restructuring in MNEs' regional strategies allow for the emergence of export-oriented ES strategies. Thus the growing prevalence of ES supply networking in MNEs' European operations would be reflected in a positive relationship between OPEN and FDI flows. This positive relationship can be expected to be most distinctive for the predicted cost-based operations in the 'periphery', whilst our speculation of the persistence of a market-responsive variant of MS in core countries, in particular, may mute the positive relationship between OPEN and FDI flows there.

Efficiency-seeking (ES)

We have just noted the implication that the movements towards a more open free-trade environment in the EU would be expected to provoke a strategic shift in MNEs' approach to the region; away from a multi-domestic (Porter, 1986) portfolio of MS subsidiaries towards a more 'coherent region-wide strategy, building individual subsidiaries into a network pursuing competitiveness across the integrating group of economies' (Dimitropoulou *et al.*, 2008, p. 52). Cost-effective supply of standardized price-competitive goods for extensive segments of the integrated EU market is clearly a key priority for such a region-wide strategy. The ES aim of MNEs is thus to generate integrated EU supply networks in which different parts of a product range are produced at different locations, for intra-group distribution throughout the community. The optimizing aim would then be to match a product's (or component's) technology, in terms of input needs, with a location's current sources of static comparative advantage. The efficiency secured by such a matching of MNE technology with host-country inputs is then amplified through the ability to achieve economies of scale through competitive access to export markets. The intuitive expectation would be that the more cost-oriented aspects of network competitiveness would be pursued most decisively in 'periphery' locations.

We have already seen how our variable OPEN can be interpreted to discriminate between the presence of MS and ES motivations in MNEs' operations. Two other proxies are used that also help test the presence of ES. Firstly, unit labor costs (ULC) provide an indicator of the cost per unit of output of an input that is centrally reflective of location competitiveness (Cushman, 1987; Culem, 1988; Veugelers, 1991; Wheeler and Mody, 1992; Barrell and Pain, 1996, 1999a, b). Pursuit of ES objectives would be reflected in a negative relationship between ULC and FDI flows.

A second broader measure of a country's revealed trade competitiveness (COMP) is also used (Filippaios *et al.*, 2004). This takes the form of 'exports divided by exports plus imports'. Thus 'the higher the value of this ratio, or the more pronounced its rise over time, the more likely it is to reflect the presence of sources of international competitiveness in any economy that may attract MNEs' (Dimitropoulou and Pearce, 2006, p. 187). Where a high value of COMP reflects very competitive inputs into standardized production processes it is likely to be attractive to ES needs (perhaps mainly in periphery economies). But strong, and especially systematically rising, values of COMP may also reflect trade performance that derives from an economy's increasing ability to generate goods of improved quality, reliability and originality. Tapping into such manifestations of an economy's innovative distinctiveness could then reflect the KS aim of modern MNEs (and perhaps be reflected in a positive relationship between COMP and FDI in 'core' economies).

Knowledge-seeking (KS)

A role for KS in the strategic networks of MNEs in Europe suggests a clear awareness of the need to not only supply mature goods competitively

(ES), but also to secure the knowledge capacities to create new sources of competitiveness to be manifested in new goods. Furthermore this is also perceived to benefit from accessing differentiated knowledge and expertise from dispersed EU locations. Thus KS represents MNEs' 'response to knowledge heterogeneity, in the understanding that, with their growth and development, individual countries have generated different capacities in terms of technology stocks, research programs and trajectories and creative human capital' (Dimitropoulou et al., 2008, p. 65). Tapping selectively into these differentiated sources of knowledge and creativity has become an increasingly significant element in MNEs' FDI location choices. Since we can also argue that these attributes become stronger and more distinctive as countries become more developed, we can expect proxies for knowledge assets to be most significant as determinants of FDI in 'core' countries.

Two variables are incorporated to provide direct indicators of the forms of science and innovation attributes that could attract KS-oriented FDI to particular economies. Firstly, total expenditure on (business and government funded) R&D as a proportion of GDP (RAD) (Wheeler and Mody, 1992; Braunerhjelm and Svensson, 1996; Barrell and Pain, 1999a). This aims to represent an input measure that would indicate forward-looking science-based potentials in an economy of types that KS-oriented MNEs would seek to internalize in laboratories or product development subsidiaries. Secondly, we use the number of patent applications to the European patent organization per million of population (PAT) as an output measure of how successful a country's national system of innovation has been in generating patentable new knowledge. Again high values of PAT are taken to suggest a dynamic and creative environment that could generate strong benefits for KS investments by MNEs.

In addition three of our other independent variables introduced with primary predictive expectations relating to MS or ES, may also embody elements of KS. Here PERCAP may be indicative of *sources* of income levels, such that higher levels of PERCAP may reflect the strong presence of high-quality human capital, embodying distinctive expertise and capacities that can feed into KS activities of MNEs. Similarly high values of ULC could represent, not uncompetitive sources of routine production labor, but rather high-skill creative labor whose extensive presence underpins the quality and originality of goods. Then, from that, as we have argued, the sources of high values of COMP may be technology-gap exports reflecting advanced and original goods rather than cost-driven supply.

Agglomeration influences – FDI stock

The regressions also incorporated the values of FDI stock in each country ($US) lagged by one year (FST). Though primarily serving as a control, we can also indicate some behavioral possibilities relating to FST. An obvious possibility here is that new investments are routinely made, in a mechanical and myopic way, in countries that have already shown the ability to attract and retain FDI. The reinvestment of their own profits by existing subsidiaries could, of course, come under this heading. But this need not be simply a reflexive and routine decision, but rather one that can be validated, within group allocation processes, as representing a logical strategic expansion that embodies a clear aim in terms of one of the motivations discussed above. With regard to new greenfield investments FST can be suggested to serve as an indicator of agglomeration potentials that derive from interactive or spillover benefits from co-location with longer-established operations of other MNEs.

Categorizing the EU-I5 countries

Traditional 'broadbrush' categorization of a core/periphery dichotomy for EU members tends to assert a convenient coalescence of geographical location and economic characteristics. But attempts to achieve a practical characterization suitable for assessing the determinants of FDI and MNE strategy in the EU-integration context project a more complex, less decisive, picture (Dimitropoulou, 2007; Dimitropoulou et al., 2008). Here a long-standing intuitive classification could clearly group Spain, Portugal, Greece and Ireland as a peripheral grouping, combining geographical location at the edge of the Community and the vulnerable 'peripheral' economic characteristics of limited industrialization and specialization in labor-intensive activity. This then leads to lower incomes, high levels of unemployment, poor productivity levels and limited scope for innovation or creativity. But convenient juxtaposition of geographical and economic marginality is immediately countered by Scandinavian countries, again on the perimeter of the community but with high levels of economic performance and few of the accepted 'peripheral' problems. This then leads us to derive an intermediate grouping of countries, whose characteristics are either somewhat ambiguous in logical core/periphery terms or which sit clearly in a status between the accepted extremes.

Policy-oriented attempts at determining an economic segmentation of the EU can be found in the patterns of support offered through the

Cohesion Fund (established in 1994) and the regional assistance provided by the Structural Funds. Here the Cohesion Fund provides support to the poorest *countries* in the EU. To be eligible for Cohesion Funds assistance a member country should have per capita GDP lower than the average EU levels. This has in practice tended to relate Cohesion Fund support with the normally accepted designation of 'periphery', with Spain, Portugal, Greece and (until recently) Ireland recording the EU's lowest per capita GDP levels and displaying many of the socio-economic characteristics routinely associated with peripherality (e.g. low incomes and productivity; high unemployment levels; weak infrastructure and poor human capital endowment). Thus only these four countries were assessed as recipients for Cohesion Funds for 2000/2006 when allocations were determined in 2000 (thus reflecting conditions through at least the latter part of the period of our study).

Allocation of Structural Funds, by contrast, has focused mainly on providing assistance for the development of regions within countries. Here funding under objectives 1 and 2 target regions with problems that could generally reflect issues of 'peripherality'. Thus objective 1 funds (which accounted for 71.5% of planned Structural Funds for 2000/2006) target regions that are considered to lag behind in terms of economic development. Then objective 2 funds (11.6% over the period) are available to regions going through socio-economic restructuring. The remaining objective 3 funds are available to regions where needed to deal with EU-wide issues, such as unemployment and modernization of agriculture, and are considered to have no innate periphery orientation (in fact 56.9% of objective 3 funds for 2000/2006 were allocated to France, Germany and UK).

Though most EU countries had some objective 1 regions in the 2000 classification an initial view of their distribution provides apparent support for some elements of received expectations of a core/periphery dichotomy. Thus Greece consisted entirely of objective 1 regions, whilst a clear majority of the population of Spain (80.7%) and Portugal (66.6%) were objective 1 or 2 regions. By contrast countries normally considered more centrally-located, such as France, Germany, the Netherlands, Austria, UK, Belgium and Luxembourg had at most one-third of their population in objective 1 and 2 regions, and therefore can be candidates for 'core' status. However, some of these categorizations may emerge as less clear-cut and, of course, some members do not allocate to these 'polar' groupings.

Ireland immediately provides an example of ambiguity in classification. In 2004 assistance to Ireland from the Cohesion Fund was terminated when its GDP per capita exceeded 90% of the EU-average threshold. Ireland had been a recipient of economic support through the Cohesion Fund from its creation in 1994 and had remained eligible in 2000 when the 2000/2006 allocation was determined.[1] Thus the notably high rates of GDP and employment growth through the 1990s clearly moved Ireland away from normally perceived peripheral characteristics. But though this removes Ireland from many of the economic characteristics and problems related to the 'periphery', the level achieved, and its dependence on exceptional patterns of growth, suggests it probably had not acceded to mature 'core' status. An intermediate classification seems logical.

Characteristics of both core and periphery can also be found in other countries. Much of Italy derives high-income levels from a significant level of industrialization, but the simultaneous presence of a considerable number of objective 1 (and a smaller number of objective 2) regions means 46.5% of the 2000 population were allocated to regions with severe economic problems or structural issues. This indicates location advantages and attractiveness to FDI that, overall, differ from 'mainstream' core and periphery. Two Scandinavian members, Sweden and Finland, from the geographic perimeters also include a significant set of vulnerable regions with low population densities needing external support. But overall GDP per capita, wage and employment rates for these economies considerably exceed those of Spain, Portugal and Greece, with stronger established industrial sectors and a notable commitment to creation of new technology and potential dynamic advantages. For those countries (Italy, Sweden, Finland) an intermediate status is indicated in terms of their position in EU regional policies.

An established area of conceptual and empirical analysis that can also help with a classification of EU members is the Investment Development Path (IDP) (Dunning, 1981; Dunning and Narula, 1996; Narula and Dunning, 2000). Here countries are classified into one of five different stages of development, with this then related to their net outward FDI position. Potentially the countries we seek to classify here are likely to fall into stages 3 to 5,[2] with the earlier of these stages most likely to be reflective of normally perceived 'periphery' conditions and movement into the latter stages concomitant with development towards 'core' characteristics. Thus in stage 3 created-type location advantages have been developed and are able to attract increasing amounts of inward FDI and also to strengthen domestic industry to a degree where outward FDI begins to emerge. In stage 4 a country's strong created assets remain location advantages (LAs) that attract significant inward FDI, but now also endow domestic firms with very strong ownership advantages (OAs). These OAs now drive outward FDI that reaches levels that exceed inward. In stage 5 countries there is very strong inward and outward FDI, whose net value fluctuates around zero.

Of the members traditionally considered as EU core the ones that are most developed in terms of FDI and IDP status are Germany, France, Netherlands and UK. These are countries which careful studies have identified as either clearly established in stage 5 or in the process of transition between IDP stages 4 and 5 (Clegg and Scott-Green, 1999; Durán and Úbeda, 2001). Of the cases of Austria and Belgium-Luxembourg, however, the limited IDP literature presents a more ambiguous picture. Here Bellak (2000) has suggested that the IDP position of small economies is determined by geographical position and by the industrial structure of their domestic sectors as well as the related policies pursued, so that this may strongly influence these cases. Though some studies (Durán and Úbeda, 2001, 2005) have associated these cases with stages 4 and 5, the FDI positions of Austria and Belgium-Luxembourg are actually quite distinctive.

Here Austria is clearly what UNCTAD would consider an 'underperformer' in terms of inward FDI, in the sense of receiving well-below the amounts that its characteristics would project. Similarly its outward, as well as inward, FDI stocks are proportionately very low compared to measures for the four core countries noted above. It can then be suggested (Bellak, 2000) that, perhaps due to weak OAs of domestic firms and related lack of dynamic LAs, Austria had not (in the period studied) yet reached stage 4 and thus, in turn, might for our purposes be most appropriately placed in the periphery grouping.

By contrast Belgium-Luxembourg can be classified as a 'frontrunner' in FDI, achieving inward levels notably above those that might have been expected from economic characteristics. Concurrently Belgium-Luxembourg recorded the highest levels of outward FDI in the EU, relative to size, in the relevant period.[3] This should place Belgium-Luxembourg in IDP stage 4 and in our intermediate country grouping. Similarly most IDP studies that cover them (Clegg and Scott-Green, 1999; Narula, 1996; Zander and Zander, 1996) place Denmark, Finland, Sweden and Italy in IDP stage 4, and these can join Belgium-Luxembourg in our intermediate group.

Ultimately we can find that IDP analysis confirms Greece, Spain and Portugal in our periphery grouping. Here Greece and Portugal certainly seem to classify to stage 3 (or perhaps between stages 3 and 4), being developed countries with relatively high per-capita income and rising wages, oriented to production of standardized goods but with a growing demand for more sophisticated products, and a rate of growth of outward FDI that is increasing relative to that of inward (Narula, 1996; Durán and Úbeda, 2005; Castro, 2004). Spain may be a more enigmatic case. Evidence (Durán and Úbeda, 2005; Alvarez, 2001; Clegg and Scott-Green, 1999; Narula, 1996) suggests Spain had moved slowly along the IDP, remaining in stage 3 as late as the early 1990s. However, analysis of its later progress (Durán and Úbeda, 2001, 2005; Verspagen, 1999; Alvarez, 2001; Zayas, 1998) debate whether Spain's later trajectory carried into stage 4, or whether it remained in stage 3. Thus Spanish outward FDI did increase substantially in the later 1990s. But key features of Spain's investment, both inward and outward, still did not seem to conform to that expected of a significantly industrialized country that had entered stage 4 on a sustainable basis. The Spanish economy did manifest high income levels and a rise in outward FDI, along with some dynamism in certain selected technology-intensive sectors (Zayas, 1998). But this was concurrent with generally much lower levels of technological capability (and limited systematic commitment to creating more), along with a lack of embeddedness of foreign firms in Spain's knowledge creating environment (Zayas, 1998). Overall this suggests Spain did not accede to IDP stage 4 during our period, and can most logically remain in our periphery grouping.

The dynamic industrial growth of Ireland in recent decades makes it another ambiguous case for our classification. In the early 1980s Ireland focused its economic development around inward FDI, and implemented policies to target this. Thus inward FDI in 2000 reached 107.1% of Gross Domestic Fixed Capital Formation, and Ireland ranked in third place as a host country for FDI in the period 1998–2000 (UNCTAD, 2002). Since Ireland's outward FDI flows over the past two decades were well below these inward magnitudes the strict IDP logic might be to place it alongside Spain and Portugal. However careful and informed IDP analysis (Clegg and Scott-Green, 1999; Durán and Úbeda, 2001, 2005; Görg and Ruane, 1999) usually suggest Ireland did reach stage 4 in the 1990s. This viewpoint reflects that the abnormally extreme values of inward investment would set unreasonably excessive targets for outward flows in assessing IDP positioning. Thus with Ireland's economic development now at a higher level than that of Spain and Portugal, and with its outward FDI in fact rising quickly by most comparative criteria,[4] it does seem reasonable to assert the essence of entry into stage 4. This then suggests a position in our intermediate grouping.

Data and methodology

The FDI data used here were obtained from the OECD International Direct Investment dataset.[5] It includes FDI into the 15 member countries of the EU from 1980 to 2001 (i.e. preceding the subsequent accession of Eastern European countries).[6] The inward direct investment data was then broken down into three sub-samples, relating to that from US, from Japan and intra-EU. This leads to a number of missing observations, since some host countries did not report full sets of data for the separate origins of their inward investments. However, as the data is used to create a panel of all recipient countries in a host-grouping for all years, for each of the three geographical origins, the number of missing observations does not provide serious problems for the regression analysis.

Careful investigation (Dimitropoulou, 2007) of the available regression techniques led to the US and intra-EU FDI samples being tested using 2SLS with two-way fixed effects.[7] For the Japanese sub-sample, testing for the panel structure and for the possibility of endogeneity indicated that the most suitable model would be two-way random effects and simple OLS regression.

Results

In the main the results for the two variables that relate most clearly to MS (GDP; PERCAP) prove to be weak and insignificant, and often counter-intuitive when significant. This is most decisively the case for Japanese FDI (Table 5.2) which is compatible with its later entry into Europe at a stage of integration that had removed any obvious need for initial location decisions to reflect market characteristics.[8]

For US FDI (Table 5.1) GDP emerges as significantly negative across the full sample and also within the core-group sub-sample. In the integrated EU context there is no obvious reason why large national markets should systematically deter US MNEs' investments. For the periphery sub-sample, however, GDP is significantly positive. With PERCAP also positively signed and approaching significance this could be interpreted as indicative of US MNEs seeking to explore distinctive new market potentials in the larger of the peripheral economies. The similar conjunction of a significant positive result for PERCAP, and a quite strongly positively signed result for GDP, in the peripheral sub-sample for intra-EU FDI (Table 5.3) can again be suggestive of exploratory market-responsiveness in the most potentially rewarding peripheral EU countries.[9] Overall, though, these results are most clearly compatible with the view that MS influences are no longer primary in FDI location decisions within the EU.

We have interpreted our variable OPEN as indicative of the extent to which MNEs' FDI location moves away from MS towards an export-oriented participation in a more open, or progressively opening, economy through ES motivation (or perhaps distinctive quality exports reflecting KS). In the US FDI core sample OPEN is significantly positive, indicating a greater presence in the more open of these economies. This is compatible here with the renunciation of MS suggested by the main MS proxies noted earlier. For the periphery group OPEN is positively signed but short of significance. This can suggest the expected presence of ES export-orientation in this group, but with this partially offset by the simultaneous presence of responsive MS as noted above. For the intermediate group of EU countries, however, OPEN emerges as significantly negative.

Table 5.1 Determinants of US FDI in Europe 1981–2001[1]

	Full sample	Core	Periphery	Intermediate
GDP	−0.019**	−0.015***	0.118**	0.001
	(−2.557)	(−3.843)	(2.634)	(0.206)
PERCAP	−0.043	−1.269	4.597	0.002
	(−0.388)	(−0.949)	(1.428)	(0.029)
OPEN	−5262.7	49351.2***	45814.1	−13568.1***
	(−1.200)	(3.094)	(0.932)	(−3.700)
COMP	14372.2	−144348.6*	−45154.3	31570.7***
	(0.943)	(−1.860)	(0.562)	(3.377)
Unit Labour Cost (ULC)	0.046**	−0.048	0.0843	−0.001
	(2.439)	(−1.612)	(0.822)	(−0.037)
Patents (PAT)	29.928**	34.962	−1.004.7	−33.572***
	(−2.095)	(0.895)	(−1.604)	(−3.893)
R&D	−7118.2***	−5327.8	−9713.7	4246.3***
	(−3.263)	(−1.246)	(−1.650)	(3.203)
FDI stock	−0.012	−0.001	−0.220**	−0.008
	(−0.872)	(−0.080)	(−2.339)	(−0.405)
No. of observations	233	76	43	114

*** significant at 1%   ** significant at 5%   * significant at 10%

Notes:
1. 2SLS regressions with two-way fixed effects. Using White's VC matrix for robust standard errors. T-ratios in brackets.

Table 5.2 Determinants of Japanese FDI in Europe 1981–2001[1]

	Full sample	Core	Periphery	Intermediate
GDP	0.000	0.000	0.000	0.000
	(0.124)	(0.431)	(0.192)	(1.491)
PERCAP	0.030	0.076	–0.047	0.005
	(1.109)	(1.033)	(–1.261)	(0.544)
OPEN	935.6**	2723.5	–894.8	348.9**
	(2.253)	(1.456)	(–1.094)	(2.423)
COMP	–2451.7	–25731.8**	–210.7	–22.4
	(–1.193)	(–2.992)	(–0.188)	(–0.028)
Unit Labour	–331.04	1026.31	320.62	–66.77
Cost (ULC)	(–0.521)	(0.943)	(0.566)	(–0.186)
Patents (PAT)	0.737	–4.530	3.176	–0.377
	(0.285)	(–0.527)	(0.870)	(–0.286)
R&D	–53.22	1970.40**	647.44*	63.03
	(–0.194)	(1.968)	(1.721)	(0.466)
FDI stock	0.000	0.001	0.000	0.000
	(0.199)	(0.461)	(0.062)	(0.229)
Constant	304.7	5353.5	621.3	–409.8
	(0.306)	(1.477)	(0.629)	(–0.888)
R^2	0.124	0.184	0.587	0.182
No. of observations	230	84	44	102

*** significant at 1%   ** significant at 5%   * significant at 10%

Notes:
1. OLS with two-way random effects. Using White's VC matrix for robust standard errors. T-ratios in brackets.

The presumption of relatively late entry into the European market by Japanese MNEs suggests the scope to make location decisions that can reflect the mature processes of integration and the established positioning of individual economies in this. The positive relationship with OPEN indicated by this is found to be significant across the full sample and intermediate countries sub-sample, and also approaches positive significance for the core group. It is, however, surprisingly negatively signed in the periphery sub-sample. For the intra-EU FDI sub-sample, on the other hand, it is for the periphery group of countries that OPEN proves a significantly positive variable.[10] For the full sample and the intermediate group of countries OPEN emerges as significantly negative, though earlier results would not suggest that this relates to the systemic presence of residual MS.

Table 5.3 Determinants of intra-EU FDI 1981–2001

	Full samples	Core	Periphery	Intermediate
GDP	0.041	0.036	0.084	−0.066
	(1.121)	(1.202)	(1.584)	(−0.997)
PERCAP	0.190	−30.922*	17.278***	−0.384
	(0.215)	(−1.984)	(3.784)	(−0.392)
OPEN	−101896.9**	−31940.0	168552.4***	−125392.9**
	(−2.458)	(−0.490)	(9.414)	(−2.187)
COMP	259721.6	−1522862.4*	−389163.9***	369099.7**
	(1.609)	(−1.817)	(−7.566)	(2.081)
Unit Labour	0.231	0.009	12.142***	0.232
Cost (ULC)	(1.548)	(0.049)	(3.540)	(0.739)
Patents (PAT)	22.678	690.725*	34.233	−234.587
	(0.320)	(1.672)	(0.060)	(−1.656)
R&D	11242.5	100423.3*	45417.5***	25776.1
	(1.076)	(1.993)	(3.658)	(1.228)
FDI stock	−0.011	−0.262	−12.363***	−0.120
	(−0.093)	(−1.243)	(−3.632)	(−0.409)
No. of observations	211	72	35	104

*** significant at 1%   ** significant at 5%   * significant at 10%

Notes:
1. 2SLS with two-way fixed effects. Using White's VC matrix for robust standard errors. T-ratios in brackets.

If we seek a negative sign on ULC as indicative of where pure-ES is most prevalent as an MNE strategic motivation then our results prove somewhat unrewarding. For US FDI the only significant result is a positive relationship with ULC across the full sample. This could then be compatible with the alternative view of how these firms read ULC as an indicator when considering locations in a region with relatively high average levels of consumer income (and consumption ambitions) and predominantly established industrialized sectors and labor force. Thus ULC could be read as indicative of availability of skill levels to support quite advanced and sophisticated production processes. Then the significant positive result for US FDI across the full sample should reflect accessing of appropriately skilled labor, rather than the lowest-cost low-skill labor for routine production.[11]

Despite the suggestion of earlier interpretation that 'late-comer' Japanese FDI may be able to pursue some degree of network optimization in European supply this is not reflected in results for ULC in this sample. Thus the negative sign for the full sample is too far from significant to be reliably indicative of an EU-wide networking of pure-ES operations. Positive signs prevail in the intra-EU sample and approaches significance for the full sample. This would broadly match the interpretation of the US result, suggesting attempts to access distinctive quality, rather than low-cost, labor. The fact that the positive sign actually achieves significance in the periphery is then surprising, however.

Our variable COMP was designed as a measure of the revealed competitiveness of an economy. This might indeed include the ability to export mature and standardized goods through very cost-effective production, but should also encompass a wider range of competitive attributes (including skilled and distinctively talented labor as suggested in the alternative interpretation of ULC). To the extent that MNE supply-side location decisions seek a wider range of competitive attributes COMP could serve as a useful catch-all proxy. This appears to be most effective within the intermediate group of countries, where COMP is significantly positive in both US and intra-EU sub-samples (though very weak for Japanese). Across the full sample COMP is also positively signed, and close to significant, for the intra-EU sub-sample and also positive, but less close to significance, for US. Elsewhere COMP is significantly negative in the 'core' group for all three 'origin' samples, and also for 'periphery' in intra-EU. In these cases the location attributes that drive economy-wide competitiveness do not appear to be those sought by MNEs as determinants of their FDI decisions.

Of our KS-related variables R&D can be interpreted as a forward-looking input measure indicative of a country's commitment to generation of new sources of competitiveness. We could, indeed, see it as proxying a country's attempt to create a national system of innovation, into which an MNE may seek to embed part of its longer-term commitment to dispersed learning and innovation. For the US FDI sample it is quite surprising then to find that R&D is significantly negative across the full sample of countries and also negative (short of significance) for both 'core' and 'periphery'. Only for the intermediate grouping is R&D significantly positive, in a way that suggests the presence of an embedded commitment to KS.

The presence of KS, as indicated by R&D, is more prevalent in the Japanese sample, being significantly positive for both 'core' and 'periphery' sub-samples. This is equally true for intra-EU with 'core' and 'periphery' again both significantly positive, and intermediate and full sample also positively signed (short of significance). This result for intra-EU may be particularly notable since there could have been a myopic tendency for European MNEs to keep KS, and learning and innovation, in their home countries, with less openness to dispersed locations than for firms from outside Europe.

The alternative, patent (PAT), KS variable is an output measure, reflective of past research and innovation success, and perhaps therefore indicative of more immediate shorter-term potentials for tapping into existing technological opportunities. Here PAT is significant across the full sample of countries for US FDI, suggesting this type of KS is activated more in technologically advanced countries (core positively signed but insignificant) than in technologically weak ones (periphery negatively signed but not significant). For the intermediate group here PAT is significantly negative (compared to significantly positive for R&D). PAT is insignificant throughout the Japanese FDI sample, which suggests the KS aims of these MNEs are of the more long-term types reflected in R&D. For intra-EU FDI the only significant result is the positive sign in the 'core' country sub-sample, supporting the similar result for R&D and thereby adding to the impression of European MNEs' willingness to disperse KS operations in the community.

The control variable of FDI stock lagged by one year is mostly insignificant throughout the tests. This suggests that FDI investment decisions are usually made in pursuit of precise strategic aims and not merely reflexive incremental extensions of existing stocks. The notable exceptions are the significant negative results for the periphery sub-samples for both US and intra-EU FDI. One element in this may be a crowding-out effect, such that MNEs from these origins see levels of FDI in these periphery countries as having reached magnitudes that remove plausible further potentials for production-cost benefits from locating there. Alongside this the presumption of existing routine cost-effective supply as the main role of established FDI in the periphery may preclude any expectation of positive agglomeration learning spillovers from locating there.

Conclusions

All three sub-samples tend to support the view that MNEs now see Europe as an integrated market, with few signs of FDI decisions responding positively to *national* market characteristics. As might be expected MS variables are most consistently insignificant for Japanese FDI, mainly entering Europe with integration and a single-market well established.[12]

There are then relatively few indicators of purely low-cost-oriented ES emerging as an alternative strategic priority, however. Thus ULC is never significantly negative. Where it is positively significant (in the full-sample for US FDI and, most surprisingly, in the periphery subsample for intra-EU FDI), we can suggest the alternative of higher-wage-cost being indicative of skilled and talented (and thus, perhaps, KS-oriented) human capital. Similarly the results for COMP are by no means suggestive of FDI entering economies with a current international competitiveness; more often the contrary in fact. This suggests that if MNE location decisions are oriented to support of their current supply the location attributes they are seeking are not those that appear to be generating economies' current trade performance.

Though the results are again somewhat mixed there is, in the main, support for an increased role for KS in MNE location decisions in the integrating, but diversified, EU. Interestingly this seems most unequivocal in the Japanese FDI sample, where the significant positive results derive from the R&D variable. We would interpret this as strategically forward-looking, focusing FDI into economies that seem committed to building up strong future competitiveness through a well-supported national system of innovation. KS is also quite strongly asserted in the intra-EU FDI sample, amongst core locations for both measures and in the periphery by the R&D measure.

As a final, somewhat heroic, generalization, from an inevitably varied set of results, we can indicate very clear support for a move away from any sort of multi-domestic approach to MNE location in the EU. However, the precise context of the more integrated strategic approach to community-wide operations is rather less clear. But systematic building of pure-ES supply-networks is by no means evident. This may suggest that to the extent that price-competitive supply of mass-market goods to EU consumers is important to MNEs they may find external locations to still be most effective. The corollary of this, to some extent supportable from our results, would be that supply operations in the EU are becoming more interrelated with KS location characteristics of host-economies, in pursuit of higher-quality and more innovative goods for a more demanding customer base.

Notes

1 Also by 2000 only 26.6% of Ireland's population was in objective 1 regions and none in objective 2. This is below obvious 'core' candidates such as UK and France.
2 The first two stages of the IDP describe countries in the early stages of development with little involvement with FDI. This would not be descriptive of any of the EU countries covered here during the period of the study.

3 Providing, for example, the highest value in the EU for FDI stocks as a percentage of gross fixed capital formation (UNCTAD, 2002).
4 Outward FDI flows as a percentage of gross fixed capital rose from 4.0% in 1991–95 to 13.8% in 1996–2000 (UNCTAD, 2002).
5 The data were transformed into US dollars from Euros using the end-of-year exchange rate (OECD International Direct Investment Statistics), and was deflated using GDP deflator (OECD online statistics: National Accounts of OECD countries).
6 The study, in practice, covers 14 locations since Belgium and Luxembourg are treated as one region.
7 Here ULC, R&D and PAT are considered to be exogenous, while two year lags of GDP, PERCAP, OPEN, COMP and FDI stock are the instruments for the rest of the endogenous factors.
8 The weakness for PERCAP suggests lack of responsiveness to *qualitative* aspects of markets (tastes, etc.) which may again reflect relatively new investments that had not had time to generate an understanding of such differences. The same may apply to reading of supply-side potentials reflected in levels of PERCAP.
9 A very speculative interpretation of the significant negative sign on PERCAP for the 'core' sub-sample for intra-EU FDI may be offered. If it is assumed that most intra-core FDI emanates from its richer countries then market-adaptive MS FDI may be more rewarding the further a host-country's PERCAP deviates from that of the MNE's home economy.
10 This despite the apparent simultaneous presence of significant elements of market responsive MS.
11 The nearly significant negative sign on ULC in the core countries' sub-sample need not contradict this. Thus US MNEs may (as suggested by the positive sign across the full sample) seek the highest skill levels in core countries (the highest average ULC in that sample compared to intermediate and periphery), but then favor core locations that provide comparably skilled labor at lower wage costs.
12 The predominance of positive signs for OPEN in the Japanese FDI sample would be consistent with the absence of traditional MS influences on location. It might, though, be difficult to interpret the occasionally significant negative result for OPEN in the other two origin samples as indicative of systematic MS decision making.

6
To 'Almost See the World': Hierarchy and Strategy in Hymer's View of the Multinational

Robert Pearce and Marina Papanastassiou

Introduction

Hymer introduces one of the key texts of his later analysis (Hymer, 1970, p. 441) by adopting Robertson's view of firms as 'islands of conscious power in an ocean of unconscious cooperation'. Thus he suggests that MNCs 'are a substitute for the market as a method of organizing international exchange'. One mode of later analysis consonant with the latter view is, of course, internalization theory (Buckley and Casson, 1976; Hennart, 2000). As recent work has argued and documented (Horaguchi and Toyne, 1990; Pitelis, 2002; Casson, 1990), Hymer (1960/76, 1968) was himself fully cognizant of the issues raised by internalization analysis and of how Coase's formulations could be co-opted to resolve this area of MNC theorizing. This, then, predominantly addresses reasons why MNCs *reject* various markets for intermediate goods. Hymer, we argue here, was also concerned with the adopted alternative, in the sense of analyzing and questioning how and to what ends the 'conscious power' was exercised. Two strands of the analysis of his later years address this, in ways that to some degree reflect ideas now seen as central to the conceptual breakthroughs of the PhD research (Hymer, 1960/1976).

Firstly, one strand of Hymer's later argument emerges in the empirical analysis of the growth of the world's leading enterprises (Hymer and Rowthorn, 1970) and its interpretation of emerging patterns of internationalized oligopoly. This can be seen (Yamin, 2000, p. 65) as relating to the 'removal of conflict' explanation for MNC expansion found in the PhD. Secondly, other perspectives emerge in papers (Hymer, 1970, 1972a, b) which trace the emergence of MNCs as an organizational form and define their format as globally-segmented hierarchies. The ability of a dominant center to control such stratified hierarchies is seen to derive from the possession of centrally-derived 'advantages', and to reflect the need to retain dominance of their dispersed use and to appropriate the benefits from doing so.

In the next section we start our interpretation of this second strand of Hymer's later work by outlining his argument that the globalized hierarchical MNC serves to impose 'core' (home-country) control over a weakened and static poor-country 'hinterland'.

The hierarchical MNC and uneven development

Hymer develops his characterization of the MNC as a centralized hierarchical system of authority and control through two complementary lines of argument; applying respectively what he terms the laws of increasing firm size and of uneven development. In the first of these laws he describes the tendency for firm size to increase as the organizational form developed from the *workshop* of the industrial revolution, through the *factory* to the *national corporation* and from the *multidivisional corporation* to the *multinational corporation* (1970, pp. 442–3; 1972a, pp. 115–22; 1979, pp. 145–7). Though quantitative size *per se* affects parts of his argument Hymer, in fact, sees the most systematically influential aspects of this growth as qualitative.

We need not trace the detail of Hymer's exposition of the ever evolving organizational structures that led to the MNC of the mid-20th century. But what is crucial to those parts of his overall argument that are assessed here is his emphasis on the persistent need for ever more complex administrative structures to coordinate diverse activities and a larger centralized planning facility ('brain' in his favorite analogy) to organize growth and survival. Thus Hymer's narrative shows that each widening of the firm's base through new dimensions of product and/or geographical diversification also adds an extra level of administration, but with a unique 'all seeing' center still retaining ultimate control.

Having outlined the historical roots of a strongly hierarchical organization operating internationally Hymer moves the analysis to the normative level and the potential for uneven development. Thus it becomes vital 'to analyze the spatial dimension of the corporate hierarchy', in terms of effect 'on international specialization, exchange and income distribution' (1972a, p. 122). To develop his view that centralization of control in MNCs imposes a matching centralization of control within the global economy Hymer (1970, p. 442; 1972a, pp. 122–5) applies location theory to Chandler and Redlich's (1961) categorization of 'three levels of business administration, three horizons, three levels of task, and three levels of decision making...and three levels of policies'.

At the bottom of the hierarchical pyramid level-III is concerned with managing day-to-day operations of the MNC, keeping it going within an established framework of competitive aims and competences that it is not expected or entitled to change. Level-III activities are, therefore, the most widespread 'according to the pull of manpower, markets, and raw materials' (Hymer, 1972a, p. 124). Hymer accepts that MNCs' command of 'capital and technology and its ability to rationalize their use on a global scale' could help spread production more evenly over the world's surface. Thus it 'may well be a force for diffusing industrialization to the less developed countries and creating new centres of production' (1972a, p. 124).

The intermediate level-II is concerned with the coordination of the managers at level-III, essentially assuring the effective regional application of a particular part of a wider strategic framework that it does not help to formulate. The need for trained and skilled white-collar workers and effective communications infrastructure tended to lead certain cities to become regional centers for MNCs' level-II activity.

Level-I is then the apex of the pyramid, where top management, concerned with goal determination and strategic planning, sets the framework within which the lower levels operate. Even more than level-II these general offices tend to be concentrated in a very limited number of metropolitan centers where they have close access 'to the capital market, the media and the government' (Hymer, 1972a, p. 124).

Such a functional hierarchy in MNCs is then innately associated with the developmental stratification of the world economy (Hymer, 1970, p. 446; 1972a, pp. 124–5; Hymer and Resnick, 1971, pp. 493–4). The unique strategic-planning centers of an MNC will be located in one of a very small number of major capital cities. The most powerful and highly-rewarded MNC personnel will, therefore, be located there, providing spillover benefits in strengthening the competitive infrastructure and cultural life of these metropolises. A wider range of still powerful and influential secondary cities will host level-II HQs of MNCs, learning the strategic priorities from level-I and organizing their implementation throughout a significant regional component of the group's operations. Personnel here still possess distinctive tactical responsibility, in that they will need to address any problems relating to applying level-I strategies to the specific (market or production) conditions of their region. Finally, at level III, a very large number of facilities routinely fulfill particular production responsibilities in a strategically totally dependent status.

In the central metaphor of this part of his analysis Hymer (1970, p. 442; 1972a, pp. 120–1) suggests that while the 19th century Marshallian capitalist had 'ruled his factory from an office on the second floor' and the turn of century president of a national corporation might have been lodged on the seventh floor of a higher building, the managers of the MNCs that emerged in the second half of the 20th century 'rule from the top of skyscrapers; on a clear day they can almost see the world'.

Alongside the obvious income implications of MNCs' global hierarchy Hymer (1970, pp. 445–6; 1972a, p. 129; 1979, pp. 161–2) also indicates the presence of social (or psychological) forces that may suppress impetus toward independent local-economy development at level-II and, certainly, at level-III. The 'subsidiaries of MNCs are typically amongst the largest corporations in their country of operations and their top executives play an influential role in the political, social and cultural life of the host country' (1972a, p. 129). But these MNC personnel themselves only occupy strategically dependent positions in their group hierarchy and, it is implied, develop attitudes and mindsets that reflect their limited authority and decision scope. Yet the local government and elites respect these MNC personnel as informed and influential leaders (reflecting the global power of their *parent* MNCs) and thereby absorb the, in fact, submissive and unenterprising middle-management attitude. Therefore, Hymer argues, 'one can hardly expect such a country to bring forth the creative imagination needed to apply science and technology to the problems of degrading poverty' (1972a, p. 129).

Strategic diversity in the contemporary MNC

In his use of the two laws Hymer firstly distinguishes growth processes in firms that led to their eventually needing to become MNCs and, secondly, asserts that the organizational structures that are innate to the effective control of such geographically-dispersed operations will be decisively hierarchical. It is this view of MNCs' *organizational* format that is dominant in this phase of Hymer's work, since from it he is able to derive particular conclusions about the way in which a geographical stratification of the firms' operations affect issues of growth, development and equality/distribution. However, we can suggest that the implications of the growth of overseas operations in MNCs derive not only from how they are controlled, but also from what they do; i.e. how they fit into the (now globalized) *strategies* of these firms.

One important facet of the development of the study of MNCs subsequent to Hymer's work has been a growing focus on the role played by individual subsidiaries. An aspect of this is that what particular subsidiaries are required to do reflects a *range* of strategic motivations encompassed within an MNC's overall program for sustained international competitiveness.

Earlier work (Behrman, 1984, pp. 101–6; Dunning, 1993a, pp. 56–61; Manea and Pearce, 2004, pp. 3–5) has distinguished four strategic motivations that can be included within the scope of a subsidiary. The predominant early motive for firms' overseas operations was *natural resource (or primary product) seeking*. Indeed, Hymer himself saw this need as central to much of a first wave of US FDI in the late 19th and early 20th centuries, though he interprets this as being mainly a support for continued home-country competitiveness rather than a systematic harbinger of any more generalized global strategy.

By the time of Hymer's writing, in the early 1970s, we would now consider (Papanastassiou and Pearce, 1999, pp. 24–30; Pearce, 2001) the major motivation of FDI (i.e. the dominant subsidiary role) to have become *market-seeking* (MS). Here an MNE would have invested in a particular economy as the most effective way of supplying its existing products to the market of that country. The dominant conditioning factors for this were the continuation of high levels of developed country protection stemming from the interwar years, and import-substitution strategies implemented by many developing countries in their early industrialization programs.

By the 1970s, however, two forces were emerging that can now be seen to have fundamentally altered the competitive context for MNCs and to have required a broadening and refocusing of their subsidiaries' strategic positioning. Firstly, the moves towards regional and global free-trade agreements removed the essential protectionist support for (usually inefficient) MS facilities. Secondly, an increasing range of countries emerged as possessors of high-quality and distinctive scientific and technological capacities alongside other types of creative scope (e.g. insightful market-research detecting unique local product needs and ideas). These two factors manifested themselves in two additional strategic motivations in MNCs.

Firstly, *efficiency-seeking* (ES) in which an MNC's operations in a particular location are expected to supply certain parts of the group product range to its international markets in a highly cost-competitive manner. Here, of course, emerging freedom of trade is now seen positively as allowing MNCs to build competitive global supply networks. Secondly, *knowledge-seeking (KS)*, in which MNCs respond to growing international scientific and market heterogeneity by decentralizing and networking their learning, technology-generation and creative processes. Central to

KS have been increasingly globalized approaches to R&D and innovation in MNCs.

The next three sections address two questions. Firstly, to what extent and in which ways did Hymer perceive the possibilities of ES and KS behavior in the periphery (level-II and level-III) operations of MNCs? Secondly, how does an MNC that encompasses significant ES and, especially, KS behavior (as well as residual elements of the two earlier motivations) differ from Hymer's hierarchy?

Global supply networks-efficiency-seeking

In a section on 'the dynamics of corporate expansion' Hymer (1972b, pp. 95–6) indicates how capitalism gains its forward momentum from the twin competitive priorities that constitute the 'dialectic of the product cycle'. Through a successful innovation a business enterprise builds its immediate growth and profitability 'around some special discovery or advantage.'[1] This new product then succeeds by both attracting new customers and by displacing other longer-established goods. This quasi-monopoly position is, however, itself inherently vulnerable to both market saturation and 'new entrants who may discover a new technology, a new product, a new form of organization, or a new supply of labour.' Once the initial profitability has attracted rivals with alternative technologies or product variants production costs begin to dominate, especially where the newcomers are prepared to accept a lower rate of profit or can utilize a source of cheaper labor.

There are then two ways of dealing with this competitive threat. Firstly, by pursuing a new source of high-profit-margin growth through new products; i.e. by, in effect, institutionalizing the process of innovation. Secondly, by prolonging the original product cycle by secrecy (i.e. slowing diffusion of the competitive advantage) and/or 'by gaining control of marketing outlets, searching for and moving to places of cheaper labor'. The latter, of course, also serves to facilitate the former, since a wider market spreads the costs of innovation and allows more to be spent on R&D. Thus successful large-scale cost-efficient supply of existing products not only moves these goods towards the vulnerable stage of their cycle but (dialectically) supports the parallel commitment to creation of their successors. For Hymer, therefore, 'the incessant revolutions in production and the depreciation of the existing capital [that] this implies spur them on to new methods and new places' (1972b, p. 96). From this Hymer defines three motives for international expansion. Firstly, the rapid growth of the *markets* for the goods in which the firm specialized. Secondly, *cheaper* (i.e. more cost-effective) *labor* which made overseas production more profitable. Thirdly, the assertive growth of *foreign competitors*.

Up to his time of writing, however, Hymer had not observed significant separation between the markets and the labor supply in US MNCs' strategies. Thus it was specifically European and Japanese markets, their competitive emergent firms and (with the transfer of people between agriculture and industry and out of declining industries) a growing and productive labor supply *in* those locations, that provided the integral focus for the initial MS expansion of these US firms. But looking forward to the 1970s and 1980s Hymer (1972b, pp. 97–8) most precisely (and presciently) predicts changes in, in particular, MNCs' strategic accessing of labor. In Europe and Japan labor shortages were beginning to emerge, whilst in the US 'resistance to work seems about to reach acute proportions from capital's point of view'.[2] In the face of this firms from all these developed regions were beginning to look towards an untapped cheap-labor supply in the Third World. This large surplus of potential industrial labor, he suggested, was readily accessible to foreign enterprise, since the local capitalist class was weak (in reflection of the restraints that had been placed on it during the colonial period.) In the early stages MNCs had employed local labor in developing countries as part of MS import-substitution strategies, thereby replicating their position in developed countries in the sense of not separating the market and efficiency objectives. But by the early 1970s Hymer saw these low-cost-labor operations turning to expansion of exports.[3] In this they were becoming parts of globalized networks through which MNCs were increasingly addressing the current-supply part of their survival strategies.

Interestingly, though, Hymer did not seem to expect the competitive exhaustion of these country-level cost advantages and then 'footloose' migration of MNCs, since they would instead exploit these 'sources of future growth...in an oligopolistic rather than a cutthroat way...[recognizing] their mutual interdependencies and [striving] to share in the pie without destroying it' (1972b, p. 98). Elsewhere in his exposition (Hymer, 1972b, p. 105), however, he does see the development of ES supply networks as a threat to *advanced country* workers, with the growth of international competition placing the burden of adjustment on labor.[4]

Innovation and R&D – knowledge-seeking

Hymer adopts a strongly centralized view of the innovation process (1970, pp. 444–5; 1972a, pp. 125–6) but then finds particular benefits to

MNCs from the way new goods 'trickle down' to dispersed markets through 'an international demonstration effect spreading outward from the metropolis to the hinterland' (1972a, p. 125). Indeed speeding this process can be a significant motive for direct investment, through MNCs' control of marketing channels and communication media. Hymer sees the companies gaining two types of benefit from this.

The first relates to the characteristics of the competitive advantage which provides the MNC with the ability to expand internationally. Thus the development of a new product, through the high expenditures of innovation and invention, is a very substantial fixed cost but, once the 'ownership advantages' that define this new source of competitiveness are fully defined, they can be applied at very low marginal cost. With the actual cost of production, therefore, usually well below selling price, the problem of growth is likely to be that of finding new markets (rather than rising costs). Then 'the marginal profit on new foreign markets is thus high, and corporations have a strong interest in maintaining a system which spreads their products widely'.

Secondly, the trickle-down system is also seen as helping the center to reinforce patterns of authority and control. Thus when, after some period of delay, people in subordinate countries in the global hierarchy do receive new goods (through MNC marketing and production) this provides them with an illusion of upward mobility, even though their *relative* position actually remains unchanged.[5] From this 'it is little wonder' (Hymer comments) 'that those at the top stress growth rather than equity' (1972a, p. 125).

In the positioning of innovation Hymer also acknowledges the Schumpeterian association of oligopoly with the dynamic dimensions of competition, in which 'creative destruction' allows for the introduction of new technology and new products. Even where an oligopolistic market structure may interfere with static optimal resource allocation it may contribute to dynamic optimum allocation in a private enterprise system. It may, thus, provide a competitive situation in which innovators can capture some of the benefits of their inventions and thereby underpin the incentives for R&D expenditures and programs. Then 'one can expect international oligopoly via MNCs to provide the same kind of dynamic environment for the world economy as a whole' (1970, p. 444). Nevertheless Hymer doubts whether this situation is likely to allow consumers to choose from the full range of inventive/innovative options possible. Only a large number of independent decision centers would allow all creative avenues to be explored.

As an alternative to 'trickle down' of centralized developed-country innovations through MNCs, Hymer envisages 'a regime of national firms (private or socialized)...[so that] the pattern of output would almost certainly be quite different than the one that is now observed. There would be more centers of innovation and probably more variety of choices offered to the consumers, as each country developed different products suited to its particular characteristics' (1970, p. 445). The scope of choice would then be further extended when the products from one country would be able to spread to other countries through trade or imitation in a manner that is 'coordinated by market competition rather than the planning decision of top management in a few corporations whose interest it is to foreclose competition, to restrict the choice offered, and to insure the survival of their own organization'. Overall Hymer believes 'it does not appear to be socially efficient to allow corporations to monopolise information on new possibilities created by science' (1970, p. 445).

Nevertheless, much of the dispersed creativity Hymer prescribes has, after all, emerged from *within MNCs* over perhaps the past three decades, as they have moved toward globalized approaches to innovation and the generation and accessing of new technology (KS behavior). Thus MNC innovation has become much more decentralized, with many locations emerging as capable of developing new products and with these new goods distributed globally within, often internally-competitive, group networks. At an idealized level this could improve the capability of countries to develop internationally competitive goods reflecting distinctive local creative capacities (R&D; technology; market-research perceptions), increase the range of goods available to consumers worldwide and, at the same time, allow for increased responsiveness to distinctive localized tastes and conditions (including regulatory regimes).[6] Of course, this geographical extension of innovation programs in MNEs only spreads into countries as and when they achieve relatively high levels of development. However, as we describe below, the competitive dynamics in contemporary MNCs can provide level-III (developing-country) subsidiaries that have ES responsibilities with the scope to pursue product upgrading and competence enriching processes that move them towards a tipping point (creative transition) where they can embrace full product development (and attain level-II positioning).

Central to MNCs' move to globalized innovation strategies has been the emergence of product mandate subsidiaries. Such product mandates (PM) receive formal authorization (the mandate)[7] from the parent company to take full responsibility for the development, initial supply, marketing and further competitive evolution of a particular product. The mandate is secured on the basis of product ideas and creative inputs (R&D; engineering; marketing) available to the subsidiary from its local environment. PMs, thereby, leverage for their MNC's global competitiveness a range of local competences. Crucial to the genesis of PMs is dynamic, perceptive and ambitious local management, pulling together the concepts and competences to back a claim for this high-value role. Indeed, whereas Marshallian owners/managers of individual factories had used their talent to secure success in their *external* markets, in the contemporary PM-type subsidiary entrepreneurial (Birkinshaw, 1997, 2000) local managers now secure their subsidiary's enhanced role and strategic positioning through successful lobbying[8] in the *internal* 'marketplace' of an heterarchical MNC (Birkinshaw, 1996, 1998b).

The emergence of PMs, usually as the result of a 'creative transition'[9] in existing MS or ES subsidiaries, has important implications for the organization and implications of MNCs. This subsidiary-level transformation moves the level-III dependency of MS or ES to the PM's acquisition of what can be considered as a more contemporary form of level-II status. The PMs take a distinct *strategic* responsibility for a particular geographic and/or product segment of an MNC's global operations. They thus do much more than the earlier level-II subsidiaries' implementation of a centrally-determined strategy. Though PMs do remain ultimately dependent on centralized permission to implement, and persist with, the generation and application of their own competences, this nevertheless changes the nature of the authority and control exercised by the level-I parent companies. Ultimately the interjection of PMs into MNCs' global networks quite fundamentally subverts the earlier three-level view of a vertical hierarchy.

In a similar vein Yamin and Forsgren (2006) note that the emergence of locally-embedded subsidiaries leads logically to 'federative' rather than hierarchical MNCs. Hymer's failure to foresee this also caused him, they suggest, to fail to perceive the threat to centralized 'power retention' and control over strategy in MNCs 'emanating from embedded subsidiaries'. Had he done so, Yamin and Forsgren argue, 'he would have recognized the rationale for limiting the MNE's geographical scope'. This leads them to an endorsement of Rugman's (2003) view of a current prevalence of 'regional' (rather than globally-federative) MNCs.

The concept of PMs involves a creative interdependence between a subsidiary and the more dynamic, development-oriented, elements of its host economy. This can counter Hymer's fear of a submissive and dependent subsidiary-level mindset inculcating and reinforcing stagnation and lack of developmental initiative in poor countries. Thus (Papanastassiou and Pearce, 1999, pp. 18–19) 'our interpretation of the contemporary MNE as a flexible and dynamic heterarchy can be seen to provide local executives with the scope to take a more positive view of host-country potentials and of their own ability to benefit from activating them within evolving group-level programs. The interface between MNE executives and local decision makers *can* then be one of mutually-supportive development rather than one of shared resignation and defeatism.'

We noted earlier that Hymer's view of anti-competitive behavior of MNCs in oligopoly removed concern about 'footloose' closure by subsidiaries in low-wage economies. However, contemporary critiques of MNC behavior in the intensified competition of globalization do raise such concerns. Thus it is suggested that though the setting up of ES subsidiaries in labor-abundant low-wage economies can initiate development by generating many new jobs this will be a transitory benefit. Once effective growth leads to full-employment and rising real wages (and other input costs), this argument suggests, MNCs will close these ES operations and exercise the footloose option to move jobs elsewhere, thereby hollowing out the development process. It can be argued though that this need not happen (Pearce, 2001). If the development process improves local capabilities, notably in terms of human capital (training, retraining, improved education systems, ultimately a strong science and technology base) then MNCs can restructure (rather than remove) their subsidiaries and become an embedded part of a sustainable evolutionary process (Young and Hood, 1994; Young *et al.*, 1988).

Alongside the growth of interest in creative subsidiaries (Pearce, 1999b) another emerging concern of the analysis of MNCs over the past 30 years has been the globalization of their R&D strategies. One strand of this emphasizes the different roles dispersed R&D labs can play for MNCs and the different types of work they can do (Ronstadt, 1977; Behrman and Fischer, 1980; Haug *et al.*, 1983; Pearce, 1999a; Pearce and Papanastassiou, 1999). Though not systematically discussed in terms of geographical hierarchy[10] Hymer (1979, pp. 156–7)[11] offers some insights on the 'peculiar features' of the research function that prefigure the later perspectives. At the lowest level some research is 'done at the plant level almost as a by-product of the manufacturing process'. At an intermediate level of scientific complexity research results need to 'be channelled into the highest levels of management where they can be coupled with marketing functions in an overall strategy for product development' (1979, p. 157). Finally, Hymer sees the 'higher levels of research' as concentrated in research centers away from firms' offices at central cities. This is to allow specialized professionals the autonomy to exercise their own scientific judgment; though, as just noted, mechanisms are also needed to pull their work towards practical innovation. In a way that anticipates later ideas on knowledge-driven clusters (Porter, 1998; Cantwell and Iammarino, 1998; Howells, 1999; Balasubramanyam and Balasubramanyam, 2000) Hymer also observes the importance in basic science of scientists being 'in contact with other scientists and act as "open cells" receiving and absorbing knowledge generated at the frontiers of science'.

Recent analysis has raised concerns regarding the implications of MNCs accessing selected elements of *national* systems of innovation as part of their global R&D and innovation strategies, whose results and benefits may then spread worldwide and not directly benefit countries (or local institutions) that contribute to them. Elements of this concern are suggested by Hymer (1979, p. 157). Even when the research function is located away from the 'high-density commercial centers' it is these centers to which it ultimately owes its allegiance and with which it communicates systematically 'rather than its local community [so that] it forms an enclave rather than an integrated part of the local economy'.

Heterarchy

The emergence of ES and PM subsidiaries can now be seen to have fundamentally changed MNCs' organizational structures. Initially, at a point in time, the coordination of variegated ES subsidiaries into a network actually makes hierarchical control more powerful and decisive than it would have been when most subsidiaries played the MS role. What goods a particular ES subsidiary produces, in what quantities and to which other part of the network it supplies them, will be determined by a regional or global (essentially, in Hymer's terms, a level-II) coordinating center. However, such supply-network centers also need a much greater awareness of heterogeneity in level-III operations (different ES subsidiaries producing different goods reflecting different capacities in their host economies) and ultimately to understand forces for change in the network's configuration. Thus, even whilst retaining generic ES-status (i.e. before any creative transition to a PM), subsidiaries can develop by taking on supply of higher-value-added parts of an MNC-group's existing product range (Pearce, 2001). As skill levels improve in a country (better education and training) an ES subsidiary can improve its position by securing higher productivity technologies to produce better quality goods. Thus the relationship between an ES management and its coordinating center should move away from submissive dependency, with subsidiaries allowed to lobby for accession to higher status *within* the existing network.

Once PM operations become part of MNCs' globalized scope the organizational challenges that took a muted status within hierarchical control of ES networks become more strident. The value of PMs to MNCs is precisely an allowance for locally-driven dynamism, the leveraging for group benefit of idiosyncratic creative capacities internalized from the local economy. This is beyond hierarchical control. Such units cannot be left totally beyond supervision, but too much control must not suppress the intrinsic generation of unique capacities that can only be effectively motivated by an entrepreneurial local management activating an internally-cohesive range of functional scopes. Thus a PM's value is its *individualism* in the form of distinctive new subsidiary-level knowledge and the managerial drive to take initiatives based around it. But this must contribute to the coherent progress of the MNC group and not proceed in directions that may unbalance overall strategic scope or that the subsidiary may not have the in-house capacities to fully develop (Pearce, 1999a). 'A degree of *interdependency* has to be retained that then supports the subsidiary and/or provides benefits to the group, but does not in the process stifle the subsidiary's capacity to exercise its creative scope' (Papanastassiou and Pearce, 1999, p. 43). The generation, supervision and monitoring of such mutually-supportive interdependencies between dispersed creative activities in MNCs becomes the new role of HQs.[12]

The new world of MNC differentiation and organization has been influentially categorized by Hedlund (1986, 1993) as a heterarchy. This has been formally defined (Hedlund and Rolander, 1990, p. 15) as constituting 'a geographical diffusion of core strategic activities and coordinating roles, a break with the notion of one uniform hierarchy of decisions as well as organization positions, and an increased focus on normative control mechanisms'. From Hedlund and Rolander's (1990, pp. 25–6) full listing of the characteristics of heterarchy, six reflect on points covered here.

Firstly, there are 'many centers, of different kinds', with traditional HQ functions increasingly 'geographically diffused, and no dimension (product, country, function) uniformly superordinate'. This dispersion of key scopes requires a 'structure that is flexible over time' so that 'the heterarchical firm does not need to worry too much about logical consistency, but instead focuses on practical coherence'. This provides the basis for the second characteristic of 'a strategic role for foreign subsidiaries', which operates 'for the corporation as a whole [so that] corporate level strategy has to be both formulated and implemented in a geographically scattered network'.

Thirdly, the heterarchical MNC uses 'a wide range of governance modes between pure market and hierarchy'. Indeed Birkinshaw and Morrison (1995, p. 737) observe that 'a heterarchical MNC could easily have certain subsidiaries that were controlled in a "hierarchical" (i.e. bureaucratic) manner'. As we noted earlier this would encompass control and coordination of subsidiaries that continue to play an ES role. Fourthly, heterarchical MNCs encourage 'coalitions with other firms and with other types of actors...in order to utilize potentials for synergy in the global environment'. Fifthly, the heterarchical MNC encourages 'radical problem orientation, rather than starting from existing resources, or from competitive positions in narrow fields of business' so that, finally, they need 'action programs for seeking and generating new firm-specific advantages through global spread'.

Elaborating the last point Hedlund and Rolander (1990, p. 26) comment that 'exploitation of given, home country based advantage is emphasized in the theory of the MNC, but this should not entrap the MNC in its action'. In a similar vein Hymer (1968, p. 24) notes a dual benefit to the internalized use of 'ownership advantages' in overseas operations. This not only achieves security and control over current sources of competitiveness, but also enables an MNC to 'at the same time get indications about future developments'. Through formation of a MNC 'the firm enters into direct and immediate communication with the foreign market and so receives a continuous flow of information about local conditions that it can use to develop new products and improve its overall position as seller, buyer and producer.'

In fact Hymer quite explicitly recognized that, by the early 1970s, the electronic and transport revolutions, which were greatly reducing the cost of communications, opened up the possibility for much more flexible, less determinate and dependent, organizational structures in MNCs. The new technology, of itself, certainly did not impose hierarchy but instead would allow communication linkages to be arranged in a grid in which all parts *could* connect to each other. The *de facto* limitation to only vertical communication links in hierarchy constituted an organizational *choice* to impose 'a ritual judicial asymmetry on the use of intrinsically symmetrical means of communications and arbitrarily creates unequal capacities to initiate and terminate exchange, to store and retrieve information, and to determine the extent of the exchange and the terms of the discussion' (Hymer, 1972a, p. 126). This centrally-determined hierarchical choice served precisely to strengthen central control[13] by (as for earlier colonial powers) weakening peripheral operations, by preventing lateral communications and inhibiting the growth of independent centers of creativity and decision making. Alternatively, Hymer predicted (1972a, p. 126), if lateral as well as vertical communication was permitted then each point in the MNC could 'become a center on its own; and the distinction between center and periphery would disappear'. This is, indeed, the heterarchical world.

Conclusions

The central breakthrough of Hymer's PhD research can be seen (Dunning and Rugman, 1985) as the inadequacy of attempts to explain FDI flows at a macro level, and the need to place explanations of the international operations of firms at the micro level. In thereby initiating the analysis of MNCs Hymer also supplied the foundation insights of 'possession of advantages' and 'removal of conflict'. In terms of the analysis of the *effects* of FDI Hymer's ideas were reflected in a movement away from a purely capital movement approach (MacDougall, 1960) to the assessment of a 'package' of resource flows. Important perceptions then emerged (e.g. Dunning, 1994a) from a 'gap-filling' approach (Pearce, 2001) in which MNCs' technology, management and marketing techniques, etc., as well as capital, provided the potential to close resource gaps that were holding back the developmental potentials of host countries. An alternative approach (Pearce, 2006) has indicated that the implications of MNCs' behavior can be traced to the understanding of *why* resources are moved; i.e. the motivations reflected in firms' global strategies. This paper has found the roots of that approach in Hymer's assessment of the MNC as a globally-stratified hierarchy.

Two key presumptions underpinning Hymer's view of MNC organizational structures were decisively-centralized innovation and a predominantly market-seeking positioning of subsidiaries (or, at least, the absence of systematically-integrated efficiency-seeking supply networks). Our interpretation of subsequent developments in MNCs focused around changes in both these circumstances, leading to the emergence of heterarchy as the overriding organizational form. But we have also indicated that Hymer was aware of at least two of these developments, at least as possibilities. Firstly, he foresaw the eventual separation of where goods were produced and where they were sold in MNCs' supply networks (i.e. ES). Secondly, he acknowledged that alternatives to the vertical referral of hierarchy were technologically available and, in effect, suppressed in the interests of a controlling center. The weakening of central control and the emergence of heterarchy, that derived from MNCs' need to internalize increasingly dispersed creative capacities (including entrepreneurial subsidiary management), was not foreseen, however.

Hymer, the preceding points suggest, sees hierarchy not as the natural or immutable form of MNC organization, but as one *chosen* and *imposed* by core country (level-I) decision makers to centralize the benefits of a stratified global economy. In this he may well have been overrating its ideological bases, and underrating the pragmatism of late 20th century capitalist enterprise. Nevertheless providing the first holistic attempt to relate MNCs to global political economy is one of the enduring and undervalued aspects of Hymer's work.

Notes

1 This, of course, correlates to Hymer's (1960/76) earlier insight that firms seeking to become MNCs would need to possess a unique form of firm-specific comparative advantage. This was developed analytically as the ownership-advantage element of Dunning's (1977, 2000) eclectic paradigm.
2 This could reflect a particularly '1960s' influence on Hymer's thinking, as may the terminology (1972b, p. 97) that 'the greening of Europe is about to begin'.
3 Hymer (1972b) explicitly prescribes the desirability of an export-oriented strategy for underdeveloped countries. If they 'aimed at producing a bundle of basic consumption goods on a mass scale, they could increase employment and reduce the worst aspects of poverty. They could use technology that has been known for decades and less capital per unit of output would be required because of long production runs and standardized output. They would have little need for multinational corporations whose special advantages for the most part lie in differentiated products and new goods'.
4 The departure of the textile industry from the Northern US led to 'a cycle of depressed areas and depopulation [that]...might now be occurring on a world scale'. When 'capital leaves one group of workers for another, in a process resembling slash and burn agriculture, the advanced group is forced to lie fallow in unemployment for use later when their resistance has been weakened' (Hymer, 1972b, p. 105).
5 Hymer comments that if subordinates 'look forward and compare their standards of living through time, things seem to be getting better; if they look upwards they see their relative position has not changed' (1972a, p. 125).
6 For more detailed evaluation of this idealized potentiality see Pearce (2002).

7   Such subsidiaries were originally detected in US firms' operations in Canada (Rugman, 1983; Rugman and Bennett, 1982; Rugman and Douglas, 1986; Poynter and Rugman, 1982; Crookell and Morrison, 1990) and subsequently included in wider typologies of subsidiary roles (D'Cruz, 1986; Pearce, 1989, 2001). Recent analyses have systematically investigated the positioning of PMs in MNCs' overall strategic development (Roth and Morrison, 1992; Birkinshaw and Morrison, 1995; Birkinshaw, 1996).
8   In an important contribution to the literature on subsidiary dynamics Birkinshaw and Hood (1997, 1998) distinguish between subsidiary, parent-company and host-country drivers in the process of subsidiary development.
9   The process of creative transition (Papanastassiou and Pearce, 1994, pp. 201–3; Chapter 2) is one where MS and ES subsidiaries, which had originally secured their role on the basis of host-country markets (MS) or supply characteristics (ES) and then been *allocated* the appropriate existing technology to play that role, then *create* their own original technology-based competences (through localized KS activity) and use this to *claim* their new individualized PM status. There is a transition from a situation (MS/ES) where the role determines the technology to one (PM/KS) where technology generates the role.
10 Though he does (1979, p. 141) comment on the competition between the middle classes of different countries for managerial and scientific jobs, including the locations of scientific facilities.
11 The quotes here are from a paper entitled 'The multinational corporation and the international division of labour', which was first published in an abridged version in French in 1971. The full English text was made available, as cited here, in the 1979 collected papers.
12 For a subsidiary to commit resources and risk its intra-group goodwill in developing and putting forward a case for PM status, it needs to expect fair and informed judgment from a central management known to be capable of taking an open and flexible view of change in the group. Thus the perceived availability of procedural justice (Kim and Mauborgne, 1991, 1993; Taggart, 1997, 1999b) is crucial.
13 This is achieved (Hymer, 1979, p. 155) by strong horizontal communication at level-I (the core of the MNC) 'so that important decision makers do not work at cross purposes but have an opportunity to exchange information and reconcile differences', and very limited horizontal links at level-III (periphery operations) 'so as to prevent alliances and interchanges that lead to actions counter to those prescribed by higher management'. Yamin and Forsgren (2006) discuss these organizational concerns of MNC, under the heading of 'divide and rule'.

7
Individualism and Interdependence in the Technological Development of MNEs: The Strategic Positioning of R&D in Overseas Subsidiaries

Marina Papanastassiou and Robert Pearce

Introduction

The growth of decentralized R&D in MNEs[1] is central to the ways these companies approach the new competitive pressures of the global economy of the late 20th century. As these companies seek to define positions for technology in the generation of sustained competitiveness, roles for overseas R&D laboratories can emerge at three distinct levels. In the short term, the pressures of global competition mean that MNEs need to produce their well-established products as effectively as possible. Laboratories operating within the subsidiaries that produce such products may support their operations by assisting in the adaptation of the manufacturing process to host-country conditions and of the products to local tastes. However, to carry competitiveness into the medium term MNEs need to substantially upgrade their product range, introducing new generations that embody new concepts that extend the industry's scope. As a weapon in global competition, such product innovation needs to embody clear international dimensions.[2] Though such radical evolution of product scope is still likely to embody substantial elements of the company's existing stock of knowledge (that is, remain within an established technological trajectory), these major operations in product development will also require the crucial addition of new technology inputs in order to operationalize this knowledge in the emerging commercial context. Since this context is now a global one, a vital role emerges for overseas R&D in taking these major steps in product development. On the supply side, overseas laboratories can provide new elements of technology that complement the group's initial stock in crucial ways, whilst on the demand side overseas laboratories work with other functions in local subsidiaries to make the process of product development responsive to specific market conditions.

Finally, in the long term, companies need to regenerate the core of their knowledge assets through substantial amounts of speculative research that is intended to provide eventually a basis for more fundamentally original new products that may perhaps ultimately even reflect an alteration in the direction of the technological trajectory of the firm or industry. In implementing programs of basic and applied research to cover such speculative possibilities, a wide range of scientific disciplines may need to be accessed, and in cases where the science bases of other countries provide the best traditions in relevant technological areas overseas laboratories in these countries will be a crucial facet of MNEs' pursuit of such knowledge expansion. Laboratories that play mainly this role often operate on a stand-alone basis, independent of any other (for example, manufacturing) activity of the parent MNE in the country in question (Pearce and Singh, 1992a).

In this chapter the predominant concern is with the first two of these levels of overseas R&D, and in particular with the way an extension of the R&D function within subsidiaries represents a key element in the transition from the dependent role of supplying established products to the individualistic (though still substantially interdependent) one of product development.[3] We investigate various aspects of the positioning of R&D in the activity of the subsidiaries of foreign MNEs operating in the UK through the results of a survey carried out in 1993/94. The questionnaire was sent to 812 such manufacturing subsidiaries, with satisfactory replies received from 190 of them.[4]

R&D and interdependent individualism

This chapter seeks to encompass two closely interrelated levels of investigation. The first of these assesses in general terms the positioning of R&D in MNE subsidiaries in the UK, looking at its prevalence, its roles and its motivation. The second focuses on the more detailed theme of the extent to which R&D contributes to the distinction between types of subsidiaries, and most explicitly its contribution to the emergence of those (world or regional mandate) subsidiaries which take responsibility for the development (as well as production and marketing) of parts of their MNE group's product range.

Whilst the quantitative intensity of international competition in most major industries places pressure on MNEs to produce their established products as cost-effectively as possible, qualitative elements of global heterogeneity also open up dynamic competitive perspectives which need to be accessed if these companies are to address the potentials of sustained progress and growth. Globally competing enterprises need to articulate their medium-term development through globalized programs of market responsiveness and knowledge acquisition and application. Overseas subsidiaries with an individualized creativity (product development mandates) can play crucial roles in the ways MNEs use global heterogeneity in a positive fashion. We may discern two ways in which this can occur. First, such subsidiaries may apply a new group-level technology to their own regional market (regional product mandate) by developing from it a distinctive product variant that fully responds to the relevant local tastes and characteristics. Though operating within a program that is defined by a new group-level technology, the subsidiaries that undertake this role need a high level of individualized R&D competence that can work with its marketing personnel to develop the distinctive product variant.

In the second alternative the subsidiary-level development may be more unique and self-contained, and therefore perhaps open up wider markets (a world product mandate). Here the new product concept, and the core elements of new technology, may emerge in an individualized subsidiary that then stakes its claim to responsibility for its full commercial development and world-wide supply. A key word here, however, may be responsibility (Pearce, 1989, 1992). Even where the crucial elements of the core technology emerge at the subsidiary level the capacity for its full elaboration is likely to be beyond the scope of most such national units. Access to supporting R&D inputs from elsewhere in the group may ensure the most effective completion of all facets of the new technology from the point of view of the subsidiary, and also encourage an optimal use of group-wide technological scope. Another factor in the use of such R&D interdependencies is that it helps to ensure that new technological possibilities can emerge, and be enthusiastically supported and nurtured at the subsidiary level, but with a clear group-level understanding of how these new dimensions relate to the MNE's overall technological trajectory.

An optimal use of these supportive elements in decentralized R&D in MNEs would allow the positive emergence and application of individualized creative scope to occur within mandated subsidiaries in ways that also augment the coherent progress of group-level technology. Valuable two-way interdependencies can be discerned. As already observed, the full elaboration of the new technological possibilities that emerge within one subsidiary may need complementary inputs from elsewhere in the group.

At the same time, elements of new subsidiary-level knowledge may not only support its own product development ambitions but also have the potential to enrich the technological scope of other subsidiaries that are working on other parts of the group's product range. Approaching globalized R&D through subsidiaries requires MNEs to be aware of the benefits of both individualism and interdependency. This also underlines that there is no longer likely to be a viable dichotomy between MNEs that adopt centralized or decentralized approaches to R&D. The logical aim now appears to be for extensive decentralized originality that remains open to centralized monitoring and evaluation in order to ensure that it supports the enrichment and coherent evolution of a clearly articulated group-level technological trajectory.

Our investigation of MNE subsidiaries in the UK discerned four possible roles that these might play.[5] Here these roles, and their relative importance in responding subsidiaries, are briefly introduced along with speculations as to their likely requirements for R&D support. The first subsidiary role was defined as 'to produce for the UK market products that are already established in our MNE group's product range' (ESTPROD/UK). Though we have suggested elsewhere (Pearce, 1999b) that, as would be expected in the context of globalized competition, this role is in relative decline, it still takes a prominent residual position amongst responding subsidiaries. Thus 8.1% of respondents felt this was their only role, 37.3% felt it took a predominant position, 27.0% believed it retained a secondary position and only 27.6% considered it played no part in their operations. In terms of the globalized technology perspectives of MNEs, these subsidiaries are likely to be highly dependent, concerned only to apply standardized (centrally created) technology to their own markets. Where in-house R&D plays a role then this is likely to be the very localized one of adapting technology that is already embodied in established products to host country conditions.

The second role was defined as 'to play a role in the MNE's European supply network by specializing in the production and export of part of the established product range' (ESTPROD/EUR). Overall this role was of similar relevance to the first with 3.2% of responding subsidiaries rating it their only one, 46.5% feeling it took a predominant position, 21.6% a secondary one and 28.6% considering it played no part in their activities. Since these ESTPROD/EUR subsidiaries operate in an externally determined position as constituents of centrally coordinated networks, in order to specialize in the production of limited parts of a well-established product range for supply to a wider geographical market area, there would seem less reason for them to have in-house R&D

than ESTPROD/UK. In the latter, reaction to a distinct local market with which they can generate close affinity is viable and beneficial. However, if individual ESTPROD/EUR subsidiaries are unlikely to need (or to be allowed – where they are expected to conform to a predetermined role in a cohesive network) R&D that is uniquely supportive of their own operations, the whole integrated European system of such facilities is likely to require such backing for adaptation of its received technology. It may then be decided to locate such network-supporting R&D units within one or more of the producing subsidiaries.[6] Overall this might suggest that ESTPROD/EUR subsidiaries are less likely to possess R&D units than ESTPROD/UK, but that where they do they may then be more substantial and powerful. Also, such R&D in ESTPROD/EUR subsidiaries would still be essentially dependent within the globalized technological perspectives of the MNE, but apply its work to regionalized aims (rather than the localized ones of ESTPROD/UK laboratories).

The third subsidiary role was defined as 'to play a role in the MNE group's European supply network by producing and exporting component parts for assembly elsewhere' (COMPART). Only 1.1% of respondents considered this their only role, and only 6.1% more felt it a predominant one, whilst 22.7% believed it was limited to a secondary role, and 70.2% did not play it at all. If this COMPART role is played within a network that is seeking cost-effective supply of well-established products it is unlikely to need in-house R&D support. However, such COMPART operations could be associated with subsidiaries that have mandates to develop new products for the European (or world) markets and may be closely involved in this creative process. In this case their own R&D unit could then be a strong asset in asserting an individualized position in supporting the operations of the mandated subsidiary.

The final subsidiary role defined for respondents was 'to develop, produce and market for the UK and/or European (or wider) markets new products additional to the MNE group's existing range' (DEVELPROD). The relative prevalence of this role is compatible with its emergence as a strong element in the heterogeneity of the contemporary MNE's approach to the global strategic environment. Thus 8.7% of respondents rated this their only role, 27.2% felt it a predominant one, 34.2% believed it took a secondary status, while 29.9% did not yet include it in their activity. We would clearly expect that the performance of the DEVELPROD role would be more likely to require in-house R&D support than any of the others. Also, in line with previous discussion, this R&D is expected to be central to the proactive positioning of these subsidiaries. Thus the ideal status of such subsidiaries may be one of interdependent individualism, fully exploiting distinctive creative attributes in (or accessible to) their operations but doing so in ways that also enhance (rather than disrupt) beneficial synergies with the logical evolution of group-wide scope. Laboratories in DEVELPROD subsidiaries thus enter the globalized technology perspectives of their MNEs in a much more positive way than those in the ESTPROD types of subsidiary, moving from dependency to the exercise of an individualism that will, to varying degrees and in various ways, be modulated by interdependencies with wider group creativity. From strong positions *within* the evolution of the group-level technological trajectory DEVELPROD laboratories may support either regionalized or globalized commercial objectives (Regional Product Mandate or World Product Mandate subsidiaries).

R&D in UK subsidiaries of MNEs

A question in the survey of UK-based MNE subsidiaries asked respondents to evaluate the importance to their operations of seven potential sources of technology.[7] One of these was defined as 'R&D carried out by our own laboratory'. As Table 7.1 shows, only 40.8% of respondents did not use the output of an in-house R&D unit as part of their technology scope, whilst 3.4% considered it the only source of their technology, 35.8% a major source and 20.1% a secondary source. Support from an in-house R&D unit emerges as least prevalent in ESTPROD/UK subsidiaries, which have the largest proportion not using such laboratories at all and the smallest proportion considering their contribution to technological scope as being a major source.

The results in Table 7.1 only validate part of our hypothesis of a dichotomous status for R&D in ESTPROD/EUR subsidiaries. Thus rather more of these, as predicted, found a strong (major or only source) position for in-house R&D than was the case for ESTPROD/UK subsidiaries but less (contrary to our expectation) operated without such support. The unexpected persistence of R&D units in ESTPROD/EUR subsidiaries may reflect the selection process through which subsidiaries acquire this role. Thus it may be that in assembling a network of facilities to play this role MNE group planners view the presence of R&D and other creative attributes as reflecting favorably on the quality and potential of a subsidiary, even though there is no obvious use for these functions in the position that the unit is expected to take. If this is so the process of rationalizing these subsidiaries into their networked role may eventually see the decline of those R&D units that may (perhaps for reasons of morale or relations with host-country governments, and so on) have

Table 7.1 In-house R&D as a source of technology in MNE subsidiaries in the UK

	Importance of in-house R & D (percentage of subsidiaries)[1]				
	Only source of technology	Major source of technology	Secondary source of technology	Not a source of technology	Total
By industry					
Food		75.0		25.0	100.0
Automobiles		38.9	5.6	55.6	100.0
Aerospace		16.7	16.7	66.7	100.0
Electronics and electrical appliances	2.2	30.4	30.4	37.0	100.0
Mechanical engineering	3.8	26.9	19.2	50.0	100.0
Instruments	9.1	45.5	9.1	36.4	100.0
Industrial and agricultural chemicals	6.9	44.8	20.7	27.6	100.0
Pharmaceuticals and consumer chemicals		50.0	30.0	20.0	100.0
Metal manufacture and products	9.1	27.3	9.1	54.5	100.0
Other manufacturing		21.4	28.6	50.0	100.0
Total	3.4	35.8	20.1	40.8	100.0
By home country					
USA	1.5	46.2	18.5	33.8	100.0
Japan	4.7	21.9	20.3	53.1	100.0
Europe	4.7	37.2	23.3	34.9	100.0
Total[2]	3.4	35.8	20.1	40.8	100.0
By subsidiary type[3]					
ESTPROD/UK		32.9	19.0	48.1	100.0
ESTPROD/EUR	3.4	36.8	24.1	35.6	100.0
COMPART		50.0	16.7	33.3	100.0
DEVELPROD	7.9	58.7	11.1	22.2	100.0

1. The percentage of respondents that graded 'R&D carried out by our own laboratory' at each level as a source of their technology.
2. Includes subsidiaries of MNEs from Australia and Canada.
3. Subsidiaries that said a particular role was either their only one or their predominant one.

Subsidiary types:
ESTPROD/UK   to produce for the UK market products that are already established in our MNE group's product range.
ESTPROD/EUR   to play a role in the MNE group's European supply network by specializing in the production and export of part of the established product range.
COMPART   to play a role in the MNE group's European supply network by producing and exporting component parts for assembly elsewhere.
DEVELPROD   to develop, produce and market for the UK and/or European (or wider) markets, new products additional to the MNE group's existing range.

Source: Authors' survey, 1993–94.

been allowed to persist into the early phases of accession to this position.

As hypothesized, the use of their own R&D lab is decisively strongest in the DEVELPROD subsidiaries, where by far the smallest proportion operate without such a facility and notably the largest proportion rate the input of one to be a major (or only) source of technology. Though one-third of COMPART subsidiaries operate without in-house R&D support, a half of them rated such labs as a major source of their technology. This suggests that there exists a clear tendency for COMPART facilities to operate interdependently with the creative activity of DEVELPROD subsidiaries, rather than dependently in support of ESTPROD/EUR networks.

In Table 7.2 the analysis of 'R&D carried out by our own laboratory' (OWNLAB) as a source of subsidiary technology is extended by placing it alongside two other types of R&D that could be accessed (as technology sources) by these operations. The first of these additional sources of R&D is 'R&D carried out for us by another R&D laboratory of our MNE group' (GROUPLAB). When these two sources of R&D are summarized into average responses in Table 7.2 it is clear that overall GROUPLAB is somewhat the more prevalent.[8] However, as hypothesized, the relative positioning of OWNLAB and GROUPLAB varies considerably between types of subsidiary. For both ESTPROD/UK and ESTPROD/EUR it is GROUPLAB that is clearly the more important source of R&D as a technological input. This reflects the fact that where in-house R&D (OWNLAB) occurs in subsidiaries producing established products, its role is merely to mediate in the effective application of technology whose use is already pervasive in the group, rather than to seek any degree of individualization of the subsidiaries' own knowledge scope. In DEVELPROD subsidiaries (and to a less clear-cut degree in COMPART facilities) the position is reversed, with OWNLAB moving into the predominant position as a source of R&D. Similarly while (as Table 7.1 also showed) OWNLAB is more important in DEVELPROD/COMPART subsidiaries than in the ESTPROD ones, GROUPLAB is stronger in the ESTPROD units than in the former pair of roles. Thus the move to the more creative roles places a priority on an increased availability of R&D scope within the subsidiary. However, while OWNLAB provides the individualistic technology momentum in such operations a quite substantial (if somewhat reduced) continued access to other R&D capacity in the group also reflects the benefits from the exercise of such distinctive scope in an interdependent fashion.

These results can provide a stylized view of R&D repositioning as subsidiaries move into more creative roles.[9] In the most technologically

Table 7.2 Sources of R&D used by MNE subsidiaries in the UK

	Source of R&D (average response)[1]		
	OWNLAB	GROUPLAB	LOCALINST
By industry			
Food	2.50	1.78	1.67
Automobiles	1.83	2.65	1.39
Aerospace	1.50	1.83	1.33
Electronics and electrical appliances	1.98	2.33	1.32
Mechanical engineering	1.85	2.00	1.62
Instruments	2.27	2.18	1.73
Industrial and agricultural chemicals	2.31	2.31	1.52
Pharmaceuticals and consumer chemicals	2.30	2.40	1.60
Metal manufacture and products	1.91	1.82	1.36
Other manufacturing	1.71	2.14	1.50
Total	2.02	2.22	1.48
By home country			
USA	2.15	2.18	1.62
Japan	1.78	2.23	1.27
Europe	2.12	2.25	1.55
Total[2]	2.02	2.22	1.48
By subsidiary type[3]			
ESTPROD/UK	1.85	2.29	1.39
ESTPROD/EUR	2.08	2.27	1.41
COMPART	2.17	2.08	1.58
DEVELPROD	2.52	2.05	1.62

1. Responding subsidiaries were asked to grade each source of R&D as (i) our only source, (ii) a major source, (iii) a secondary source, (iv) not a source. The average response is calculated by allocating a value of 4 to 'our only source', 3 to a 'major source', 2 to a 'secondary source', 1 to 'not a source'.
2. Includes subsidiaries of MNEs from Australia and Canada.
3. Subsidiaries that said a particular role was either their only one or their predominant one. For definitions of subsidiary types see Table 7.1.

Sources of R&D:
OWNLAB   R&D carried out by our own laboratory.
GROUPLAB R&D carried out for us by another R&D laboratory of our MNE group.
LOCALINST R&D carried out for us by local scientific institutions (e.g. universities; independent laboratories; industry laboratories).

Source: Authors' survey 1993–94.

dependent phases of an ESTPROD role, subsidiaries may not incorporate an in-house R&D unit, instead securing any necessary work on the adaptation of the relevant group technology from other MNE laboratories that perhaps already have experience of it. Here GROUPLAB *substitutes* for work that OWNLAB would have carried out. If subsidiary-level individualization increases the amount of technological work that is needed then eventually an in-house laboratory may emerge. At first this may mainly do the types of work that would earlier have been secured from other group laboratories. However, if the subsidiary makes the full creative transition (Papanastassiou, 1995; Papanastassiou and Pearce, 1994; Chapter 2) to a DEVELPROD role the proactive position of OWNLAB also finds a new status for GROUPLAB inputs. Now the in-house laboratory articulates a program of R&D to support its subsidiary's product development objectives, but may not feel it necessary (or viable) to perform all of this itself. Instead, it may commission such additional R&D from other group laboratories, so that GROUPLAB now *complements* (rather than, as earlier, substitutes) OWNLAB activity. We have already indicated that the individualization of a subsidiary's scope through its own R&D may benefit the MNE group most when still exercised through such types of creative interdependence.

The second of the additional R&D sources covered in Table 7.2 was defined as 'R&D carried out for us by local scientific institutions (e.g. universities; independent laboratories; industry laboratories)' (LOCALINST). If the scope of the local science base is a factor in attracting the more creative types of MNE subsidiary to a particular country, then there are two ways that this indigenous technology scope can be accessed. First, it may be internalized in the type of OWNLAB units already evaluated. Secondly, it can be secured through externalized contractual routes in the form of collaborative R&D arrangements with local institutions. As Table 7.2 shows, the LOCALINST means of securing R&D inputs initially appears relatively underdeveloped in the MNE subsidiaries' operations in the UK, with only 44% of respondents making any use of such collaborations and only 3% considering that this was more than a secondary source of technology. However, it is likely that such collaborative R&D with independent local laboratories would be most effectively implemented through an in-house MNE laboratory and would then be logically interpreted as a secondary technology source mediated through the OWNLAB (as a lead source). Then, if we now assume that LOCALINST R&D can *only* be accessed through an in-house lab, we can suggest that up to 75% of subsidiaries with OWNLAB R&D allowed their laboratories to supplement their work through such collaborations. Table 7.2 confirms, to a moderate degree, that LOCALINST is more prevalent as a technology source in the more creatively ambitious (DEVELPROD/COMPART) subsidiaries.

Responding subsidiaries that possessed R&D laboratories were asked to report if they expected growth or decline in these facilities in the near future. The results reported in Table 7.3 generally underwrite a con-

Table 7.3 Anticipated changes in size of R&D laboratories of MNE subsidiaries in the UK, by industry and home country[1]

	Anticipated change (percentage of respondents)	
	Growth	Decline
By industry		
Food	42.9	14.3
Automobiles	42.9	0
Electronics and electrical appliances	55.6	0
Mechanical engineering	46.7	0
Instruments	0	50.0
Industrial and agricultural chemicals	19.0	30.0
Pharmaceuticals and consumer chemicals	37.5	25.0
Other manufacturing	50.0	0
Total	39.8	11.9
By home country		
USA	42.8	4.7
Japan	59.3	7.4
Europe	21.4	29.6
Total[2]	39.8	11.9

1. Responding MNE subsidiaries that possessed an R&D laboratory were asked if they anticipated its growth or decline in the near future.
2. Indicates laboratories of MNEs from Australia and Canada.

Source: Authors' survey 1993–94.

tinued momentum in decentralized R&D in these companies, with 39.8% of respondents anticipating laboratory growth and only 11.9% expecting laboratory decline. Both Japanese and US subsidiaries recorded a decisive net expectation of growth in their R&D laboratories, but subsidiaries of European MNEs did provide a net expectation of decline. For the Japanese and US subsidiaries the reported expectation is compatible with growing intra-subsidiary creativity as they aim to claim leading positions in their group's strategic approach to the European market (that is regionalized dimensions replace localized ones and require more R&D support to do so). In the European subsidiaries' case there may also be a growing consciousness of specific need for a regional technology strategy, with a decision to focus the key creative elements of this on home-country (that is, Continental parent) operations. This then results in a decline in decentralized (for example, UK-based) R&D within Europe.[10]

Regressions were run using replies to these questions as dependent variables (Table 7.4). These tests included dummy variables for industry and

Table 7.4 Regressions with anticipated changes in size of R&D laboratories as dependent variables

	Dependent variable	
	Anticipated growth	Anticipated decline
Intercept	−0.1869 (−0.60)	0.1648 (0.87)
Food	0.0713 (1.23)	0.0390 (1.12)
Automobiles	0.0900 (0.31)	0.0592 (0.33)
Electronics and electrical appliances	0.1037* (1.77)	−0.0096 (−0.27)
Mechanical engineering	0.0553 (1.52)	−0.0014 (−0.06)
Instruments	−0.0511 (−0.97)	0.1501*** (4.72)
Industrial and agricultural chemicals	0.0434 (0.54)	0.1028** (2.11)
Pharmaceuticals and consumer chemicals	0.0452 (1.45)	0.0212 (1.13)
USA	0.0266** (2.37)	−0.0210*** (−2.98)
Japan	0.0404*** (3.35)	−0.0083 (−1.13)
ESTPROD/UK	0.0077 (0.12)	−0.0332 (−0.84)
ESTPROD/EUR	−0.0713 (−1.09)	0.0575 (1.44)
COMPART	−0.0327 (−0.41)	0.0397 (0.82)
DEVELPROD	0.1098* (1.78)	−0.0744* (−1.93)
R^2	0.2820	0.4323
F	2.17**	4.11***
n	99	97

*** significant at 1% ** significant at 5% * significant at 10%
n = number of observations

home-country[11] and the roles of subsidiaries as independent variables. Apart from confirming anticipated growth in Japanese and US subsidiaries the tests also provided significant results for the DEVELPROD role. This further substantiates the view that increasing commitment to product development in a subsidiary is positively related to the incorporation of R&D capacity within its scope. Though in neither case reaching significance, the signs on ESTPROD/EUR do suggest that the more prevalent is this role in a subsidiary the more likely is a decline in its R&D capacity. This would be compatible with our suggestion earlier that many ESTPROD/EUR subsidiaries may be carrying R&D capacity in excess of their needs. Though this scenario is necessarily speculative, it may have some worrying implications for host countries (for example, the UK in this case). Thus subsidiaries with a certain degree of creative (high-value-added) scope may gain the essentially cost-based ESTPROD/EUR role and then later shed those characteristics that could individualize their situation in the MNE. Once this R&D has gone, the subsidiary can only sustain its networked position by low-cost supply of standardized inputs. The need to avoid 'unnecessary' overheads in retaining the ESTPROD/EUR position then makes it increasingly difficult to set up the potential to accede to the DEVELPROD role.

Roles of MNE subsidiaries' R&D laboratories

A question in the survey asked those manufacturing subsidiaries that possessed R&D units to evaluate the relative importance of four roles in their activity. Somewhat the most pervasive of these roles (Table 7.5) was the one aimed at providing an individualized product scope and creative competence to the subsidiary, that is 'to play a role in the development of new products for our distinctive markets'. This was rated their laboratory's only role by 5.9% of responding subsidiaries, a major role by 75.2%, a secondary one by 15.8% and not part of its role by only 3.0%. The other prevalent role also involved the laboratories providing direct support to the production unit with which they were associated, though here perhaps more to help them to perform effectively an externally-determined role in group supply programs (either to local or regional markets) than to create original scope within the subsidiary itself. Thus 'adaptation of existing products and/or processes to make them suitable to our market and conditions' was reported as the only role of 2.0% of subsidiaries' laboratories, a major one for 65.3%, a secondary one in 25.7% of cases and not part of the role in 6.9%.

Table 7.5 Roles of R&D laboratories of MNE subsidiaries in the UK

	Importance of laboratory roles[1] (average response[2])			
	A	B	C	D
By industry				
Food	2.71	3.00	2.57	1.57
Automobiles	2.86	3.00	1.86	1.43
Electronics and electrical appliances	2.59	2.73	1.89	1.54
Mechanical engineering	2.60	3.00	1.87	1.40
Instruments	2.20	3.17	1.80	1.60
Industrial and agricultural chemicals	2.81	2.81	2.38	1.86
Pharmaceuticals and consumer chemicals	2.38	2.50	1.75	2.38
Other manufacturing	2.54	2.82	1.73	1.45
Total	2.62	2.84	2.00	1.64
By home country				
USA	2.52	2.90	2.19	1.76
Japan	2.78	2.93	1.74	1.54
Europe	2.59	2.63	1.96	1.56
Total[3]	2.62	2.84	2.00	1.64
By subsidiary type[4]				
ESTPROD/UK	2.53	2.81	2.08	1.81
ESTPROD/EUR	2.68	2.83	2.11	1.73
COMPART	2.57	3.00	2.86	2.29
DEVELPROD	2.67	2.94	1.98	1.60

1. Respondents were asked to evaluate each laboratory role as (i) its only role, (ii) a major role, (iii) a secondary role, (iv) not a part of its role.
2. The average response is calculated by allocating a value of 4 to 'its only role', 3 to 'a major role', 2 to ' a secondary role', and 1 to 'not a part of its role'.
3. Includes laboratories of MNEs from Australia and Canada.
4. Subsidiaries that said a particular role was either their only one or their predominant one. For definitions of subsidiary types see Table 7.1.

Roles of laboratories:
A – adaptation of existing products and/or processes to make them suitable to our market and conditions.
B – to play a role in the development of new products for our distinctive markets.
C – to provide advice on adaptation and/or development to other producing subsidiaries of our MNE group.
D – to carry out basic research (not directly related to our current products) as part of a wider MNE-group-level research programme.

Source: Authors' survey 1993–94.

It is interesting to note (Table 7.5) that where subsidiaries that played predominantly one or other of the ESTPROD roles had an R&D unit its activity seems likely to be rather more oriented to product development than to adaptation of established technology. This suggests that in such cases the subsidiaries feel that in order to defend their possession of R&D, and to generate a positive perspective on the future evolution of the overall operation, their laboratories should particularly support emerging product development scope. By contrast where subsidiaries predominantly encompass the DEVELPROD role their laboratories still retain a substantial secondary commitment to adaptation of established technology.

The third laboratory role evaluated by subsidiaries was defined as 'to provide advice on adaptation and/or development to other producing subsidiaries of our MNE group'. Table 7.5 indicates that while clearly less important than direct support of their own subsidiaries, this manifestation of MNEs' technological interdependency was quite pervasive.[12] This laboratory role was decisively most important within the operations of the COMPART subsidiaries. Taken with the strong commitment of the COMPART subsidiaries' laboratories to product development, we find a further indication that a significant element in this component supply role is to work creatively with DEVELPROD operations. Thus here the strong involvement of COMPART subsidiaries in providing advice to other subsidiaries seems likely to be part of a mutually supportive product development operation to which, ultimately, they will provide custom-created component parts. This third role is most strongly incorporated in US subsidiaries' laboratories, perhaps indicating a more ingrained tradition of networked integration and interdependence in these MNEs' European operations. By contrast it is very weak in Japanese subsidiaries compared to their strong commitment to the two in-house roles, suggesting that in the absence so far of fully-fledged European networks these companies' UK-based operations act as bridgeheads for the regional application of existing products (adaptation) and technology (development).[13] The weak position of this role in European-MNE laboratories in the UK, alongside the also limited position of product development, is compatible with the suggestion that growing regionalized dimensions in these companies involve increased centralization of core technology operations in their Continental parent facilities.

The final laboratory role was defined as 'to carry out basic research (not directly related our current products) as part of a wider MNE-group-level research programme'. This relates to the third (long-term) aim of globalized technology programs of MNEs that we distinguish in the introduction, seeking to tap into distinctive research scope and scientific traditions of host countries. The separation of the precompetitive aims of this role from current commercial technology make it likely that where a host-country's potential inputs to this type of work are powerful they can be most effectively applied in laboratories that operate independently from producing subsidiaries. Nevertheless, cases could plausibly emerge where the skills and resources put into place to support the wider objectives of subsidiaries' laboratories might also usefully provide supplementary inputs into their groups' pure research programs. This type of work emerged as completely absent from the activity of 57.0% of the labs of responding subsidiaries. On the other hand where it did occur it often asserted a more than spin-off or residual position, being reported as a major (or only) role in 20.0% of cases.

Absence of R&D

Two questions in the survey were addressed to those responding production subsidiaries that did not have an in-house R&D facility. The first of these (Table 7.6) asked the respondents to say whether or not they believed each of six possible factors had contributed to the decision not to have an R&D unit. A majority (53%) of these subsidiaries endorsed the view that a significant factor in not having a laboratory was that 'our operations do not require enough adaptation or development to need one'. Alongside this even more (66%) believed 'we can obtain adequate adaptation/development advice from other laboratories of our MNE group.' Bearing in mind that the majority of the subsidiaries without laboratories are those predominantly taking the ESTPROD roles these results suggest that, as supply of such established products becomes an increasingly specialized and networked position, there is likely to be decreasing need for in-house R&D to support such production units. Taken with the evidence of pressure towards decline of existing R&D in ESTPROD/EUR subsidiaries these perspectives again suggest that if subsidiaries do not actively target the enhancement of a product development role within their operations they may suffer a 'hollowing out' of functional scope that reduces them to a technologically-limited and strategically-vulnerable cost-based position.

Another well-supported reason for not having R&D (53% of responding subsidiaries) was that 'R&D economies of scale in our industry mean our operations are not large enough to justify a laboratory of effective size'. Though earlier discussion (Pearce, 1989, pp. 38–43) and the general growth of decentralized R&D suggests that interdependent approaches to the internationalization of technology in MNEs can often provide means of overcoming the potential constraints of economies of scale, these results also indicate that there can be limits to this with some

Table 7.6 Evaluation by MNE subsidiaries in the UK that do not have an R&D laboratory of reasons for not having one, by industry and home country[1]

	Reason for not having a laboratory (percentage of respondents)					
	A	B	C	D	E	F
By industry						
Automobiles	33.3	83.3	58.3	0	16.7	8.3
Electronics and electrical appliances	44.0	52.0	48.0	4.0	16.0	8.0
Mechanical engineering	63.6	63.6	45.5	0	27.3	0
Industrial and agricultural chemicals	45.5	72.7	81.8	18.2	9.1	0
Other manufacturing	66.7	70.0	46.7	13.3	16.7	3.3
Total	52.8	66.3	52.8	7.9	16.9	4.5
By home country						
USA	58.6	62.1	44.8	10.3	24.1	6.9
Japan	46.3	63.4	53.7	4.9	14.6	4.9
Europe	58.8	76.5	64.7	11.8	11.8	0
Total[2]	52.8	66.3	52.8	7.9	16.9	4.5

Reasons for not having an R & D laboratory:

A – our operations do not require enough adaptation or development to need one.
B – we can obtain adequate adaptation/development advice from other laboratories of our MNE group.
C – R&D economies of scale in our industry mean our operations are not large enough to justify a laboratory of effective size.
D – our group believes technology is too sensitive to risk decentralization of important scientific work.
E – our group centralizes creative work because it believes communications and coordination problems make decentralization of R&D ineffective.
F – we believe it would be difficult to recruit adequate local personnel to staff a laboratory to meet our needs.

1. MNE subsidiaries without an R&D laboratory were asked to indicate which of the offered reasons they believed were relevant to the decision to omit such a facility from their operations.
2. Includes subsidiaries of MNEs from Australia and Canada.

national operations still being too small to justify a separate R&D scope.

Two other somewhat traditional arguments against overseas R&D in MNEs did not receive much support as reasons behind the continued absence of laboratories in UK-based subsidiaries. Thus only 8% of respondents endorsed 'our group believes technology is too sensitive to risk decentralization of important scientific work' and 17% considered 'our group centralizes creative work because it believes communications and coordination problems make decentralization of R&D

ineffective'. Though both these factors may well constitute matters of valid concern for MNEs it seems likely that the benefits of decentralized approaches to technology are such that organizational procedures have been developed to mitigate these concerns and minimize the risks. Finally only 5% of respondents believed they did not have R&D because 'it would be difficult to recruit adequate local personnel to staff a laboratory to meet our needs'.

The second of these questions to subsidiaries without in-house R&D asked them to consider whether or not each of four factors might influence them to set up a laboratory in the future (Table 7.7). Here there was widespread support (69% of responding subsidiaries) for the

Table 7.7 Evaluation by MNE subsidiaries in the UK that do not have an R&D laboratory of factors that could influence them to set one up, by industry and home country[1]

	Influence (percentage of respondents)			
	A	B	C	D
By industry				
Automobiles	50.0	16.7	0	0
Electronics and electrical appliances	80.0	25.0	5.0	10.0
Mechanical engineering	87.5	25.0	25.0	0
Industrial and agricultural chemicals	66.7	33.3	50.0	16.7
Other manufacturing	53.3	33.3	6.7	0
Total	69.1	27.3	12.7	5.5
By home country				
USA	46.7	26.7	13.3	13.3
Japan	83.9	29.0	9.7	3.2
Europe	71.4	28.6	28.6	0
Total[2]	69.1	27.3	12.7	5.5

Reasons for considering setting up an R&D laboratory:

A – our subsidiary wishes to increase the degree of independence it can exercise within the MNE group.

B – we feel the creative potential of our personnel (e.g. in management, marketing, engineering) is currently stifled and could be better used for the group if combined with additional local technological inputs (i.e. our own scientists).

C – the UK has a strong science-base in our industry and we could use this on behalf of the MNE group if we had our own laboratory.

D – we would recommend our MNE group to use talented local scientists in a basic-research-oriented laboratory, even if this does not contribute to this subsidiary's current operations.

1. MNE subsidiaries without an R&D laboratory were asked to indicate which of the offered reasons they felt might influence them to set one up in the near future.
2. Includes subsidiaries of MNEs from Australia and Canada.

view that a factor that could positively affect the desire for an R&D laboratory was that 'our subsidiary wishes to increase the degree of independence it can exercise within the MNE group'. Recalling again that most of these subsidiaries currently play ESTPROD roles this response shows a strong awareness of the vulnerability that can arise from the functionally-constrained dependency of this position and therefore the desirability of in-house R&D as a crucial element in individualizing their scope. That a formal commitment to R&D may be a key factor in operationalizing under-employed subsidiary-level competences was quite strongly endorsed (27% of replies) in the view that 'we feel the creative potential of our personnel (for example in management, marketing, engineering) is currently stifled and could be better used for the group if combined with additional local technological inputs (that is, our own scientists)'.

The addition of in-house R&D therefore appears to be viewed by many subsidiaries as a key way in which they can augment their scope sufficiently to accede to a less dependent role within the creative programs of their MNE group. However, these ambitious producing subsidiaries usually wish their new position to be one that is interdependent with the evolution of the mainstream of their MNE's technology trajectory, rather than one which helps the group to access more radical new scientific inputs. Thus only 13% of respondents considered that 'the UK has a strong science base in our industry and we could use this on behalf of the MNE group if we had our own laboratory' was a factor that might encourage them to set up a laboratory. Similarly only 6% viewed 'we would recommend our MNE group to use talented local scientists in a basic-research-oriented laboratory, even if this does not contribute to this subsidiary's current operations' as being a viable reason for a future R&D unit. This generally confirms that within the globalized technological activities of MNEs, accessing the basic and applied scientific inputs that underwrite the long-term (precompetitive) progress of these groups' technological trajectories constitutes a program that is operationally distinct from the medium-term evolution of these trajectories into new product generations. Retaining logical coherence between these phases in the technological progress of MNEs is therefore a major challenge to their knowledge management programs.

Conclusions

Technology has always had a strong influence on analytical thinking on the MNE. The early perception (Hymer, 1960/76) that national firms seeking to compete internationally would need a very distinctive source of competitive advantage in order to do so quickly targeted knowledge as an obvious example of such an asset. Again, the understanding (Buckley and Casson, 1976) that firms entering into overseas production were taking a decision to internalize (rather than externalize through a market) the internationalized use of a key source of their competitive advantage found the characteristics of technology to provide a clear illustrative case. Thus knowledge could be transferred relatively cheaply and effectively[14] between parts (albeit in different countries) of the same firm, while external markets for knowledge were subject to very significant elements of inherent failure.[15]

However, complementing this understanding of the role of technology as a crucial motivating factor in the emergence of MNEs was the perception (Vernon, 1966; Hirsch, 1967) that within these companies the creation of knowledge, and its innovation into successful commercial products, was likely to be a highly centralized activity. An obvious implication of this was then that all the really creative R&D activity in MNEs would also be centralized.[16] Only rather routine adaptation of products (and manufacturing processes) to local conditions was believed to provide any role for overseas R&D units.

The arguments of this chapter suggest that the contemporary MNE (reacting to the intensified nature of global competition) is still motivated by the same attributes and characteristics of technology, but now needs to operationalize its response in a much more decentralized and differentiated fashion. The persistent evolution of their core stock of technology remains central to the sustained long-term competitiveness of leading companies. At the same time the ability to apply the current commercial manifestation of this knowledge as effectively as possible throughout the global marketplace is also a crucial element in MNEs' technology programs. However, the globalized dimensions that are now increasingly interjected not only intensify and deepen the *challenges* to technology creation and application in MNEs but also provide new *potentials* for the enrichment of the programs through which they pursue these objectives. The expanding scope of decentralized R&D in these companies is central to meeting these challenges and embracing these potentials.

It is, therefore, a key managerial challenge in the contemporary MNE to achieve decentralized access to, and creative use of, technology in ways that can thus enrich both the knowledge available to the group and the effectiveness with which it is applied commercially. In a global environment that increasingly demands decisive response to both market and technological heterogeneity, the use of creative (product development) subsidiaries seems the best way of monitoring such aspects of competitive knowledge on behalf of the MNE group. Allowing them to develop their own individualized scope around their perceptions is then the best way to motivate such subsidiaries to do this job well. From this positioning they should benefit the group in two ways: first, through their own innovative operations (that is product development), which then directly increase the current scope of the group, and second, by making their original perceptions on market trends and technological progress available to the group so that, more indirectly, they can also influence decisions on the group's overall evolution.

By looking at the technological dimension of their creative subsidiaries in this light MNE central management should understand that they need to be encouraged to *individualize* their knowledge scope and creative skills in ways that still retain valuable *interdependencies* with the group's overall technological progress. Usually this will mean enriching the group's technological scope in *evolutionary* ways. Occasionally, however, it could challenge the scope and limits of core technology in more radical or *revolutionary* ways. When this happens it becomes a key responsibility of central technological planning to decide if it should be attempted to decisively assimilate these challenging new perspectives into group progress, to suppress them, or to allow them a certain degree of further investigation as a tentative and provisional independent strand. Such radical possibilities should usually not be allowed to proceed in more or less unsupervised ways that may disrupt other parts of creative programs, reduce the degree of cohesion and coherence of technological progress and, at an extreme, lead to technological anarchy.

A useful viewpoint from which MNE central planners can evaluate these dimensions of the ways in which creative subsidiaries individualize their technology is to understand that they do so (particularly through in-house R&D units) by deriving distinctive perspectives from positions in two technological communities. The first of these is that of the MNE group itself, whilst the second is the scientific-heritage and research-base of the host country. Where the first of these prevails the local element may strengthen the subsidiary's scope in valuable ways that nevertheless remain securely anchored in the mainstream technology of the group. Usefully enhanced application of core technology emerges, but with limited contributions to longer-term progress (but also with less danger of reducing coherence and balance in group operations). Where it is the second community that prevails the subsidiary's distinctive technology may be much more radical and much less firmly grounded in current group technology. There is a bigger potential here (substantial reinforcing of the longer-term technological development of the group) but also a greater danger in terms of loss of control over key areas of knowledge evolution. The most successful MNEs, in terms of central management of technology, may ultimately be those that can harness even the more radical of decentralized creative perceptions to group-level evolutionary processes without thereby lessening the incentives to overseas subsidiaries and laboratories to pursue the more idiosyncratic possibilities of their local environments.

Notes

1. For evidence and analysis of R&D in MNEs see Dunning (1994b), Dunning and Narula (1995), Fors (1996), Håkanson and Nobel (1993a, b), Howells and Wood (1993), Papanastassiou (1995), Pearce (1989), Pearce and Singh (1992a, b).
2. For analysis of approaches to innovation in a global context see Ghoshal and Bartlett (1988), Bartlett and Ghoshal (1989, 1990), Papanastassiou and Pearce (1996a), Pearce and Papanastassiou (1996a).
3. Other studies that include discussion of the position of R&D in the operations of MNE subsidiaries include Hood *et al.* (1994), Molero and Buesa (1993), Molero *et al.* (1995), Roth and Morrison (1992).
4. The survey was carried out as part of a project financed by the ESRC. It was intended to survey all relevant manufacturing subsidiaries that could be found in the National Register Publishing Company's *International Directory of Corporate Affiliations*.
5. For more detailed discussion of these roles see Pearce and Papanastassiou (1996b), Papanastassiou and Pearce (1997a).
6. An alternative might be to set up a laboratory independent from any production unit. This would establish its neutrality and mitigate tensions that could arise from co-location with one production subsidiary.
7. See Papanastassiou and Pearce (1997a, b), for detailed discussion of the full scope of this question.
8. To some extent this reflects the fact that more subsidiaries use GROUPLAB inputs than greater intensity of use when it is accessed. Thus only 27% of subsidiaries had no use for GROUPLAB compared with 41% that did not use OWNLAB. By contrast 66% of subsidiaries that used OWNLAB at all felt it took a major (or only) position as a source of technology, whilst only 57% of those using GROUPLAB felt it took this position.
9. Of course causation is indeterminate here. Thus subsidiaries may acquire R&D that is unnecessary for their current role in order to generate the scope to claim a move to a higher-value-added role.
10. A global technology strategy for these companies (within which the European element operates) may then simultaneously involve R&D growth outside Europe (e.g. in North America and Asia).
11. The miscellaneous other manufacturing group served as omitted industry dummy and European MNE subsidiaries as omitted home-country dummy.

12 It was never rated as a lab's only role and a major one in only 27.7% of cases, but 44.6% of subsidiaries did consider it a secondary role of their labs.
13 Defense of this high-value-added position as Japanese companies widen their European-networked dimensions will be a significant challenge for UK government inward investment policy.
14 Though Teece's work (1976, 1977) did demonstrate that internal technology transfer was far from costless and that, therefore, it should not be construed as a public good within MNEs.
15 For a review of the empirical investigation of technology as a determinant of overseas production see Pearce (1993, pp. 32–4).
16 More explicit reasons for this view stemmed from arguments relating to economies of scale in R&D, security risks in decentralized knowledge-based operations, and problems of control and coordination. Evidence in this chapter suggests that only the first of these is now perceived as a matter of any real concern.

8
Multinationals and National Systems of Innovation: Strategy and Policy Issues

Robert Pearce and Marina Papanastassiou

Introduction

One of the most significant journeys in our understanding of international business has been that from an essentially centralized view of innovation in MNEs towards one that encompasses an increasing range of decentralized inputs and strategic postures. This change in perspective can then be seen as decisively embodied within comparable changes in the way in which the *effects* of international business on individual host countries has been analyzed. Here we can see a refocusing from an FDI-based interpretation of flows of separate firm attributes (increasingly technology and other intangible assets rather than finance capital *per se*) towards a more MNE-strategy oriented evaluation of how firms position their operations in a specific location within wider globalized programs (Pearce, 2001, 2006). The aim of this chapter is, then, to generate a methodology for the assessment of the ways in which MNEs' globalized strategies for innovation involve themselves with the attempts of national economies to generate and operationalize innovation competences as a source of growth and international competitiveness.

An extremely valuable platform on which to build an understanding of these changes and their current implications remains Vernon's (1966) original product cycle model (PCM). In the next section, therefore, we show how external and internal forces altered the environment for MNE innovation from the home-country focus of the PCM towards the need for more decentralized approaches to innovation. From this the third section derives the elements of a stylized global innovation strategy (GIS). This postulates MNEs approaching a decentralized innovation strategy by drawing distinctive capabilities and attributes from several different countries into an integrated program that enhances their *global* competitiveness, and thus raises vital questions about how the individual *national* economies are rewarded. The core aim of the chapter is then to provide some insights on these questions. To further facilitate this, section four outlines a very simplified linear or sequential national system of innovation (NSI). The following section then investigates the implications of the ways in which components of MNEs' GIS interact with different elements of countries' NSI. Policy interpretation of this is provided in the concluding section.

From the product cycle to global innovation strategies

It is not necessary to recapitulate here the full detail of Vernon's (1966, 1979) PCM, but facets of the argument that are relevant to our own analysis can be drawn out. At the initial product development (innovation) stage it is, in effect, assumed that the firm is not yet an MNE.[1] In Vernon's exposition the key implication of this is to support the centralized home-country focus of the (essentially market-driven) innovation process. Thus it is not innate to the PCM that only the firm's home-country could possibly manifest the distinctive tastes and new product ideas to drive an innovation, but rather that without even marketing operations in other countries the firm has no reliable means of accessing such alternative insights and perceptions. Vernon also notes the benefits that centralization offers by providing the environment for close day-to-day contact between the key top-level functional participants in innovation (scientists, market researchers, engineers, entrepreneurial strategic management). The tension between the persisting benefits of close interfunctional proximity and alternative efficiency/ specialization gains from dispersing functional inputs to different locations can then be seen to be reflected in later MNE innovation strategies.

At the start of the second (mature product) stage of the PCM overseas demand for the good emerges in an *ad hoc* fashion, beyond the traditional strategic horizons of the firm. Thus, at some time after the initial innovation, at least the more prosperous and cosmopolitan citizens of other countries begin to aspire to ownership of the good and take the initiative to secure its import.[2] Initially this new market is then brought within the planned scope of the firm through an exporting responsibility. This will then be, sooner or later, superseded by market-seeking production in some of the more significant of the foreign markets. Though conventional cost factors can influence the decision to initiate overseas production, Vernon places more emphasis on strategic-competition forces. Thus a benefit of starting production in a particular foreign market may be that it can, at least, slow down the growth of emergent local suppliers of rival versions of the product. Though incipient local suppliers will have less experience of the core technologies (and face the cost and risk of having to design around the more proprietary of the original investor's capabilities) they may have a potentially compensating latecomer advantage in being able to create product variants that can respond to distinctive local tastes (ignored by imports) or production conditions. However, if the original innovator begins local production it can then also access the benefits of localization, by adapting its technologies to the different tastes and environment.

Having explained how the centralized creation of unique competitive capabilities allows firms to become MNEs by initially expanding into major foreign markets Vernon then, in the PCM's third (standardized product) stage, predicted a further dimension of these firms' strategic development in the form of an efficiency-seeking priority. Thus, once it has ultimately failed to prevent the emergence of rival suppliers of its good, the basis of competitive positioning will have to move from originality/quality to price and, therefore, to cost-effective supply. From this Vernon predicted MNEs' increasing use of the emerging free-trade environment to locate export-oriented supply subsidiaries in low-cost countries for their standardized mass-market goods. We can now see that this points towards the growth of integrated international supply-networks to allow MNEs to pursue one of their two core strategic priorities, i.e. efficient supply of well-established price-cost-competitive parts of their product range. Whilst one change in the global environment (freer-trade) allowed better pursuit of this objective, we can also argue that other changes (one external to the MNE and one internal to the firm and, in fact, endemic to the original PCM process itself) led to reorientation in its approach to the other core priority, in the form of generation of new products and the sourcing of new competitive attributes. Thus the PCM's process of centralized innovation followed by a relaxed and gradual diffusion of new goods into overseas markets needed to be replaced by more proactive and internationalized approaches to technology generation and product development.

The external change that we see as conditioning the need for new approaches to innovation in MNEs is that, through most of the last third of the 20th century, the spread of sustained economic growth led to an increased number of countries at quite similar and high levels of income. Taken with increased numbers of firms competing internationally and the shortening of product life cycles[3] this means that, even if the essence of a new innovation emerged in one location, firms would need to get the new good into all key markets with the greatest possible speed.

Internal to the firm, once it has been through the PCM the assumption that it is not an MNE has been removed and this alters its organizational structure in a way that, in effect, provides it with the mechanism to deal with the new competitive need provoked by the external change. Thus the second stage of the original PCM saw the establishment of local-market-focused subsidiaries in other high-income markets. These can provide the vehicle for getting new goods into key markets very promptly. Indeed it would be an expectation of internal competition in MNEs that ambitious subsidiaries in major markets would *demand* early access to important new products emerging elsewhere. If these subsidiaries had, as suggested by our interpretation of the second stage of the PCM, already developed in-house capacity to individualize established products to meet specific distinctive characteristics of their local market and production conditions, they could then become, in effect, part of new innovation processes. Thus rather than adapting well-established goods in an *ex post* fashion, they could acquire early access to a development process whose essence (new technology and market ideas) is emerging elsewhere in the MNE and complete its own version of the innovation that responds to aspects of its own competitive context. This would, in some ways, collapse the first two stages of the original PCM into one internationally-differentiated innovation process.[4]

From the viewpoints previously outlined we can distil three aims for the global innovation strategy that we describe in the next section and that becomes central to the subsequent analysis. Firstly, the MNE needs to secure the key ground-breaking inputs into a major new innovation in the most effective manner possible. Importantly the emphasis of this effectiveness does not relate primarily to costs, though it must be accepted that adequate budgeting for these expenditures becomes a delicate balancing act in firms facing the myopic short-termism of immediate profitability and support for the share price (with a problematic concomitant reluctance to allow for the need to reinforce future sources of profitability and, ultimately, competitive survival). Instead the primary aim of this effectiveness is to maximize the possibilities for securing access to important new scientific knowledge (adding science-driven potentials to the likely origins of major innovations) and customer-originated ideas for radical extensions of an industry's competitive scope. Since we would see increasing technological- and market-heterogeneity as a central feature of the evolving global economy the implication of this first aim of the GIS is a need to monitor, and secure first-mover access to, potential sources of the primary inputs that drive major innovations, through internationalized approaches to precompetitive R&D and market research.

If the MNE does put together the fundamental components of a major new innovation (the 'new product concept' that we elaborate in the next section) then the second aim of the GIS will be to get it into all key markets as quickly as possible. Thus the intensity of globalized competition, and the ability of rival firms to quickly generate their own variants of the new good, means that the innovating MNE needs to maximize returns during its period of monopoly supply and therefore must target all relevant markets as an integral part of the innovation process. The third aim then adds an important dimension to this by suggesting that the new good should enter all segments of the global market place not only quickly but responsively. In many industries it is accepted that differences in economic conditions, regulations and tastes, mean that extensive variation of products yields competitive advantage in different segments of the global economy. Responding to such differences *ex ante*, within the innovation process of new goods, can then represent a significant step forward compared to earlier *ex post* adaptation of mature products.

A global innovation strategy

In this section we outline an idealized approach to a GIS available to a contemporary MNE[5] (Pearce and Papanastassiou, 1996a, pp. 38–40; Pearce, 1997, pp. 17–21; Papanastassiou and Pearce, 1999, pp. 93–5). We see this as implemented through two stages, each of which is articulated around a different type of R&D laboratory.[6] Thus the first, precompetitive, stage of the GIS is positioned (Figure 8.1) around a network of internationally interdependent laboratories (IIL),[7] and seeks to contribute to achieving the first aim (or benefit) of globalizing innovation activity. Thus MNEs with a perception of a range of separate scientific disciplines that could provide new results that contribute to a technology-driven component of innovation, acknowledge technological heterogeneity (i.e. that different countries' science-bases provide frontier-quality research capabilities in different areas of specialization) and set up a portfolio of IILs to tap into the distinctive potentials of different NSIs. Though the set of IILs can be seen as seeking to be a balanced portfolio, in the sense that each aims to take independent responsibility for covering research in a potentially important area of science (that reflects a strong distinctive capacity of its host NSI), the MNE also needs them to generate at least *ad hoc* networking (inter-

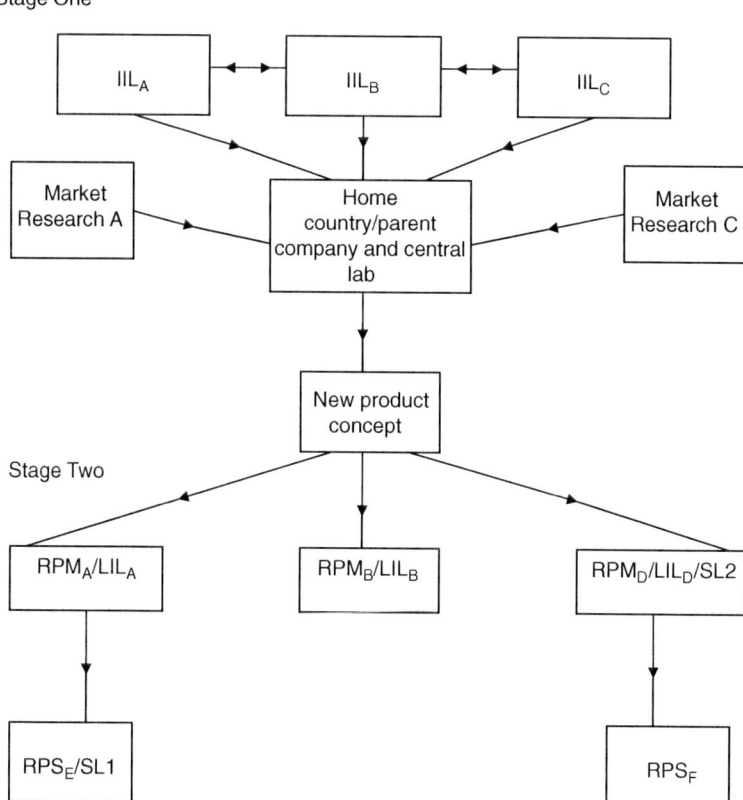

Figure 8.1 Global Innovation Strategy

dependency) in terms of exchange of results, questions and opinions. Thus the perception of potentials for future commercial innovation emerging from basic research may well derive from insights representing synergistic combinations of results from different projects in different IILs, and the further progress of these potentials may then benefit from the building in of complementary research reflecting the specialized disciplines of additional parts of an IIL network.[8] Thus Figure 8.1 includes lines and arrows connecting IILs, reflecting the benefits of knowledge flows that can enrich and condition the work of individual labs in terms of their contribution to the ultimate strengthening of the MNE group's core scientific competences. Crucially arrows also depict a more persistent and routine reporting of results and details of ongoing programs from each IIL to a central coordinating 'parent' laboratory (along with similar flows from complementary market-research groups).

The preceeding point leads us to the coordinating role of a 'parent' laboratory in a GIS, and indeed of the status of a home-country parent HQ in an MNE which is now placing significant emphasis on the decentralization of much of its creative and innovative strategic activity. The centralization of innovation in Vernon's original PCM also implied that, at least in its early life, the MNE that emerged would be a hierarchy, perhaps extended (through the PCM's third stage) to the dependency of the core-periphery stratification critiqued by Hymer (1970, 1972a; Chapter 6). Once the forces outlined earlier undermined such a center-dominated hierarchy and allowed dynamic forces into dispersed operations, however, the center remains pre-eminent but in a rather reformulated fashion. Thus we can now see a 'center' as no longer generating all the key competitive competences and taking full responsibility for the planning of their use throughout the group. Instead, in this more heterarchical (Hedlund, 1986, 1993; Birkinshaw, 1994) context, it is the HQ that aspires to the fullest *understanding* of what is evolving in dispersed operations and, from this, of securing an effective balance in networks of both supply and creative units (Papanastassiou and Pearce, 1999, pp. 90–2; Pearce, 1999b).

Then, in a fully-developed GIS scenario, we can see a central or parent laboratory as coordinating a group of IIL projects, with their potential for overlaps and synergies, and then collating the outputs of these separate units. One responsibility of this central lab may be to nurture and facilitate interdependence between IILs by encouraging the sharing of results and by inculcating a non-defensive culture in which it is routinely acceptable for one IIL to see its work taken up by another.[9] Crucially it may also be such a central lab that is most naturally committed to discerning applied research potentials in the basic research output. Thus the commercial potentials of precompetitive work may often not be perceived from individual isolated basic research projects, but only when various results are brought together and evaluated dialectically in terms of their resonances (consistencies, inconsistencies, overlaps and interdependencies). The parent lab may then allocate back into the appropriate parts of the precompetitive IIL network responsibilities for necessary applied research that is needed to complete the technological basis for possible commercial innovations.

In the GIS the first stage is completed when the center (bringing together market research perceptions as well as scientific results) is able to fully define the essential elements of a new product concept (NPC).

This NPC does two things. Firstly, it fully defines the essential nature of the major new service through which the innovation will extend the competitive scope of the firm and industry. Secondly, it puts into place (from basic and applied research of stage one) all the technologies necessary to secure effective supply of a prototype of the good. However, to secure the second and third aims of a GIS this new good needs to be got into each segment of the global market place quickly and in forms which fully respond to particular localized tastes and conditions. Thus the remaining responsibility of the 'center' in a GIS is to allocate product development responsibilities to particular subsidiaries, and to provide them with the core details of the NPC (i.e. to articulate and organize stage two of a GIS).

As depicted in Figure 8.1 the second stage of a GIS is implemented through product mandate (PM) subsidiaries and associated locally integrated laboratories (LIL). Thus a PM gains, from its MNE parent, full responsibility for developing a product (here by filling in the locally-responsive details of a NPC), its initial production, marketing and further competitive evolution. To do this a PM builds a strong functional scope, including R&D, market research and assertive marketing, creative engineering and an impetus from an ambitious management that is committed to the unit's individualized competitive status in the MNE. An LIL is a central element in the PM's creativity, and essentially mediates new science emerging from applied research to the other functions (i.e. those with which it works in a closely *integrated* fashion) involved in the innovation process. Thus an LIL will not itself carry out further pure scientific investigation, but instead learn a core new technology, interpret it to associated functions (marketing, engineering) and thereby play a key role in its practical manifestation in new goods, services and production techniques.

In a fully-developed GIS an MNE will authorize a separate PM/LIL nexus in *each* of several regional markets to generate a distinctive variant of the NPC that responds to all the idiosyncratic tastes and needs of its regional customer base and optimizes the production technology in its use of the input environment (availability and price of factors) of the host country. A subsidiary operating in this manner can be designated as having a *regional* product mandate (RPM).

With the completion of separate product developments in its group of RPMs the GIS provides its contribution to *one* of the MNE's two core strategic priorities, by providing major additions to the product scope that are based on new knowledge competences. In a way presaged within the PCM these new products will eventually lose the competitive edge of originality and uniqueness, so that they may fall within the purview of MNEs' second strategic priority, i.e. the need to supply maturing products in more cost-competitive ways. At this point some supply of these goods may be relocated to cost-based rationalized product subsidiaries (RPS) elsewhere in the group. The role of an RPS is to take on production of well-established goods of the MNE in a cost-effective manner. Thus Figure 8.1 shows an RPS in country E taking on production of a good originally developed in RPM_a and one in country F similarly inheriting supply responsibility for a good created in RPM_d.

This efficiency-seeking behavior takes us back into the worlds of hierarchy and technology transfer, in the sense that the roles of RPS_c and RPS_f depend on using technologies finalized by RPM_a and RPM_d. Such technology transfer we see as mediated by another type of R&D unit, the support laboratory (SL). Two variants of the SL role are depicted. Thus RPS_c includes an SL1-type unit, whose aim is to learn the technology from RPM_a and secure its effective assimilation and activation in the RPS's supply. Alternatively SL2 activity is depicted as a supplementary aim of the LIL in RPM_d, seeking to organize the outward transfer of those parts of the RPM/LIL's technology that will be used in RPS_f. In effect the SL2 teaches RPS_f to apply and use its new technology.

The emergence of this efficiency-seeking priority emphasizes the vulnerability of any innovation-based unit to product-life-cycle forces. In the case of PM/LIL operations the question of the ability to sustain dynamic creativity is enhanced in a GIS scenario where it is dependent on access to group technology and new product ideas (the NPC). Thus the persistence of PM/LIL units often depends (externally) on the parent MNE group's ability to generate new innovation potentials, and (internally) on the host-country's ability to support those aspects of its NSI that enable the facility to continue to attract elements of the group's creative programs. The presumed ideal of a PM would in fact be to escape from a GIS and internalize more local inputs (science, market research, etc.) into a fully localized creation of a unique new good with world market scope (i.e. become a world product mandate, WPM).

A national system of innovation

For the purposes of this analysis we adopt a highly simplified linear NSI with four stages (Figure 8.2). Referring to the separate facets as 'stages' does not imply an immutable sequential behavior, however, merely that the intuitive logic is for the defined activity of, for example, applied research to follow basic research or product development to

| BASIC RESEARCH | APPLIED RESEARCH | PRODUCT DEVELOPMENT (Including market research) | ADAPTATION AND MARKETING |

Figure 8.2 National System of Innovation

follow applied research. This does not presume that successful product adaptation (stage four) must be predicated on knowledge that has evolved through all three previous stages. It also does not preclude reversal of 'stages' where, for example, product development operations request extra applied research to resolve, scientifically, a gap in their knowledge. Most crucially, for our purposes, we have suggested that MNEs approach NSIs selectively and may then focus different stages of a GIS in different countries. Whether this selective MNE intervention increases or diminishes the value of a country's NSI to its wider developmental concerns is the theme of our questioning here.[10] We now introduce the four stages of our NSI.

Basic research is carried out purely to resolve scientific issues, defined by scientists whose commitment is entirely to the enhancement of the body of knowledge delineating their discipline. There is no predetermined perception in the articulation or implementation of basic research projects of any specific commercial application, or of the work as being an attempt to resolve a question defined by a particular problem within a firm's current product development or engineering operations. To commercial enterprise basic research is a purely speculative scientific abstraction. However, private companies will in some way support basic research, in the view that ultimately the longer-term perspectives of competitive development will need to be fuelled by radical new perceptions driven by new dimensions of scientific understanding. Unique, or favored, access to results of a major scientific breakthrough can then be the crucial factor enhancing an enterprise's competitive revitalization and underpinning its scope for long-term survival. Similarly, countries see basic research as an important element of a balanced and sustainable NSI, as a central driver of the wider economic aims of technologically-oriented competitive progress. The particular projects implemented in a country's basic research programs will be predominantly evolutionary, with a current generation of research scientists deriving the impetus to their ongoing investigative agendas from their background in the body of knowledge currently defining distinctive scopes of that country's science base.

Horizontally, in our schematization of the NSI, currently successful enterprises will be, to some degree, based on use of scientific knowledge that is now part of the country's technological heritage and, therefore, will be willing to support further speculative research aiming to deepen understanding of those disciplines (now defining the country's internationally-perceived areas of scientific leadership). We can consider a particular piece of investigation to have reached the end of its basic research stage when it starts to be perceived as embodying potentials of specific commercial value.

Applied research then continues to be based around the investigation of specific *scientific* questions. Now, however, these questions are defined in the light of potential practical applications (e.g. in radical new generations of products, or the substantial qualitative enrichment of existing ones), that have been discerned within the results of basic research. Whilst applied research is still *done* by scientists the articulation of the problems, and the full comprehension and evaluation of results, now depends on inputs from the more creative elements in other functions (market researchers, engineers, strategic planners). Thus an enterprise with a strong innovative culture is one with well-developed and mutually-creative inter-functional communications, in which research scientists can achieve valuable and uncompromised originality with this ultimately able to support competitive commercial progress. Governments with the commitment to a full NSI, that includes basic research, would then support such complementary applied research, not by downgrading or isolating the basic work (potential threats to such purist investigation), but by generating mechanisms for the detection and activation of its potential applications. The end of the applied research stage is reached when a much clearer view of the commercial potential is available and, crucially, all the essentially scientific issues are resolved.

Product development addresses the need to turn the potentials emerging from applied research into fully-realized commercial attributes. Thus, in our terms, it uses talented marketing personnel to define the most viable commercialized form of the broad product concept and creative engineers to generate the most cost-effective supply technology in the relevant production location. Scientists remain central to the product development stage of the NSI, both in communicating the new technology to its users and, perhaps, through more applied research to resolve any unexpected residual issues. But the balance within the multi-functional product development stage has changed, with the impetus now deriving from marketing and engineering under an increasingly involved strategic management. These groups now address competitive responsiveness in specific environments, with new goods and services, defined to meet needs of particular customers, supplied in a way to optimize cost-efficiency under given impact constraints.

Adaptation of products and production processes represents the last of the creative, competitiveness-enhancing, activities encompassed in our categorization of an NSI. Over time, within a national context, a successful mature product may benefit from competitive refinement (adaptation of details and peripheral characteristics) as income levels rise and other influences provoke changes in tastes. Also, as development proceeds, changing costs and qualities of inputs (notably labor) may lead to adjustments of production techniques. Similarly, and notably relevant to our concerns here, when a firm seeks to interject production of a successful established good into a new geographical market area a suitable concern for competitive responsiveness may again lead to adaptation of the detail of product characteristics, packaging and marketing techniques, and to the way in which the good or service is produced. Again this element of global strategy denies homogeneity, and creative activity (responding to diversity) becomes part of the process of competitive spread.

MNEs' participation in NSIs

This section uses the concept of a GIS to evaluate how MNEs participate in individual NSIs. For each stage of an NSI we indicate the institutions (subsidiaries and/or laboratories) through which MNEs operate, what they interject into the NSI through such units, and the ways in which they co-opt and utilize the relevant outputs.

(i) Basic research

The institutional arrangement through which MNEs' GIS enters the basic research components of an NSI is the IIL (Figure 8.3). This provides inputs into the NSI in two ways: funding and new dimensions of technology. As we have defined it an IIL is a wholly-owned and fully-controlled research facility of an MNE operating within another country's NSI. The aim is to generate new research results whose value is likely to be perceived in a manner that is synergistic with other results (or supportive of ongoing research agendas) elsewhere in the group. An MNE's financial commitment to an IIL is likely to be manifest, firstly, in expanded scientific infrastructure, through the building of new labs or the extensive refurbishment and re-equipment of existing ones.

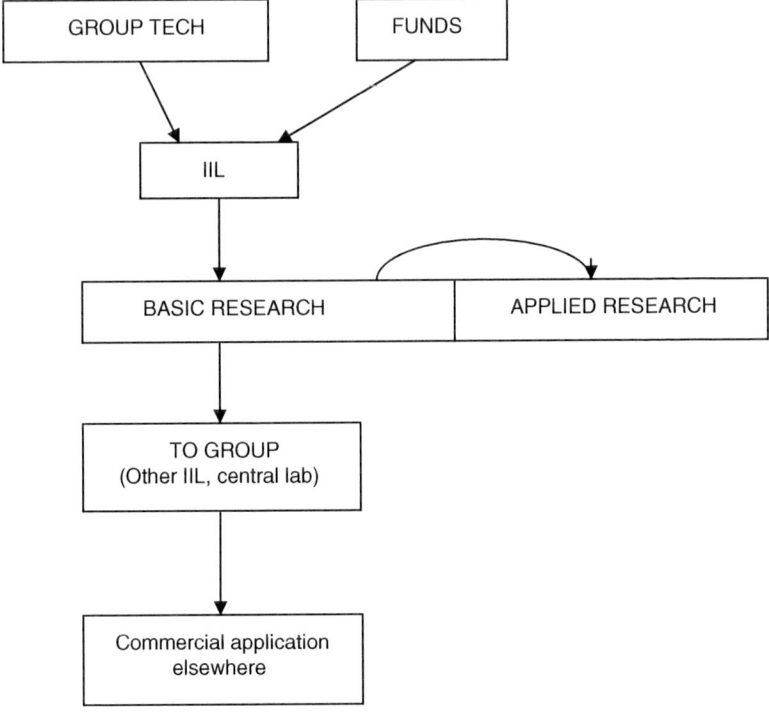

Figure 8.3 Basic Research

The second funding component of an IIL will take the form of salaries to locally-trained scientists. Thus the distinctive research capacity that emerges in an IIL is expected to derive from the recruitment of a balanced team of local scientists, who possess specialist capabilities that reflect their education, training and previous research work within the country's science base. This immediately raises the crucial point that these are potentially scientists (experienced and successful researchers and, perhaps, their emerging 'star' protégées) with a very high opportunity cost to those local institutions that fail to retain their services. MNE funding through salaries may, therefore, be merely crowding-out some of the higher-quality possibilities in local labs.[11] This must be acknowledged as an important factor, albeit one that is hard to evaluate practically since it invokes a particularly complex version of the counterfactual situation. Two positive possibilities of the IIL can be suggested, though.

Firstly, the work the scientists do in the IIL may be more productive (in terms of strengthening local technology scope and then, perhaps, feeding through to better performance of the wider local economy) than they could have achieved in a host-country institution. How this might eventuate is a key element in the analysis here.

Secondly, the top local scientists recruited by IILs might *not* have perceived the continued development of their careers in the research units of the firms and Universities of their country of origin. They may have been candidates for the international migration that is increasingly common in high-quality human capital, with the improved funding (their salaries and project support) and/or the renewed and extended research stimulus of an IIL instead now retaining their local commitment. This is likely to have positive externalities, or spillovers, into the local scientific community beyond their direct benefits to the (admittedly 'foreign') lab they now work for. This may include charismatic stimulus (through public lectures, University visits, contributions to broader controversies and intellectual debates, etc.) to younger scientists outside their own institution (the IIL), or inputs to the formulation of wider scientific policies and programs (serving on government advisory boards, funding bodies, committees of enquiry, etc.)

The second input into an NSI deriving from the operation of an IIL can be seen as technology itself, in the sense of new research options emerging from access to an additional, but essentially complementary, body of scientific knowledge and competence (i.e. that of the parent MNE). Thus *where* an IIL is located is determined by the ability of the host-country's technological heritage and current research capacity to support the type of investigations required. But *what* that research is is determined by the MNE's own technology trajectory (Papanastassiou and Pearce, 1999, pp. 91–2). This trajectory can be seen to comprise the MNE's current stock of core technology and its embodiment in a product range, and a broadly understood view of the directions in which these are expected to evolve through basic research (IILs) and product innovation (LILs). Thus the perceived needs of extending and enriching the technological trajectory will determine the range of scientific disciplines to be researched in IILs. The essentially evolutionary nature of this will also indicate that particular IIL projects, whilst clearly seeking to benefit distinctively from the specific strengths of the host-country inputs, are likely to also be defined in the light of existing MNE technologies (those seen as potential bases for valuable progress) and indeed, to some degree, will use these technologies amongst the building blocks from which research programs are generated.

An idealized interpretation of the effects of IILs on the basic research component of an NSI is that they can both deepen and widen the scope of the work undertaken. Access to improved funding, and to a body of complementary technologies, can reinforce the scope for the NSI to further pursue those lines of basic investigation that are dictated by its own technological heritage and established specialisms. Here the IIL supports the processes of agglomeration that deepen the focus on particular areas of science for which the NSI already has an established reputation of world research leadership. But an IIL's agenda may, to some degree, also work against these agglomerative forces, without necessarily weakening the ability of distinctive basic research to benefit the rest of an NSI (and economy).

Thus research issues and current technologies of MNEs may ask somewhat different questions of the NSI's strengths than would have been articulated by purely local scientific and commercial interests. If the symbiotic process between the two scientific communities (MNE and NSI) works effectively the IIL research agenda will then differ from that which is purely locally driven, but be no less logical as an evolution of the research programs. Compared to what would have happened in their absence, IILs may widen the basic research agenda of the host country, but in ways which remain coherent and cohesive with the balanced and logical progress of the NSI. Ideally IILs carry out projects that would not otherwise have been undertaken but which, nevertheless, make distinctive use of the defining strengths of the local science base and research community.

Within the concept of a purely *national* innovation system the justification for support (financial and institutional) for *pre*competitive basic research is that ultimately some of the output *will* fuel commercial progress and supply part of the basis for the competitive evolution of the economy. However, whilst the networked position of MNEs' GIS participation may bring in resources that enrich and stimulate the basic research component of an NSI, these interdependencies may also influence the future application of their results in ways that diminish the contribution to the rest of the NSI. The international linkages and aims of GIS programs may mean that the innate tendency is to see the output of IILs more in terms of potential 'lateral' flows to other elements of the group than 'horizontal' to another phase of the NSI.[12]

There is, of course, a very real potential for MNE basic research output to move into applied research in the same NSI (indeed, almost inevitably, in the same unit). Thus the perception of possible eventual commercial use for particular basic research results may emerge in the IIL that carried out the project, and this may secure for it the permission to accede to the appropriate applied research. A strong IIL can internalize the crucial basic/applied research transition. Thus Figure 8.3 provides an arrow indicating the possible horizontal transfer of IIL output within the same NSI.

But the scope for leakage out of the NSI is, as observed, also very strong. Basic research results of an IIL may be transferred to another part of the MNE science community in two forms. In the first, possible commercial applications may, again, have been perceived in the basic researching IIL, but permission for further applied research may this time be denied. Here a group-level decision determines that another IIL, in another country, is better equipped to perform the type of applied research that appears necessary. The second case is the GIS scenario where research results flow to, and are assimilated by, a central/parent laboratory.

(ii) Applied research

An MNE's applied research in a particular NSI still takes place mainly within an IIL-type facility and still targets the solution of an essentially scientific problem. From the point of view of the GIS, however, the investigation is now less purely speculative, in the sense that the need to answer a more specifically-defined scientific question *is* perceived in terms of an emerging commercial possibility. The applied research problems posed here are now likely to derive extensively from a new body of knowledge, and thus be positioned within a complementary range of questions, that resulted from antecedent basic research in the MNE and the perception of possible competitive uses for it.

Additional funding clearly remains a routinely significant input of MNEs to the applied research component of an NSI. However, it is the ability to now ask very specific and potentially highly-rewarding questions, that are defined within a complementary body of supportive new research, that becomes relatively more important. Thus Figure 8.4 designates 'basic results' as a key MNE input. This, it is suggested, can arrive in two ways. Firstly, as part of the wider group-defined GIS program. Secondly, in a more self-contained (horizontal) fashion, where the IIL is able to carry through to an applied research context the investigation of issues deriving from its own basic work.

In ways that closely resemble those indicated earlier for basic research the MNE inputs can both enrich generally, and refocus the content of, the applied research component of an NSI. However, the latter element may have particularly significant consequences here. Whilst MNEs' involvement may well increase the amount and scientific quality of the applied research done in an NSI it will mean that an increased proportion of output is likely to be diverted away from support of the local economy

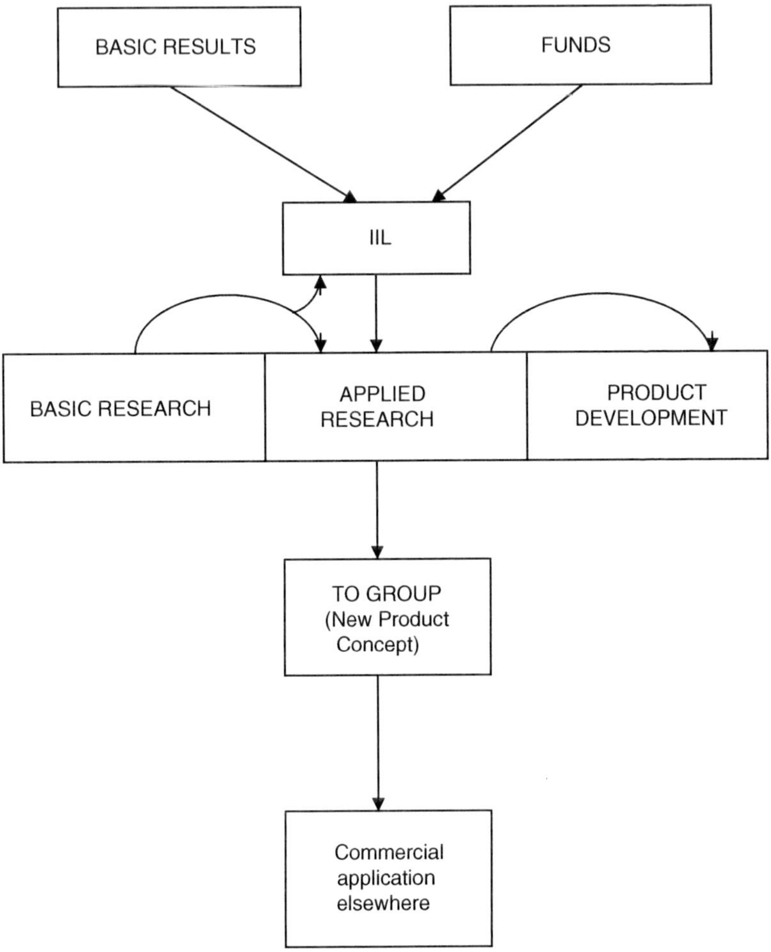

Figure 8.4 Applied Research

towards the global technological and innovation programs of the sponsoring companies.

Of course it remains possible that an MNE's important applied research results could feed forward into product development operations in the same NSI. Two factors endemic to the global aims and options of MNEs can mitigate against this, however. Firstly, even if an IIL has resolved all the scientific questions relating to an innovation (or, at least, has access to all the needed technology) it may still be that the MNE's operations in the same country do not provide the ideal context for the fulfillment of the commercial innovation process. Thus the other functional inputs that complement science in the process of innovation may be perceived as better equipped to take forward the commercial activation of the applied work in another location. Even where an innovation is self-contained around a small body of new science from one precompetitive research location, the parent group's evaluation of its range of options in other functional inputs may provoke the outward leakage of the new knowledge to the benefit of other NSIs. Second, the applied research done in an IIL may in fact be far from self-contained, and it is then innate to its role in a GIS that the results will flow from the NSI to feed into a broader program that is coordinated elsewhere. Though the results may ultimately be a significant component in building the technological base of a NPC this cannot influence the country's participation in the eventual commercialization process. Thus Figure 8.4 indicates a significant outward flow of applied results from an NSI into the dispersed GIS processes of the group.

(iii) Product development

MNEs' involvement in the product development facet of an NSI is operationalized through two institutions (Figure 8.5); a product mandate (PM) subsidiary and an associated locally integrated laboratory (LIL). The PM, we recall, takes full responsibility for the innovation, initial production, marketing and subsequent competitive evolution of a product. The LIL is a central element in the PM's creativity, and essentially mediates the new science emerging from applied research to the other functions involved in the innovation process. The framework envisages two scenarios through which new technology enters an MNE's operations in the product development stage of an NSI.

Firstly, the PM's innovation process may be predominantly driven by the results of applied research secured through the internalized (horizontal) transfer of scientific output from precompetitive IIL-type work in the same country. This independent and self-contained subsidiary-level approach to innovation will also need, and be partly defined by, top-quality marketing inputs, since it will derive locally the broad new product concept (NPC) as well as then fill in the precise details of its commercialized form. Although the scientists recruited for the LIL will embody less distinctive capacities than the basic researchers of IILs, they will still need the talent to comprehend, articulate and apply new results and often, therefore, represent a significant opportunity cost in terms of their non-availability to indigenous enterprise. As suggested, the PM's market researchers are certainly also likely to be amongst the

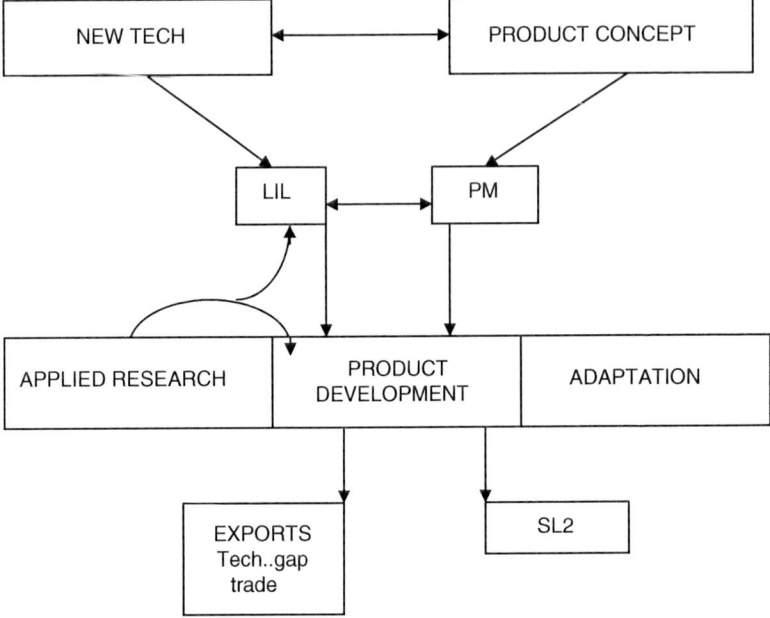

Figure 8.5 Product Development

most creative available and their recruitment, again, represents a significant opportunity cost to local firms.

Against this (and subject to the usual counterfactual uncertainties) this scenario has powerful potential to enrich the product innovation phase of an NSI. Notably it means that where an MNE's involvement in the previous stages has generated distinctive outputs in precompetitive science these are co-opted to secure equally distinctive outcomes in market competitiveness. Also it means that a product innovation secured in a PM can have greater competitive impact than would a comparable one in a local enterprise, since its markets may be determined by the MNE's wider global perspectives. Thus, we can suggest, if a new good is derived essentially within one NSI it is likely to represent a unique addition to the group's product range and potentially have access to all the world's markets. We can thus designate the subsidiary activating this self-contained scenario as a *world* product mandate (WPM).

The alternative GIS scenario determining the role of the RPM/LIL nexus in innovation involves it in the completion of a process begun elsewhere in the MNE group, by picking up an outline NPC and its associated science and generating from it a fully market-responsive and efficiently-produced good.

Where an RPM wins the responsibility to fill in the competitive detail of an NPC it is likely to do so by asserting the capacity of its host NSI to supply the necessary creative inputs (scientists, marketing, engineering), rather than potentials for low-cost production possessed by the wider local economy.[13] To do this, we have noted, it will be seeking to recruit top quality local personnel with potentially high opportunity cost to indigenous firms' innovation activity.[14] Against this, potential external benefits or spillovers may also be discerned in an enhanced learning scope available to local personnel that are recruited for the RPM/LIL's operations. Thus the process of assimilating the technology and ideas underpinning the NPC will involve these personnel in interaction with the high-level creative activity of the MNE group, which may inculcate valuable new attitudes and perceptions on the organizational procedures of efficient innovation. This will immediately strengthen the NSI by deepening the LIL's in-house ability to retain and enhance its position in its group's innovation network. Beyond this the increased experience of these personnel in the formulation and operationalization of innovation processes (additional to an enhanced competence in their specialized functional area) may be of immense value if they decide to move back into indigenous enterprise.[15]

Overall there are realistic reasons for an expectation that MNEs' use of the RPM/LIL nexus in a globalized approach to innovation can interject knowledge and resources into individual NSIs in a manner that can result in enhanced competitiveness of the local economy. The sources of this competitiveness in technology and creative personnel imputes to these MNE operations a role in generating a country's dynamic comparative advantage. Within the host economy the immediate benefits of this competitiveness may take the form of new and higher-quality products available to consumers and an upgraded employment structure encompassing higher-value jobs. However, the innate involvement of RPM/LIL operations in MNEs' global strategies also implies the benefit of improved *international* competitiveness. In Figure 8.5 we indicate the key manifestation of success for the MNE taking the form of significant exports from the host country, as the PM fulfills its responsibility to supply new goods to, at least, parts of the company's global markets. The origins of this in successful innovation characterizes this as technology gap trade.

(iv) Adaptation

Whilst the previous stage of our NSI involved the generation of the original competitive use of an initially disembodied new source of technology, here the final stage addresses the frequent need to adapt technologies that are already successfully embodied in established competitive goods in order to sharpen their value in the specific context of a particular national economy (Figure 8.6). Our understanding of the global competition strategies of MNEs suggests that production of an existing good may commence in a new country for two possible reasons.

Firstly, a market-seeking truncated miniature replica (TMR) subsidiary pursues the objective of increasing the returns from supply of the good to local consumers.[16] Traditionally a dominant factor provoking this was avoidance of restraints on trade, leading to the interpretation (Kojima, 1978) of such a relocation of production as sub-optimal,

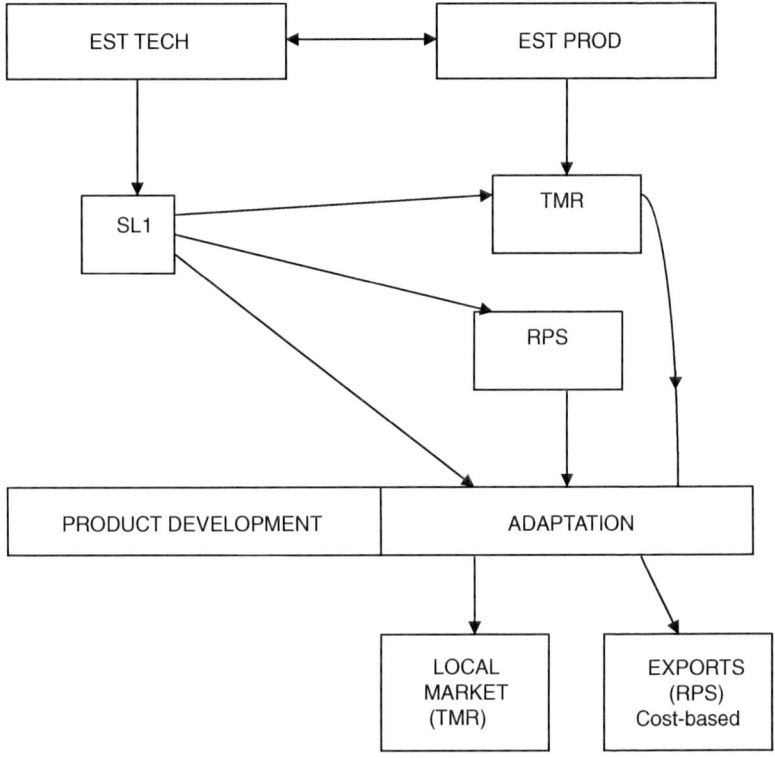

Figure 8.6 Adaptation

trade-destroying, behavior. In more recent perspectives of competitive strategy this localization of supply may, instead, acknowledge the distinctiveness of certain important markets and the advantage to then be obtained from individualized responsiveness to their idiosyncratic needs. Thus the TMR, working with an SL1 lab and a strong marketing group, will adapt the goods (and perhaps, as a result, also the production technology) to enhance their competitiveness in the perception of local consumers. The core benefit to the host economy is then manifest in greater consumer satisfaction. To the extent that this then results in greater demand, successful TMR/SL1 activity can also expand employment and tax revenues.

The second motivation (included in the GIS of Figure 8.1) for starting production of an established good in a new location is the efficiency-seeking one of securing an additional low-cost source of supply to an increasingly price-competitive international market. Thus an RPS is expected to realize economies of scale and utilize the host-country's most abundant inputs, in order to assert itself as a specialized low-cost location in an MNE's supply network for successful mature products. The importance, in an MNE's supply network rationalization process, of locating manufacture of mature goods in countries where the abundant inputs fit the existing production techniques underpins a trade-orientation that helps activate these countries' sources of static comparative advantage (Pearce, 2001). Thus it is construed (Kojima, 1978) as a welfare-enhancing trade-creating mode of behavior. In some cases MNEs may feel the need to optimize this process by adapting the production technique to further sharpen its match with available local inputs. This may be done locally (in-house) through an SL1 or externally through advice from an SL2 that is already familiar with the process technology.

Conclusions

The key theme of this analysis is that contemporary MNEs address globalization as a strengthening of the context in which they can leverage *difference* between economic areas[17] in terms of tastes, production capacities and technological and research scope. Paralleling this is the view that as countries' development proceeds the strength and distinctiveness of their NSIs increasingly defines the extent and form of their international competitiveness. The scenarios reviewed here indicate the generalized way in which the interjection of MNEs' global programs for technological and competitive enrichment can strengthen individual NSIs, but also that the GIS's tendency to do this on a selective basis can alter the balance of an NSI (between stages) and its content (what is done in a particular stage). It is the need to understand the qualitative detail of MNEs' participation, rather than quantitative extent of attraction, that is the basic policy recommendation here. This can take the form of two, complementary, warnings.

The first is a warning against a short-termist over-emphasis on attracting PM/LIL operations as a key element in a country's product development activities. Though this can strengthen the immediate scope for innovation-based trade success it often does so in a way that diminishes the depths of the roots of such competitiveness in the host economy's wider capabilities. Thus basing localized innovation on technology and product concepts already generated by the MNE can shortcut aspects of the development sequence, but also makes it extremely dependent and with a diminished reflection of distinctive localized science and competences. Sacrificing 'backward' roots in the NSI's precompetitive activity increases the dependency of the country's competitive development (innovation) on both the ability of MNEs' wider GIS to generate new product concepts, and the ability of the economy to supply the types of skills needed to *play a role* within a mainly externally-driven creative process. Lack of real roots could make MNEs' product development activity in a country almost as potentially 'footloose' as cost-based supply operations.

The second warning is the corollary of the above, suggesting that governments should normally also welcome MNE participation in basic and applied research activity. Three factors in our analysis could lead governments to display a reluctance in attracting IIL-type operations. Firstly, that the results of successful IIL research may leak from the NSI (to fuel MNEs' operations elsewhere). Secondly, that precompetitive work is *per se* expensive, unpredictable and high-risk. Thirdly, and opportunistically, that the product development stage can now depend on MNEs' global operations as sources for key scientific inputs.[18] As observed above, allowing the emergence of an imbalance in an NSI (towards product development) has innate short-termist risks by diminishing potential sources of creative sustainability. With explicit regard to IILs we have suggested that, even where the next *use* of powerful research results may be elsewhere in the MNE's network, these units can still strengthen an NSI in significant ways.

Notes

1 This is implied in Vernon's exposition of the first stage, but becomes more clear when the second stage analysis focuses on explaining how the sources of competitiveness generated in the home country innovation process

provide the firm with the capability to enter overseas markets for the first time (i.e. become MNEs).
2. In the practicalities of Vernon's modeling the product will have been innovated in the US and eventually have come within the income and taste compass of (mainly) European consumers.
3. See, for example, Granstrand and Sjolander (1992).
4. As early as the late 1970s Giddy (1978) noted that the product cycle was becoming 'highly compressed' into a series of near simultaneous innovations in several major markets.
5. We do not argue that this represents an approach that is pervasive in its full articulation amongst current MNEs. Rather it is intended to serve, for analytical purposes, as a summary of various institutional forms (e.g. laboratories) and organizational approaches and linkages that we *do* believe have been validated in the wider literature and in our own research results.
6. The main focus of our analysis here is built around the science and technology inputs as pursued through different types of R&D units. This is not to play down the importance of market research in both seeking out new product ideas and needs from customers as early inputs into innovation (stage one) or in later helping to develop the optimal variants of new products for the tastes and conditions of particular market areas (stage two). However, it is the R&D networks that we see as being consciously articulated by MNEs as a response to *ex ante* perceptions of *different* scientific potentials and technological competences of particular NSIs. Similarly it is the policy commitment to scientific and technological progress that generates the distinctive strengths of NSIs as sources of potential economic development pursued by governments.
7. For elaboration of the typology of MNE laboratories used here see Papanastassiou and Pearce (1999, pp. 149–59), Pearce (1999a). It is originally derived from Hood and Young (1982) and Haug *et al.* (1983).
8. This reflects one manifestation of the importance of interdependent individualism (chapter 7) in the innovation programs of MNEs (also relevant to PM subsidiaries and their LILs). Here one element (laboratory or subsidiary) seeks to build up a core of individualized competitive competences, but is also willing to operate interdependently by seeking supplementary advice from other parts of the group when needed, and similarly to provide support to other parts of the group from its own specialized competences.
9. Thus part of the central laboratory's responsibility can be seen as the generation of a sense of the operation of procedural justice (Kim and Mauborgne, 1991, 1993; Taggart, 1997b, 1999b) within the collaborative R&D network.
10. Of course the detail of fully-developed analyses of NSIs (Lundvall, 1992; Nelson 1993) focuses on the social institutions, competitive organizations and collaborative arrangements whose interdependencies comprise the activity at the different stages. However, we can then present our analysis as, in essence, focusing on the activity and effects of one subset of these institutions and systems, in the form of those involved in GISs of MNEs.
11. Though an element of crowding-out may also apply to the physical capital (infrastructure), it is likely to be more precise for human capital (scientists). Thus for infrastructure (laboratory capacity) net expansion is clearly feasible.

162 *Multinationals and National Systems of Innovation*

> The host-country stock of the quality of researchers sought by MNEs is, however, fixed at a particular point in time.

12. For discussion of project mobility in MNEs' science and innovation programs see Pearce and Singh (1992a, pp. 73–5, 144–5). The associated ideas of 'reverse transfer' of technology in MNEs has been analyzed by Håkanson and Nobel (2000, 2001) and Yamin (1999).
13. In fact this does not imply *inefficient* production of the new goods because the innovation process can seek to engineer production technologies that are oriented to use of the available input mix and competences.
14. The demands of local marketing personnel will be less here, however, since they do not create the truly pathbreaking aspects of an NPC but only focus on its locally-responsive refinement.
15. Indeed a certain frustration with the somewhat dependent position of an MNE's PM/LIL activity could encourage such personnel to pursue more individualized creative scope in a local enterprise once they have acquired the confidence to do so.
16. A truncated miniature replica is expected to supply most of the product range of the group (as a 'miniature replica' of the parent) to its local host-country market, but will be functionally 'truncated' through the absence of creative scope (no role in innovation) and strategic decision making.
17. Discussed for convenience during the exposition as national economies, but also applicable to wider (integrated) areas or sub-regions (clusters).
18. In fact if all, or most, developed industrial economies adopted the same opportunistic approach and lowered support for basic/applied research the ultimate result would be a slowing of technology-driven economic progress worldwide. It could then be MNEs that perceive this first and most clearly. A response could then be an attempt to reinvigorate precompetitive investigation through commitment to IIL networks.

9
Externalization and Individualism: MNE Laboratories' R&D Collaborations

Robert Pearce and Marina Papanastassiou

Introduction

A key element in the modeling of the MNE as a heterarchy (Hedlund, 1986, 1993; Hedlund and Rolander, 1990; Birkinshaw, 1994) is to discern the presence in these companies of an increasing variety of types of subsidiaries.[1] Within this the most radical perception has been of the emergence of new forms of subsidiaries, which undertake product development based round individualized in-house creative competences.[2] Another quite decisive perception is that a key factor discriminating between types of subsidiaries, and playing a strong role in defining the characteristics of the creative (product development) subsidiaries, is the degree of in-house commitment to R&D. In this way the subsidiary evolution literature parallels another strongly emerging area of investigation, i.e. that relating to the decentralization of R&D in MNEs.[3] Within this literature it is now frequently argued that 'supply-side' factors are becoming increasingly relevant, i.e. that the presence and role of MNE labs in a particular country reflects the ability of that country to supply distinctive and high-quality scientific inputs (Florida, 1997; Cantwell, 1991; Cantwell and Janne, 1999; Kuemmerle, 1999a; Granstrand, 1999). Supporting this it is then argued that a vital factor affecting the value of these MNE labs is the extent and richness of their interaction with the host-country science-base and technological community.[4] This chapter seeks to analyze certain aspects of such scientific collaborative links between foreign MNE labs operating in the UK and institutions external to the company.

It is a long-standing theme of investigation of overseas R&D in MNEs that such decentralized labs can play two very different types of roles in terms of the ways in which they can affect the technological evolution of their groups.[5] Firstly, they can work closely with an associated production subsidiary in order to support its immediate effectiveness (through adaptation of the established product it is expected to supply) or enhance its (and its group's) medium-term competitiveness by creating new products (or substantially evolutionary product variants) from the knowledge that defines the current state of the MNE's technological trajectory (Pearce, 1999b).

Secondly, such a decentralized lab could work predominantly on pre-competitive research (often totally separate from any production unit in the same country) in order to provide inputs into programs of research (often articulated and coordinated by a central laboratory) that are ultimately aimed to secure the MNE's long-term competitive development by reinforcing, in quite radical ways, the core scientific knowledge that defines the distinctive evolution of the technological trajectory itself. We have argued elsewhere (Chapter 7) that the effective positioning of labs (and where relevant the subsidiaries that embody them) to support such strategic aims invokes a process of interdependent individualism. In this the lab develops individualized competences that secure its position as a distinctive creative element in the MNE group, but still finds that it is most effectively able to fully develop and apply such distinctive abilities when exercised in ways that are interdependent with other constituents of the company's overall global operations. Thus we have suggested (Pearce and Papanastassiou, 1996b) that the creative richness of such labs derives from a careful positioning within two scientific communities, that of the parent MNE group and that of the host country. Previously (Papanastassiou, 1995, 1999; Papanastassiou and Pearce, 1997a, 1997b; Pearce, 1999a; Pearce and Papanastassiou, 1996a, 1996b, 1999) we have analyzed aspects of the former interactive positioning. Here we turn attention to the latter by reviewing evidence on the extent and nature of external research collaborations of foreign-controlled MNE labs based in the UK.

The information to be reviewed derives from a survey of foreign MNEs' laboratories operating in the UK. A questionnaire was sent to 180 such facilities and satisfactory replies were received from 48 of these.[6] The respondents include 17 in pharmaceuticals, nine in industrial chemicals, 11 in electronics and 11 in miscellaneous other industries. Nineteen had a Japanese parent company, 13 were from the US and 16 from Continental European MNEs. Four questions in the survey related directly to aspects of the labs' relations with scientific institutions outside of their MNEs' ownership or control. Analysis of these questions provides sections 2 to 5 of this chapter. Since these scientific links are here perceived as integral to the ways that decentralized labs in MNEs serve various purposes in the strategic technological programs of their group, they may vary in nature or content according to the wider positioning of the implementing labs in their MNEs' aims. To enrich discussion of the collaborations we therefore cross relate evidence on them to two other aspects of the questionnaire; i.e. those relating to the roles of UK-based labs and to the types of work done in them. This introduction concludes by briefly introducing these categorizations.

Firstly, the analysis distinguished four roles that the labs may play. The first of these was defined as 'to support UK-based production operations of the MNE by assisting in the adaptation of the products to be produced or processes to be used'. This type of support laboratory (SL1) helps solve problems that UK production subsidiaries may encounter in applying established group technology that is already embodied in products and processes. The second role was then 'to support non-UK production operations of the MNE by advising on the adaptation of the product to be produced or processes to be used'. This too is clearly a support laboratory (SL2) in that it plays an *ad hoc* troubleshooting role, rather than being an integral part of a sustained product development or knowledge generation process. However, because the SL2 serves a wider (international) constituency than the SL1 it is likely to possess a broader technological scope, to allow it to address a potentially greater range of problems, and will benefit from superior knowledge of emerging group technologies as well as possessing better communication skills (than the nationally-introverted SL1). Potentially these extra attributes may enable the SL2 to articulate, and discern circumstances where it benefits from, collaborations with local scientific institutions in ways that a SL1 might not.

Moving to a more systematically creative positioning the third lab role (the locally integrated laboratory – LIL) was defined as 'to work with the UK subsidiary's other functions (i.e. management, marketing, engineering, etc.) to develop a distinctive new product that it will produce for its markets'. Compared with the SLs the LIL takes a clearly defined *ex ante* position in a sustained product development process, rather than a sporadic *ex post* troubleshooting role relating to problems in the extension of the market and production environments for established products. The final (internationally interdependent laboratory – IIL) role is to take positions in group-level precompetitive research projects, being defined as 'to operate independently of any producing subsidiary to carry out basic or applied research (not associated with current producing operations) as part of a program of precompetitive R&D implemented and coordinated by the MNE group.'

The second classification that is intended to inform our subsequent analysis covers the types of work done in the MNE labs. The first two of these relate to what we may broadly consider as the precompetitive phase of investigation leading up to the point of the initial derivation of a generalized commercial possibility, but before the invocation of a full product development commitment. Thus these encompass 'basic research' (BASIC) and 'applied research aimed at creating a possible commercially applicable concept from basic results available in the group' (APPLIED).

The next two types of lab work represent variants within the product development stage itself. The first of these (DEV/LAB) was defined as 'development work aimed at helping to create a commercial product for particular markets from new ideas resulting from our own laboratory's applied research'. Here the development process builds on earlier work within the same laboratory, so that its associated subsidiary implements a self-contained innovation aimed at generating a relatively individualized position in its group's operations. The alternative (DEV/GROUP) takes the form of 'development work aimed at helping to create a commercial product for particular markets from new ideas resulting from applied research carried out in other laboratories in the MNE group.' Here the lab helps to position its subsidiary within an MNE's global innovation strategy (Chapter 8), in which a new product concept is to be innovated worldwide through the derivation of a number of variants that respond to the differentiated consumer tastes and production conditions of key geographical market segments. Thus a laboratory doing DEV/GROUP picks up the core group-level technology of the new product and works with local marketing and engineering units to create the distinctive variants that are most responsive to local needs. The final two types of work cover the troubleshooting objectives of SLs in the form of 'work to adapt current products for particular markets' (ADAPT/PROD) and 'work to adapt current production processes to particular conditions' (ADAPT/PROC).

Extent of MNE laboratories' scientific collaborations

In this section our main purpose is to evaluate the extent of MNE labs' collaborative associations with external scientific institutions, using evidence from the questionnaire that was sent directly to those R&D facilities. As a preface to this, however, we look briefly at information derived from a complementary questionnaire survey, involving MNEs' producing subsidiaries in the UK.[7] Here respondents were asked to evaluate seven sources of technology in terms of their importance to their operations. In this analysis the 'front-line' sources of technology emerged as existing group technology (either as already embodied in established products or in a disembodied form ready for development into new products by the subsidiary), in-house R&D within the subsidiary or R&D inputs secured from elsewhere in the group (these perspectives thereby supporting the overall view of interdependence alongside the individualism of the subsidiary). However, local scientific links did emerge as a quite prevalent, albeit predominantly secondary or supportive, source of their current technology as perceived by the manufacturing subsidiaries. Thus whereas only 3.3% of respondents deemed 'R&D carried out for us by local scientific institutions (e.g. universities, independent labs, industry labs)' to be a 'major' source of their technology, a further 40.3% did consider such inputs to be a 'secondary' source.

The first type of collaborative link addressed in the survey of the labs themselves was those with 'Universities in the UK'. Here 14 (29.2%) of respondents said that such collaborations were 'extensive', 25 (52.1%) rated them as 'moderate' and only 9 (18.7%) considered that they were 'non-existent'. When converted into an average response in Table 9.1 this indicates that collaborations with universities were the most prevalent type for these MNE labs. That this suggests a stronger perception of scientific links than reported by the production subsidiaries (in the complementary survey noted above) may be due to two factors. Firstly, the lab survey includes cases of MNE labs which are independent from production subsidiaries (and therefore not covered by that questionnaire) and which, it may be hypothesized, are the most likely to value the high-quality and scientifically-distinctive inputs from local facilities to support their usually more ambitious (basic and applied research) aims. Secondly, when the replies derive from production subsidiaries they may be able to clearly evaluate any technology inputs they receive directly from their in-house labs, but be much less aware of any component in this knowledge that was contributed by the lab's association with a UK university.

An expectation here would be that university labs are likely to do work of a predominantly precompetitive nature (i.e. with no immediate commercial problem or market potential in mind)[8] in particular technological disciplines that reflect a distinctive long-term area of specialization in the country's science base. From this we expect that such collaborations would be strongest for MNE labs whose own specialization and role is towards the longer-term aims of strengthening the group's technological

Table 9.1 Extent of collaboration between MNE laboratories in the UK and other scientific institutions

	Institution (average response[1])						
	A	B	C	D	E	F	G
By industry							
Electronics	1.82	1.18	1.45	1.64	1.82	1.27	1.27
Pharmaceuticals	2.29	1.65	1.29	1.41	1.47	1.29	1.29
Chemicals[2]	2.33	1.89	1.44	1.67	1.44	1.44	1.56
Other	1.91	1.55	1.73	1.27	1.36	1.27	1.45
Total	2.10	1.56	1.46	1.48	1.52	1.31	1.38
By home country							
USA	2.08	1.69	1.54	1.38	1.46	1.23	1.31
Japan	2.05	1.37	1.32	1.42	1.74	1.16	1.21
Europe	2.19	1.69	1.56	1.63	1.31	1.56	1.63
Total	2.10	1.56	1.46	1.48	1.52	1.31	1.38
By type of laboratory[3,5]							
SL1	1.83	1.58	1.42	1.42	1.58	1.17	1.58
SL2	2.14	1.71	1.29	1.57	1.71	1.43	1.57
LIL	2.12	1.53	1.47	1.65	1.59	1.18	1.24
IIL	2.20	1.55	1.35	1.25	1.30	1.50	1.40
By type of R & D [4,5]							
BASIC	2.22	1.56	1.44	1.33	1.44	1.44	1.44
APPLIED	2.24	1.71	1.47	1.47	1.47	1.47	1.59
DEV/LAB	2.18	1.55	1.59	1.68	1.55	1.32	1.41
DEV/GROUP	1.93	1.40	1.27	1.40	1.73	1.13	1.00
ADAPT/PROD	1.88	1.50	1.25	1.38	1.63	1.00	1.25
ADAPT/PROC	2.00	2.00	1.33	1.33	1.67	1.00	1.33

Institutions:
A – Universities in the UK.
B – Independent research laboratories in the UK.
C – Industry research laboratories in the UK.
D – Other UK firms.
E – Other independent firms overseas.
F – Universities overseas (e.g. as part of an EU supported programme).
G – Government and other public laboratories.

Notes:
1. Respondents were asked to grade collaborations with particular institutions as (i) extensive, (ii) moderate, (iii) non-existent. The average response was calculated by allocating extensive the value of 3, moderate the value of 2, non-existent the value of 1.
2. Includes petrochemicals and petroleum.
3. Average response calculated for labs that said they were 'predominantly' or 'only' that type.
4. Average response calculated for labs that said the type of R&D was their 'only' or 'predominant' work.
5. For definitions of lab types and types of R&D see text.

trajectory through a precompetitive research focus.[9] Thus university collaborations emerge as strongest (Table 9.1) for those MNE labs where basic and/or applied research are a strong priority. Such links are, however, also very important for labs that help subsidiaries to develop products based on their own research (DEV/LAB), with this notably exceeding their relevance to labs that help with the creation of new products based on group-level research (DEV/GROUP). So where MNE subsidiaries create products based on a sustained in-house (subsidiary-level) scientific effort this does seem to reflect an interaction with local knowledge specialisms (as embodied in university research traditions) that is continued on into the actual product development process. But when the subsidiary picks-up new group-level technology as the basis for its product development the local technology heritage is then less relevant to support of the innovation process, so that university links are rather less prevalent. University collaborations are also of relatively limited significance for labs doing mainly adaptive work.

Reflecting the previous results and interpretation university collaborations are most relevant to IIL type units and least so to the SL1 type. Such university links also support LILs quite strongly (probably especially those with DEV/LAB product creation focus) and also SL2 type units. The latter result suggests that support of a wider constituency by SL2s, compared to SL1s, demands higher-quality work, and perhaps the solving of *ad hoc* problems that are beyond the scope of their immediate in-house knowledge or research competence. Labs of European MNEs and those in chemicals and pharmaceuticals were the most likely to have formulated collaborative arrangements with UK universities.

Our expectation is that 'independent research labs in the UK' would base their ability to market themselves to potential customers/collaborators through a heritage of research experience within the acknowledged technological specialization of the host country. Though this might allow for slightly less flexibility of scope than university laboratories, it would involve the same precompetitive-research-related appeal to potential MNE collaborators. Such links with independent labs are overall much less prevalent than with universities. Thus only one MNE respondent reported that such links are extensive, 25 (52.1%) rated them as moderate and 22 (45.8%) considered them to be non-existent. As with the case for universities, collaborations with independent labs are most prevalent for chemicals and pharmaceuticals and in European-controlled labs, though here US labs also use these links to an above average degree.

In the main (the strong result for ADAPT/PROC excepted) the results in Table 9.1 are compatible with the view that independent labs provide high-quality locally-specialized technological inputs, though perhaps applied somewhat closer to commercial problems and priorities than hypothesized. Thus MNE labs that are focusing on applied work now clearly prevail over those doing basic research, in terms of their collaborations with UK independent labs, whilst those developing products locally in a technologically self-contained fashion (DEV/LAB) continue to prevail over those creating products in a group innovation program (DEV/GROUP). Here IILs, LILs and SL1-type units differ little in their propensity for collaborations (which represents a relative enhancement of the SL1 position compared to that with university labs), whilst SL2s emerge as most likely to establish such associations with independent labs. It may be the case, therefore, that independent labs are able to provide specialized inputs that complement the competences of the MNE facilities, but these are then accessed and exercised in a relatively more *ad hoc* problem-solving fashion (i.e. in the more ambitious types of SL2 activity) than as integral parts of ongoing programs of product development (LIL) or precompetitive (IIL) work.

The third scientific institution that the survey offered for evaluation, in terms of degree of collaboration with MNE labs, was 'industry research laboratories in the UK'. This envisages local labs that have a tradition of (often significantly industry funded) support for particularly focused areas of science. These, therefore, are labs that are likely to have a strong background in those scientific disciplines that are especially relevant to 'their' industry, but which also have a greater knowledge of, and commitment (compared with university and independent labs) to, the problems and potentials of the commercial application of this specialized competence. No MNE labs felt they had extensive collaborations with industry labs in the UK, but 45.8% did perceive such associations to exist to a moderate degree. Pharmaceuticals is the industry that is distinctively the least oriented to this type of collaboration (Table 9.1). This then reflects its generally stronger commitment to those more purely scientific elements of precompetitive investigation that are better articulated through research links with universities and independent labs. As was also the case with independent labs (though less decisively so for universities) Japanese MNEs are least likely to establish associations with industry labs. This may reflect either unfamiliarity with such institutions in an environment to which they are relatively new, or a perceived lack of need to seek outside advice on their currently very effective commercial technologies and product.

LILs show relatively strong links with industry labs. This is compatible with the latter's anticipated expertise in the commercial application of technology. In a similar way the stronger links of SL1s, relative to SL2s and thus reversing the position for independent labs, seems to reflect a particular knowledge of the localized (here UK) market conditions for commercial applications of technology as a distinctive capacity of these industry labs. The leading position of MNE labs doing DEV/LAB work, in terms of degree of links with industry labs, is again likely to reflect the ability of these local facilities to assist these MNE labs (and their associated producing subsidiaries) in not only the nurturing of distinctive technological capacities (that derive from the local scientific tradition) but also, most crucially, its applications to a process of product development that is responsive to local conditions.

MNE labs' research collaborations with 'other UK firms' were rated as extensive by two (4.2%) respondents and as moderate by another 19 (39.6%). The relative prevalence of such collaborations in labs focusing on DEV/LAB and APPLIED work, and those substantially taking on the LIL role, suggests these links are entered into as an element of a product development process. Since we have shown elsewhere (Papanastassiou and Pearce, 1997a) that MNEs' product development subsidiaries in the UK make substantial use of independent UK input suppliers, we may suggest that this creative relationship underpins many of the interfirm research collaborations found here. Pure scientific research on the other hand seems sparse in such collaborations (low values for BASIC and IILs). Though there has been much discussion of inter-firm collaboration in this phase of research, in terms of strategic technology alliances (Dunning, 1993b; Chesnais, 1988; Hagedoorn, 1993), it seems likely that such relationships (precisely because of their often strategic implications) are most clearly articulated at the parent (rather than subsidiary) level.

Two types of overseas collaborations for MNEs' UK labs were suggested. Firstly, 'other independent firms overseas' provided extensive research associations for four (8.3%) of the responding labs and moderate links for 17 (35.4%) more. Once again precompetitive research appears to be of little relevance to the formulation of such links (low values for IILs, BASIC and APPLIED). Instead these collaborations were relatively strongest in the SL2 type of lab that is defined to have an international commitment and where work involves an interdependent position in a group-level innovation program (DEV/GROUP). Though the associations defined for SL2s and DEV/GROUP work are intra-group (with sister labs or subsidiaries of the same group) it appears that their expertise in international communications, and their generally more extrovert and cosmopolitan outlook, also provides them with the competences to generate research collaborations with independent firms outside the UK.

Secondly, the MNE labs felt that R&D links with 'universities overseas' (e.g. as part of EU supported programs) were extensive in two (4.2%) cases and moderate in 11 (22.9%) more, but absent from 35 (72.9%). That links were most prevalent for labs of European MNEs may, indeed, reflect the presence of EU support. A strong precompetitive element in such programs would also be compatible with the relative prevalence of such links in IILs and in those labs oriented towards BASIC and APPLIED work.

Finally, respondents were asked to evaluate their research collaborations with 'government and other public laboratories'. None assessed these as being extensive, and only 18 (37.5%) believed they were even of moderate relevance. The relatively strong response of European MNEs' labs alongside quite strong collaborations of IILs and BASIC and APPLIED work, could again suggest the presence of relationships that are generated within the context of EU supported programs. The strong results for both types of SL are, however, neither compatible with this possible institutional influence nor with the types of work that provoke such collaborations (e.g. low values for adaptation).

Content of R&D collaborations

We have suggested in earlier sections that the collaborative R&D arrangements analyzed here involve MNEs tapping into distinctive knowledge and skill competences of host countries in order to secure, in various ways, the enhancement of their own technological scope to support their global competitiveness. The MNE programs to both create new core technology (precompetitive research), and to apply it effectively commercially (through globalized approaches to innovation), are increasingly articulated through international networks that involve strong intra-group research interdependencies and knowledge transfers.[10] This means it is no longer at all inevitable that high-quality inputs and scientific work that are secured in one country will automatically boost the immediate competitiveness of that economy. Therefore significant issues may be seen to arise concerning the value to host countries of allowing MNEs the scope to access and work with institutions within their scientific community (Pearce, 1989, 1997; Pearce and Papanastassiou, 1996a; Dunning, 1993b). An important discriminating element in understanding the issues that are involved here is the nature of work done within collaborations between MNEs and host-country institutions (Chapter 8). Therefore the questionnaire that was sent to MNE labs asked them to state whether each of five different types of work played a role in their collaborations with UK-based scientific institutions.

The types of issues raised above perhaps take their most stark form in the case of basic research. The strong prevalence of the types of subsidiary-level product development (LAB/DEV) that embody ideas and technology uniquely accessed or created by that subsidiary suggests that on occasion locally-derived basic research results can feed through to self-contained in-house product innovation. But this is by no means the only likely scenario. Alternatively basic research that is done at the subsidiary lab level (supported by local collaborations) may be only a specialized part of an MNE's global program, with other complementary research done in labs in other countries. The ultimate output may then be derived centrally (in a 'parent' lab) through a synthetic overview of all the decentralized elements of the extended and dispersed program. Though this should lead to vital new product concepts being implemented globally by the MNE, the extent to which its operations in any country might receive a competitive boost through this will not be automatically related in any systematic way to the contribution that country might have made to the earlier phases of the MNE's research.

Nevertheless, whilst the basic research element in collaborations may well not result in a direct or immediate boost to a host-country's competitiveness, it could have important indirect longer-term benefits. These could accrue if host-country scientific institutions improve their scope, knowledge and experience through collaborations with MNEs. Improved funding, entry into the alternative knowledge community of the MNE and experience of how it organizes and implements its wider R&D programs may all enhance the scope of host-country institutions and their researchers and planners. This can then engender ultimate improvements in the ability of the local scientific community to contribute to the growth of competitiveness of locally-based industry. It becomes relevant, therefore, to look at the degree of presence of basic research in collaborations and, in particular, at the context within which it occurs.

Overall Table 9.2 shows that one-third of MNE labs that had links with UK scientific institutions included basic research in such collaborative work. As would be expected basic research was most prevalent in the collaborations of those MNE labs that themselves had a predominant focus on this type of work, though 37.5% of them only used the association with the UK institutions for applied work. This may suggest that the local institution here gets an early acquaintance with new basic research output that has been derived entirely within the MNE laboratory and therefore provides an example of how such links can enrich the knowledge available to the local technological community. In addition half of

Table 9.2 Types of R&D involved in collaborations of MNE laboratories with other UK scientific institutions

	Types of work (percentage of respondents[1])				
	Basic Research	Applied Research	Product Development	Product Adaptation	Process Adaptation
By industry					
Electronics	14.3	57.1	28.6	14.3	57.1
Pharmaceuticals	41.2	70.6	29.4	5.9	0
Chemicals[2]	28.6	71.4	14.3	0	28.6
Other	36.4	63.6	27.3	18.2	36.4
Total	33.3	66.7	26.2	9.5	23.8
By home country					
USA	33.3	75.0	41.7	16.7	25.0
Japan	26.7	46.7	20.0	13.3	13.3
Europe	40.0	80.0	20.0	0	33.3
Total	33.3	66.7	26.2	9.5	23.8
By type of laboratory[3,5]					
SL1	33.3	88.9	11.1	22.2	33.3
SL2	14.3	71.4	28.6	14.3	28.6
LIL	33.3	75.0	41.7	25.0	33.3
IIL	50.0	60.0	10.0	5.0	15.0
By type of R&D[4,5]					
BASIC	62.5	62.5	0	0	0
APPLIED	50.0	81.3	12.5	6.3	12.5
DEV/LAB	38.1	57.1	38.1	14.3	23.8
DEV/GROUP	27.3	54.5	27.3	18.2	18.2
ADAPT/PROD	0	60.0	20.0	40.0	60.0
ADAPT/PROC	0	33.3	33.3	33.3	66.7

Notes:
1. Percentage of respondents who considered that at least part of their collaboration with another scientific institution was to assist with a particular type of work.
2. Includes petrochemicals and petroleum.
3. Figures for labs that said they were 'predominantly' or 'only' that type.
4. Figures for labs that said the type of R&D was their 'only' or 'predominant' work.
5. For definitions of lab types and types of R&D see text.

the labs that focused their work mainly on applied research sought inputs of basic work from local collaborations. These two results parallel the greatest prevalence of basic research in the local links of IILs. Nevertheless both LILs and SLs, and labs doing the DEV/LAB variants of product creation, also incorporated basic research to a substantial degree in their collaborations. This points to the presence of a certain amount of UK-based product development by MNEs that derives from semi-autonomous sequentially-integrated scientific work that is contained within subsidiaries and builds on local basic research. Thus it appears that whereas a very clear potential for basic research results derived within MNEs' collaborations to 'leak' out of the UK through IILs does exist, the alternative possibility of 'capturing' such results for localized product development through LILs (and DEV/LAB work) is also indicated in the results.

The phase of applied research may be considered to run from the point where the purely scientific results of basic research begin to be perceived to have possible commercial possibilities to the point where such potentials have been refined to the state of a new product concept. The product concept then defines the broad service that the new good will provide and puts into place all the technology needed to produce it, but without the full development of its commercial format. Successful applied research at the subsidiary level may obviously lead to locally-integrated product development (commercial refinement of the product concept, i.e. DEV/LAB within the host country). However, given the technological networking and globalized-innovation perspectives of contemporary MNEs, applied research results (like basic ones) may migrate for further development elsewhere in the group[11] (i.e. the host country may not get the full benefit of the extra value-added scope its technological inputs help create). Since Table 9.2 shows that two-thirds of MNE lab collaborations with UK scientific institutions involved applied research it is again relevant to scrutinize closely the contexts where this occurs.

Perhaps predictably applied research is most prominent in the collaborations of those MNE labs that themselves focus on such work as their own predominant motivation. However, its prevalence in the links of basic research labs, and as the most prominent element in the local associations of IILs, opens up the possibility that in some cases the further development of collaborative applied research may occur elsewhere in the MNE group. Nevertheless the fact that applied research occurs in three-quarters of LILs' collaborations, and in over half of those of labs that focused on DEV/LAB (and even DEV/GROUP), does suggest the successful localized appropriation of the results of such research associations in many cases.

There is also a strong position for applied research in the collaborations of SLs and of labs focusing on product adaptation. This may have an explanation in the processes of subsidiary evolution in modern MNEs. Thus we have noted elsewhere (Chapter 7) that subsidiaries producing standardized products, that traditionally employ SL1s, feel vulnerable in the contemporary MNE and seek to use their labs (whose own survival would otherwise be in doubt) to upgrade and individualize their competences in order to secure a move to a high-value-added product-development status. Working with local labs on applied research (which would be beyond the initially limited in-house scope of SLs) may secure distinctive new knowledge for the ambitious subsidiary. This is pursued away from the (potentially disapproving) scrutiny of the parent company, and can also provide a learning environment within which the SL's personnel can enhance their own research scope and perspectives. In this way SLs implementing such externalized applied research collaborations hope to upgrade their own status to LIL, by enriching their own knowledge base and research scope and by endowing their related subsidiary with the technological capacity for individualized product development.

Work on product development only occurs in just over one-quarter of the collaborations in Table 9.2. This reflects the fact that the technological input into this type of work needs to be very closely integrated with other in-house functions (e.g. marketing, engineering, financial management) and also that the specialized competences of many local institutions (e.g. university labs) are more focused on the pre-competitive research phases. Nevertheless product development collaborations were most prevalent where they would be predicted (i.e. in LILs and those labs whose work focused on DEV/LAB and DEV/GROUP). Also it should be recalled that these labs, with a predominant product development mandate, did have strong collaborations involving basic and, especially, applied research, thereby building their own technological competences prior to the more widely-functioned and coordinated in-house development process.

As would be anticipated work on adaptation of products was a rare constituent of the research collaborations covered here, occurring in less than one-tenth of all cases. Even those MNE labs for which product adaptation was the main function only included such work in four-tenths of their own collaborations, instead focusing on rather more ambitious work for reasons suggested above. However, process adaptation laboratories did incorporate work of the same type in two-thirds of their collaborations which, along with its strong complementary presence in product adaptation labs, meant process adaptation work was included in almost one-quarter of all links.

Motivations for collaborations

The questionnaire also investigated some of the reasons behind R&D collaborations between MNE labs and UK scientific institutions. As

Table 9.3 indicates the vast majority of the labs (91.9%) felt that such scientific links served *inter alia* to simply extend the scope of their operations by enabling them 'to secure inputs that we do not have in our own laboratory'. The pervasiveness of this motivation means that it does not vary at all systematically in relevance between types of lab or the nature of the work that they do. It does, however, underline a more general point about the decentralization of R&D in MNEs. Thus it suggests that the types of MNE labs covered here do not attempt to internalize all the knowledge or skills that they require, but have an innate willingness to complete their scope through externalized relationships with other elements of the host-country science base. The collaborations can therefore be seen as strongly indicative of the way that decentralized R&D labs in MNEs serve to mediate between these companies' overall scientific needs and an increasingly geographically-differentiated and permanently-evolving range of sources. Initially these qualitative aspects of the local science base help to determine what roles an MNE operation there can claim within its group's programs. The lab can then decide (with various degrees of parent company intrusion) what elements are best brought within its permanent in-house scope and what may be better performed within the types of supporting collaborations that are surveyed here.

Just over half (51.4%) of responding labs felt that their collaborations also served 'to improve our knowledge of the direction of scientific activity in our research field'. This is again part of a crucial monitoring function that is played by decentralized R&D in MNEs. As innovation-oriented MNEs find that they need inputs from a wider range of scientific disciplines to support their effective technological evolution, and as an increasing range of countries move to the frontiers of specialized areas (i.e. as individual national science bases narrow in terms of their true world class specialisms (Cantwell, 1991), but more countries have *some* such leading-edge competences), these companies need means of retaining a sustained contact with the sources of scientific progress in all relevant locations (e.g. university and other specialist labs). Their overseas R&D labs and, in turn, their collaborations with relevant local institutions seem to serve this purpose. The potential pure research (precompetitive) orientation of this behavior seems to be reflected in the fact that this motivation is endorsed most strongly by IILs and labs doing basic and applied work.

Only two of the other reasons for collaboration covered in the survey (Table 9.3) received more than negligible support. First 16.2% of respondents felt that work within such collaborations enabled them 'to help in

Table 9.3 Reasons for collaboration of MNE laboratories in the UK with other scientific institutions

	Reasons for collaboration (percentage of respondents[1])							
	A	B	C	D	E	F	G	H
By industry								
Electronics	75.0	50.0	12.5	12.5	12.5	0	0	12.5
Pharmaceuticals	92.9	42.9	0	0	7.1	0	0	7.1
Chemicals[2]	100.0	71.4	14.3	0	28.6	0	0	28.6
Other	100.0	50.0	0	0	12.5	12.5	12.5	25.0
Total	91.9	51.4	5.4	2.7	13.5	2.7	2.7	16.2
By home country								
USA	100.0	40.0	0	0	10.0	10.0	10.0	20.0
Japan	78.6	42.9	0	0	14.3	0	0	14.3
Europe	100.0	69.2	15.4	7.7	15.4	0	0	15.4
Total	91.9	51.4	5.4	2.7	13.5	2.7	2.7	16.2
By type of laboratory[3,5]								
SL1	87.5	50.0	0	0	12.5	12.5	12.5	37.5
SL2	100.0	62.5	0	0	0	0	0	12.5
LIL	100.0	41.7	0	0	8.3	8.3	8.3	25.0
IIL	87.5	68.8	6.3	0	18.8	0	0	6.3
By type of R & D[4,5]								
BASIC	75.0	62.5	0	0	0	0	0	12.5
APPLIED	87.5	68.8	6.3	0	12.5	0	0	12.5
DEV/LAB	83.3	44.4	5.6	0	22.2	0	0	27.8
DEV/GROUP	88.9	44.4	0	0	11.1	0	0	22.2
ADAPT/PROD	75.0	0	0	0	0	25.0	25.0	50.0
ADAPT/PROC	100.0	0	0	0	0	0	0	0

Reasons for collaboration:
A – to secure inputs that we do not have in our own laboratory.
B – to improve our knowledge of the direction of scientific activity in our research field.
C – to improve our production subsidiary's image.
D – for financial/tax reasons.
E – in response to our group's policy.
F – in response to government pressures.
G – in response to government incentives.
H – to help in the improvement of the quality of life (e.g. environment, nutrition, other social concerns).

Notes:
1. Percentage of respondents who considered that a particular reason played a role in the implementation of their collaboration(s).
2. Includes petrochemicals and petroleum.
3. Figures for labs that said they were 'predominantly' or 'only' that type.
4. Figures for labs that said the type of R&D was their 'only' or 'predominant' work.
5. For definitions of lab types and types of R&D see text.

the improvement of the quality of life' by addressing issues relating to the environment, nutrition and other social concerns. The concerns were of greatest relevance in labs involved with product adaptation and product development and that were most likely to be locally responsive (i.e. LILs and SL1s). Thus it may be that the MNE subsidiaries and their labs feel a social and marketing-related need to help address particular issues of local public concern. They may do this through collaborations both because local institutions already have a background in the problems and because announcement of such associations provide good public relations.

Secondly, 13.5% of respondents felt their implementation of collaborations was 'in response to our group's policy'. The earlier discussion suggested reasons why MNEs might feel potential benefits from their decentralized R&D units' interactions with the local science base. But only a small number of these overseas labs seem to be aware of this as a forcefully articulated group policy. Though absent from the perception of basic research labs this motivation tends to otherwise occur where it would seem to be most relevant (i.e. in IILs, applied research labs and in units with a product development orientation). These types of units have a level of in-house orientation that provides them with the ability to read and evaluate local scientific trends through collaborative work.

Forms of collaborations and universities

The final question investigated the nature of MNE labs' collaborations with UK universities. The first of the possibilities related to the presence of 'work proposed and carried out by the university, and funded by us'. Overall 38.1% of responding MNE labs felt that such a situation occurred within their collaborations (Table 9.4). By type of MNE lab IILs were clearly the most likely to adopt this type of collaboration and SL1s notably least so. Furthermore those labs mainly doing basic or applied work used such associations most, followed by both types of product development unit, whilst this form of agreement was absent from labs with an adaptation orientation. Clearly the further the natural concerns of the MNE labs are from the solution of short-term problems relating to current commercial technology, and the closer they are to the longer-term pure scientific investigation needed to reinforce their group's core knowledge, the more they rely on host-country universities to discern the most promising lines of (mainly basic) research. This reinforces the view that though precompetitive research is accepted by MNEs as needing to be fully addressed if they are to achieve sustained competitiveness, the natural environment for the proper articulation, and purely

Table 9.4 Nature of collaboration with UK universities of MNE laboratories in the UK

	Form of collaboration (percentage of respondents[1])				
	A	B	C	D	E
By industry					
Electronics	57.1	57.1	28.6	28.6	71.4
Pharmaceuticals	47.1	82.4	23.5	41.2	58.8
Chemicals[2]	37.5	75.0	25.0	62.5	62.5
Other	10.0	60.0	40.0	40.0	60.0
Total	38.1	71.4	28.6	42.9	64.3
By home country					
USA	16.7	66.7	25.0	50.0	91.7
Japan	50.0	64.3	14.3	21.4	35.7
Europe	43.8	81.3	43.8	56.3	68.8
Total	38.1	71.4	28.6	42.9	64.3
By type of laboratory[3,5]					
SL1	22.2	77.8	33.3	44.4	55.5
SL2	42.9	85.7	14.3	28.6	57.1
LIL	38.5	76.9	38.5	30.8	61.5
IIL	52.6	68.4	31.6	52.6	57.9
By type of R & D[4,5]					
BASIC	44.4	77.8	33.3	44.4	55.5
APPLIED	41.2	76.4	23.5	52.9	64.7
DEV/LAB	28.6	71.4	38.1	52.4	61.9
DEV/GROUP	27.3	72.7	18.2	45.5	45.5
ADAPT/PROD	0	80.0	0	20.0	60.0
ADAPT/PROC	0	66.7	0	33.3	66.7

Form of collaboration:
A – work proposed and carried out by the university, and funded by us.
B – work proposed and funded by us, but carried out by the university.
C – participation in, and coordination of, wider research projects involving several universities.
D – provision of scholarships for research students at universities.
E – employing students in our laboratory as interns.

Notes:
1. Percentage of respondents that endorsed the relevance of a particular form of collaboration to their university links.
2. Includes petrochemicals and petroleum.
3. Figures for labs that said they were 'predominantly' or 'only' that type.
4. Figures for labs that said the type of R&D was their 'only' or 'predominant' work.
5. For definitions of lab types and types of R&D see text.

scientifically-motivated performance, of much of the work of this type is within universities.

As previously observed a significant role of many overseas R&D units in MNEs is to monitor and tap into precompetitive work where it is being done in their host country, reflecting the increasing tendency for particular countries to generate areas of world leadership in specialized scientific disciplines. In order to evaluate likely local collaborations effectively, and to benefit most decisively from a coherent working relationship with them, the MNE labs themselves usually need to incorporate a certain level of in-house basic and, especially, applied research commitment. Though such in-house performance of precompetitive work by MNEs' overseas labs is itself significant, the evidence here also suggests that it understates the importance of internationalized access to this type of research and knowledge as an element in the globalized technology programs of these companies.

The complementary type of collaboration, in the form of 'work proposed and funded by us, but carried out by the university', was used by 71.4% of responding MNE labs. In absolute terms this format was again very strongly used by IILs and by labs with a basic or applied research focus (Table 9.4). This again suggests that labs with in-house precompetitive competences and priorities can also use this part of their background to articulate, in a more pre-emptive way, programs of work that can embody complementary expertise of local labs. The MNE labs are again seen to be acting as a crucial medium for the creative interaction of their group's current technology trajectory with those national science bases that can provide key precompetitive research inputs to the longer-term enrichment and reinforcement of the core technology. This then helps to define the form taken by the future evolution of the MNE's technology trajectory.

However, by contrast with the earlier form of association, development and adaptation oriented labs also make very extensive use of this second type of collaboration. In many such cases the problems to be addressed within the university collaboration emerge initially from the inter-functional associations of the MNE labs (e.g. with associated marketing and/or engineering groups within a production subsidiary). Elements of technology problems that are detected in this way may then devolve onto the labs' local collaborative links. This may take different forms, however. In the case of LILs addressing local product development high-quality in-house abilities may be matched to strong university lab competences in a confidently proactive attempt to secure the capacity for sustained localized knowledge input into MNE innovation processes.

Here the MNE lab has a skill in discerning the technological needs of a subsidiary that is seeking to build an individualized product development competence, and can skilfully mix internal and external capabilities in sustained dynamic programs that support their aims. On the other hand where SL1s address difficulties in local application of existing products and processes they may be most adept at defining the technological issues (good inter-functional communications), but sometimes lack the scope to actually solve problems that then arise. Where they cannot get an answer from elsewhere in the MNE (due to a strongly localized element in the problem or, perhaps, a reluctance to expose their own limitations within the group) they may invoke a more *ad hoc* association with a host-country university.

A broader context for these collaborations, in the form of 'participation in, and coordination of, wider research projects involving several universities' was recognized by only 28.6% of responding labs. The projects articulated by labs in this way seem to address both pre-competitive and product development aims. The last two forms of scientific link that were evaluated involved support of students. Though the direct work of such young scientists is unlikely to immediately boost the MNE's technology in uniquely distinctive ways, support of them may provide a key basis for the creation of a mutual confidence in its position in the local science base. It also fits with the types of spillovers that may enable MNE labs to play a positive role in the broader development of the host-country science base and its technology scope. Here 64.3% of labs reported that they were 'employing students in our labs as interns' and 42.9% supported the 'provision of scholarships for research students at universities'.

Conclusion

An essential element in governments' attempts to build the bases of sustainable development in recent decades has been the generation of national systems of innovation (NSI). Descriptions of these (Nelson, 1993; Lundvall, 1992) emphasize the range of institutions and agents that play roles in NSI and draw attention to the importance, often the key factor discriminating between failure and success, of the linkages and interdependencies generated between these components. MNEs' attraction to various NSI reflect the distinctive strengths and heterogeneous learning and creative potentials offered by them. Through subsidiaries mandated to create products, and laboratories encouraged to pursue distinctive research agendas, MNEs insert their own components into particular NSI.

These subsidiaries and laboratories seek to secure strong individualized positions (Chapter 7) in their MNE groups through what may be considered to be processes of strategic internalization (Chapter 3). Here the subsidiaries and laboratories assert their intra-group status through the internalization into owned and controlled operations of distinctive aspects (scientists; other talented creative personnel; existing technology; ongoing research agendas informed by the science-base's established strengths) of the NSI.

However, these MNE R&D laboratories also position themselves in an NSI, and seek to co-opt its unique capacities, through means that fall short of full internalization. Thus, in line with the familiar insight of Cohen and Levinthal (1989, p. 593) MNEs 'invest in R&D not only to pursue directly new process and product innovation, but also to develop and maintain their broader capabilities to assimilate and exploit externally available information'. But in the light of the familiar limitations to a market for technology (Buckley and Casson, 1976), especially in its more speculative and not-fully-formulated stages, MNEs' externalized tapping into the individualized potentials of an NSI needs to be articulated through formalized contractual collaborative agreements. These are often generated through the in-house laboratories in a country, which then have a fairly clear view of the aims and content of such R&D collaborations. This chapter has analyzed this in the context of MNE labs and collaborations in the UK.

A significant generalization from the results is that the more speculative scientific investigation of precompetitive research (basic and applied) is *relatively* more prevalent in MNE laboratories' collaborations with UK institutions than in their own in-house work. Nevertheless MNE labs that themselves have a strong precompetitive research commitment are amongst those most likely to establish collaborations whose target is similar types of work. This fits with the MNEs' need to monitor, access and assimilate those unique areas of investigative specialization that define an NSI's distinctive potentials. Thus, when operationalized by IILs, these basic/applied research collaborations are part of these labs' role as individualized contributors to the group-level programs of precompetitive research whose aim is to enrich MNEs' overall technology scopes.

However, basic and, especially, applied research are also very prominent in collaborations activated by MNE labs whose own focus is more towards product development within production subsidiaries (notably product mandates). Here the LILs playing this role may focus their in-house capacities on mediating the new technological inputs to an innovation process as a joint problem solving exercise with other creative functions at the subsidiary level (marketing, engineering, entrepreneurial management). But whilst this often means limited scope for *creating* new technology internally the LILs will have a major role in accessing, learning and explaining (to other functions) technologies which are new (or to be applied in a new context). Whilst some of these may come from intragroup transfers (e.g. DEV/GROUP) a more decisively individualized source would be from basic/applied research in the host NSI. Thus LILs' externalized research collaborations may be a crucial source of an individualized knowledge scope in product developing subsidiaries, which allows them to assert their distinctive position in their parent MNEs' globalized innovation program.

The evidence reviewed here can clearly be interpreted as representative of a distinctive and important component of learning and creative processes in heterarchical MNEs. This externalization of knowledge-seeking aims in a particular NSI then emerges as a vital mechanism for accessing the most individualized aspects of host-country's research and technological trajectories, before mediating them into the wider creative agendas of innovation-driven MNE operations.

Notes

1 Aspects of the transnational (Bartlett and Ghoshal, 1989, 1990) and the horizontal organization (White and Poynter, 1990) are also relevant to the types of strategic developments in MNEs that condition the technological positioning discussed here.
2 This has been formalized in the literature on product mandate subsidiaries (Roth and Morrison, 1992; Birkinshaw and Morrison, 1995; Pearce, 1992, 1999b; Birkinshaw, 1996; papers in Etemad and Séguin Dulude, 1986). The expansion of subsidiary scope into creative activity also takes a key position in the emergence of differentiated networks (Ghoshal and Nohria, 1989).
3 For reviews of earlier work in this area see Pearce (1989, 1999a).
4 Though not a direct analytical concern of this chapter there are clear resonances between the types of collaborations addressed here and the literature on the knowledge generation and diffusion content of regional clusters (Cantwell and Iammarino, 1998; Porter, 1998; Howells, 1999).
5 The distinction was originally suggested by Cordell (1971, 1973) and elaborated within the typology of Ronstadt (1977, 1978). It has been usefully activated, in the context of the strategic needs of the contemporary MNE, by Kuemmerle (1997, 1999a, 1999b). Here the distinction is made between overseas R&D that is home-base exploiting (i.e. 'established to help a company to effectively commercialize its R&D in foreign markets') and home-base augmenting (i.e. 'designed to gather new knowledge for the company').
6 The survey was carried out in 1994 as part of a project financed by the ESRC. The questionnaire was sent to all UK-based R&D units of foreign MNEs that could be identified from the Longman's *Directory of European Research Centres*.

7 The questionnaire was sent to 812 producing subsidiaries in the UK in 1993–94 and 190 replies were received. For more detailed discussion of parts of this questionnaire that are relevant to the themes of this chapter see Pearce (1999a, 1999b), Papanastassiou and Pearce (1997a, 1997b).
8 For detailed analysis of the position of US universities *vis-à-vis* the knowledge needs of commercial enterprises see Rosenberg and Nelson (1994). They conclude (p. 340) that 'what university research often does today is to stimulate and enhance the power of R&D done in industry, as contrasted with providing a substitute for it'.
9 An important area of analysis here concerns the issue of whether such technological expansion through overseas R&D seeks to *build on* home-country strength or *compensate for* home-country weakness (Patel and Vega, 1999; Fors, 1996; Zander, 1999a). Zander (1999b) generates a typology of innovation networks that discriminates along the lines of technological duplication and technological differentiation of advanced technological capabilities.
10 The growth of collaborative interdependency in the processes of knowledge generation in MNEs is exemplified in the analysis of reverse technology transfer (Håkanson and Nobel, 2000, 2001; Yamin, 1995, 1999). The networking of knowledge flows is also addressed by Randøy and Li (1998) and Howells (1998).
11 An extensive potential for international mobility of product-development and knowledge-creating projects within MNEs is documented by Pearce and Singh (1992a).

10
Funding Sources and the Strategic Roles of Decentralized R&D in Multinationals

Marina Papanastassiou and Robert Pearce

Introduction

A key implication of the growth of decentralized R&D in MNEs has been a comparable increase in the extent and diversity of knowledge flows within these companies. Early views of the MNE saw knowledge flow as almost uniquely a matter of many separate and distinct, bilateral and unidirectional, routes *from* the home-country parent *to* individual subsidiaries. This provided the basis of the only role then perceived as routinely available for overseas R&D laboratories, in the form of helping to assimilate and operationalize those group technologies on which subsidiaries were essentially dependent. However, as the changing competitive environment imposed increasing strategic diversity on MNEs an important manifestation of this took the form of a notable growth in dispersed R&D, with this playing an enhanced range of roles within not just the application but also the generation of these companies' core technologies. A crucial implication of this was, in turn, the ability of decentralized labs to supply as well as receive technology and, therefore, the growth of multidirectional knowledge flows in MNEs.[1]

In line with this perception of the increased diversity in use and creation of technology in MNEs, the influential typology of subsidiaries derived by Gupta and Govindarajan (1991, 1994) explicitly defined their status according to the extent to which they involve inflows and/or outflows of knowledge. In a similar way recent research has begun to explicitly investigate 'reverse technology transfer' (Håkanson and Nobel, 2000, 2001; Yamin, 1995, 1999) and knowledge networking in MNEs (Randøy and Li, 1998; Howells, 1998). In terms of the status of overseas R&D labs in MNEs their net position with respect to knowledge flows can be seen to reflect two factors, their individualism and their interdependence (see Chapter 7).

The more the quality and originality of local scientific inputs allows an R&D laboratory to generate distinctive in-house competences the more it can manifest a position of individualism within the group's technological scope. In principle this individualism could then be exercised autonomously through a local subsidiary (e.g. in a self-contained product development operation) or in a fashion that is still highly dependent (e.g. as one specialized element in a wider networked program of precompetitive research organized and coordinated by the MNE group). In practice labs can operate with varying degrees of interdependence, in terms of their association with technological activity elsewhere in their MNE group.[2] Thus a lab's degree of individualized competence, and the extent and nature of intra-group interdependency, will define its precise strategic role and determine its position with regard to knowledge transfer. In turn these factors can be expected to be crucially reflected in the sources of funding from which a laboratory operates.

This chapter seeks to investigate the relevance of five sources of funding in MNEs' labs in the UK, in the light of the prevalence in their operations of four possible roles. The data derives from a survey of foreign enterprises' R&D units in the UK carried out in 1994. The questionnaire was sent to the 180 R&D units of foreign MNEs in the UK, that could be distinguished from the *Longman's Directory of European Research Centres*. Replies were received from 48 of these. The respondents include 17 in pharmaceuticals, nine in industrial chemicals, 11 in electronics and 11 more in miscellaneous other industries. Nineteen had a Japanese parent company, 13 were from the USA and 16 from continental European MNEs.

The aim of the chapter is not to provide a guide to contemporary management practice, as reflected in MNE R&D funding patterns. Rather it seeks to indicate how detailed analysis of the interaction between funding patterns and differentiated R&D laboratory roles can provide insights into the strategic nature of the modern MNE. Economists would now view both technological progress and the internationalized dimensions of business (i.e. the MNE) as core elements in understanding and influencing the performance of the contemporary global economy. Thus the strategic positioning and status of the generation and use of technology in MNEs and, therefore, the organization of these companies' R&D, are matters of considerable relevance and concern.

As indicated above, and amplified systematically in later discussion, MNEs locate labs in particular countries to improve the competitiveness of their operations there and/or to access specific technological strengths of that country (the forces of *individualism*). This has clear potentials to strengthen both local industry and local science (e.g. by, indeed, providing extra funding, as well as new challenges and access to additional technologies and perspectives), but does so by enhancing *interdependency* with other globalized needs and priorities of MNEs.

Does the dispersion of R&D operations reflect a fragmentation of technological activity, to mainly support localized subsidiary needs and aims, or does it comprise differentiated but integral parts of the competitive evolution of an MNE's overall global strategic perspectives? The latter possibility raises issues about the ability to appropriate the benefits of improved research scope and about the balance of specialisms within a national system of innovation (Chapter 8). An understanding of how funding practices reflect on the localization/globalization tension in particular types of MNE lab is, therefore, the core concern of this analysis.

Our data from 1994 can be seen to provide a picture of MNE R&D strategy in a technologically strong and mature economy (UK) at a particular point in its evolution. As the analysis here suggests the operations of US and European MNEs are likely to have reached a point of well-developed familiarity with the UK science base and to have taken a fully-articulated positioning that, nevertheless, remains open to evolutionary adjustment. By contrast the Japanese MNEs' operations are interpreted as at an early stage of quite speculative implementation and, therefore, open to a more significant short-term refocusing that would reflect major learning processes deriving from growing operational familiarity. The study therefore combines a realized analysis of aspects of the strategic positioning of MNEs' R&D with a benchmarking from which evolutionary change or more basic restructuring can be tested in subsequent surveys.

In the next section we introduce four roles that MNEs' decentralized R&D labs may play and broadly suggest how the positioning of these roles may affect the sources from which their operations are funded. Section 3 then reviews the degree of presence of five funding sources in these labs' budgets and relates these to the roles that they play.

Roles of laboratories

Respondents to the survey were asked to evaluate the extent to which their laboratories' activity involved each of four potential roles.[3] The first of these was defined as 'to support UK-based production operations of the MNE by assisting in the adaptation of the products to be produced or processes to be used'. This is clearly the traditional support laboratory (SL1) role, in that its aim is to assist an associated production subsidiary to assimilate, and optimize the effectiveness with which it uses, imported group-level technologies.

Performance of the SL1 role is likely to require the work of highly competent lab personnel, but does not need highly distinctive or original research capabilities. Effective SL1 work will help the associated production subsidiary to operate to the fullest potential of the imported technology, but in no sense seeks to generate new capabilities that go beyond those limits. The SL1 asserts no distinctive individualized capabilities within the MNE group's scope. The production subsidiary will remain essentially dependent on technological progress elsewhere in the group for any substantial future development of its product scope, but how it uses current technologies becomes its own, predominantly independent, responsibility, to which any SL1 unit it possesses makes its contribution. Though the production subsidiary is likely to pay the parent group a royalty for the technologies it imports, any separate effort of localization through SL1 work is its own independent responsibility. Thus the predominant source of funding for the SL1 role is likely to be from an associated production subsidiary. The SL1 role was reported as its 'only' one by one laboratory (2.1% of respondents), as a 'predominant' one by 11 (22.9%), and a 'secondary' one by 18 (37.5%), whilst another 18 felt it played no part in their activity.

A second type of laboratory whose role focuses on the technological scope and competitive operations of its 'own' subsidiary is the locally integrated laboratory (LIL), which was defined for survey respondents as 'to work with the UK subsidiary's other functions (i.e. management, marketing, engineering, etc.) to develop a distinctive new product that it will produce for its markets'. The LIL is thus a key element in a nexus of creative functions that helps to secure a product mandate (PM) for its subsidiary. This mandate then provides parent HQ validation for a product development process operationalized at the subsidiary level. In terms of both the wider subsidiary scope and responsibilities and of the level of competence expected of an LIL, this process represents a major manifestation of the benefits MNEs' now expect to get from the generation and activation of individualism in their dispersed operations. How the PM/LIL operates in terms of intra-group interdependencies is open to possible variation however.

Though the early (mainly Canadian) literature on PMs clearly demonstrated a range of quite idiosyncratic origins for such subsidiaries,[4] we have suggested two more systematic scenarios for the emergence of PM scope in subsidiaries (Pearce, 1999b, pp. 128–30) and the concomitant product development commitments of LILs (Pearce and Papanastassiou, 1999, pp. 33–4). In the first the process is initially very self-contained at the subsidiary level (avoidance of substantial interdependency). The new product concept is itself initiated by the subsidiary, perhaps as a result of an original perception from its marketing unit or to build on a new technology that is derived in its own laboratory or accessed through a collaborative arrangement with a local university (or other independent) lab. As pursuit of a new PM is usually seen as quite an aggressive act within the competitive network of MNE subsidiaries, initial development of the prospective idea may be contained within the subsidiary in a quite covert fashion. Once its potentials are clarified, however, validation (the formal mandate) will be sought from the parent company. At this stage the LIL may begin to liaise with the central R&D unit of the group in order to sharpen (refine or redefine) some elements of the new good's technology from the wider scope of the MNE's core technologies. The main funding for the LIL's participation in this form of product development is likely to be the associated subsidiary (especially in the more exploratory and pre-mandate stage), though supplementary finance might become available from the parent company in the later more interdependent stages. The latter would certainly be true if the local technologies being generated by the LIL are seen to have potential value to aspects of the group's operations beyond the specified and mandated product development process.

The alternative procedure involves group-level interdependency from its initiation and has been described elsewhere as positioning in a global innovation strategy (Pearce and Papanastassiou, 1996a; Pearce, 1997; Chapter 8). Here the new product concept emerges at the group level. Where tastes and other differentiating elements make it appropriate, the MNE may then wish to see the new product and/or its associated production process taking different forms for different environments and use local PM/LIL operations to secure this. For example, the UK LIL of a US or Japanese MNE may have responsibility for securing the European variant (significantly different from other variants in North America and Asia) of the new product concept. The LIL will here be responsible for acquiring the underlying technology of the new good from central R&D and will then work with other functions in the product mandate subsidiary (engineering; marketing; management) to secure its most effective local implementation. Though the substantial benefits that the subsidiary will obtain from producing and selling the new good may involve it to some degree in the financing of the LIL, the intra-group positioning of the operation is likely to secure substantial parent funding (especially in the earlier stage of the localization of the new technology). Though none of the responding laboratories felt that they only played the LIL role, 17 (35.4%) rated it a predominant one and 11 (22.9%) more considered that it took a secondary position in their operation.

The third role that responding UK-based laboratories were invited to evaluate was described as 'to support non-UK production operations of the MNE by advising on the adaptation of the products to be produced or processes to be used'. The emergence of this version of the support laboratory role (SL2) can be seen as reflecting two particular developments within MNEs' supply networks. One facet of this has been the systematic rationalization of the product range supplied by individual subsidiaries, as these are moved towards a specialized position in coordinated supply networks. Thus the intensification of competition in the markets for most mature standardized goods has resulted in subsidiaries that once supplied a substantial product range to, mainly, their national host-country market being increasingly required to move to a focus on a more cost-effective supply of only a subset of these goods (but to do so for a wider market space, i.e. mainly Europe in the case of the UK-based subsidiaries). Those products that exit the supply profile of one subsidiary will then become the specialized responsibility of another subsidiary, elsewhere in the same coordinated supply network. This rationalization process may impart SL2 responsibilities onto UK-based MNE labs in two ways (Pearce and Papanastassiou, 1999, pp. 30–1).

Firstly, a production subsidiary in another part of the network may be expected to take on lead supply responsibility for a good that the UK operation had previously established competence in, but which it is now required to drop from its range. If the new supplier faces initial problems with this inherited responsibility these may be solved by consultation with the UK subsidiary's lab, which can apply its well-rooted experience of the product in question. Mutual support of this SL2 type, between laboratories, in the process of relocation and application of these forms of tacit knowledge of established goods, may play a crucial *ad hoc* role in the MNE's transition to more integrated supply networks.

The second positioning of SL2 type labs may then occur once the rationalization process is mostly complete and the supply network is more or less stabilized. At this point an MNE group may decide that many of the network's production sites no longer need the type of (SL1) in-house R&D that securing the responsiveness of a large product range to specific local-market needs could earlier have justified. Instead, with the generation of good communications and increasingly well-honed experience of intra-group networking, it may become possible to use a limited number of high-quality SL2 units to supply the R&D needs of the whole rationalized system (at least as far as the optimally effective supply of existing goods is concerned). Such enhanced SL2 units thus aim to back up a wide constituency of dispersed supply facilities and often, to avoid group politics and accusations of favoritism, may be located independently of any particular production unit (perhaps as a supplementary responsibility of the type of stand-alone precompetitive R&D units that play the fourth role, discussed below).

The other major factor in the strategic evolution of MNEs that may generate a position for the SL2 role, is the emergence of product mandate subsidiaries and their associated locally integrated laboratories. Once a product is successfully innovated by the PM/LIL, and its production stabilized, it may be that its competitive supply (for some markets at least) is best achieved through other subsidiaries in foreign locations. Helping these new suppliers to assimilate and operationalize the technology in question can be seen as a logical and potentially significant SL2-type responsibility for the mandate subsidiary's laboratory (alongside a continued LIL commitment to further product development operations).

The key definitional difference between the SL1 and SL2 roles is the innate intra-group interdependency through which the latter is expected to operate, by contrast with the containment of the former within the functional scope of a particular subsidiary in order to support its specific operations. The three contexts we have outlined for SL2 behavior also point to more individualized capabilities (though ultimately still activated only to support the effective application of existing technology). In the first and third of these situations it is knowledge of specific products and processes that makes the laboratory the competitive supplier of precise advice needed elsewhere in the MNE. In the second case a network operating through a wide geographical area is to be serviced by a small number of SL2 units of quite wide ranging scope. Securing the SL role in these circumstances is thus likely to reflect a demonstrated ability to carry out this trouble-shooting function through a flexible initiative that indicates possession of more than routine competences. The SL2 role differs from that of the LIL in two respects. Firstly, it is only concerned with the *transfer* of technology that is already embodied in established products, whilst the LIL is concerned with the primary *operationalization* of new technologies in an innovation process. Secondly, it is only concerned with the outward flow of technology, whilst the LIL can have a secondary use for both inward and outward flows.

The positioning of the SL2 role clearly indicates that, compared to SL1, it is likely to be substantially funded by sources other than a subsidiary with which it is routinely associated on a day-to-day basis. Two possibilities then emerge. Firstly, that the status of the SL2 is sufficiently precisely defined within the MNE's strategic scope and needs that it is substantially funded through a predetermined annual budgetary allocation from the parent company. Secondly, that its role is basically more *ad hoc* and involves a wide range of occasional and sporadic associations with other parts of the group, each of which provides one-off payments for fulfillment of specific tasks. Some supplementary funding from an associated UK production subsidiary could emerge in the budgets of SL2s in two ways, however. In line with one potential positioning of SL2 work, this could occur if the relevant production subsidiary is a successful product development facility and the SL2 is helping subsidiaries in other countries to acquire the capability to supply a good that has been innovated by the associated UK subsidiary. Alternatively a local subsidiary may provide a SL2 with funding to help it sustain a high level of capability in that role, in the hope of sharing in any intra-group credibility earned by its successful operation in providing quality advice to a wide constituency.

The fact that, in terms of the average responses (ARs) reported in Table 10.1, the SL2 role emerges as the least significant of the four reflects, in a fashion that is compatible with the types of contexts that we have suggested for it above, a mainly secondary, rather than lead, position in laboratories' operations. Thus with just one laboratory rating it as its only role, and only seven more (14.6% of respondents) a predominant one, SL2 activity is notably the rarest at this lead level of prominence. However, the 21 (43.8%) respondents that evaluated SL2 as a secondary part of their activity was clearly the highest.

The final lab role offered for consideration was defined as 'to operate independently of any production subsidiary to carry out basic or applied research (not associated with current producing operations) as part of a program of precompetitive R&D implemented and coordinated by the MNE group'. Thus this internationally interdependent laboratory (IIL) role avoids any immediate systematic integration with other functions (notably those related to the competitiveness of current products and technologies) and instead operates interdependently with similar labs in other countries to pursue the regeneration of the group's core technologies. Here MNEs are seen as being aware of a need to regenerate and extend their core technologies in order to secure the basis for subsequent programs of product innovation that can be sustained into the longer

194 Funding Sources and Roles of MNE R&D Laboratories

Table 10.1 Roles of MNE laboratories in the UK

	Roles of laboratory (average response)[1]			
	SL1	SL2	LIL	IIL
By industry				
Electronics	2.18	1.73	2.09	1.64
Pharmaceuticals	1.35	1.53	1.59	3.00
Chemicals[2]	1.89	2.11	2.00	2.00
Other	2.45	2.00	2.27	1.82
Total	1.90	1.79	1.94	2.23
By home country				
USA	1.92	1.85	2.23	2.00
Japan	1.84	1.68	1.68	2.16
Europe	1.94	1.88	2.00	2.44
Total	1.90	1.79	1.94	2.23

Roles of laboratories:

SL1 – to support UK-based production operations of the MNE by assisting in the adaptation of the products to be produced or processes to be used.

SL2 – to support non-UK production operations of the MNE by advising on the adaptation of the products to be produced or processes to be used.

LIL – to work with the UK subsidiary's other functions (i.e. management, marketing, engineering, etc.) to develop a distinctive new product that it will produce for its markets.

IIL – to operate independently of any producing subsidiary to carry out basic or applied research (not associated with current producing operations) as part of a program of precompetitive R&D implemented and coordinated by the MNE group.

Notes:
1. Respondents were asked to grade each role as (i) our only role, (ii) a predominant role, (iii) a secondary part of our role, (iv) not a part of our role. The average response was calculated by allocating only role a value of 4, predominant role a value of 3, secondary role a value of 2, and not part of role a value of 1.
2. Includes petrochemicals and petroleum.

term. However, the range of scientific disciplines that are perceived as needing to be accessed in order to build this new body of regenerative technological competence is widening for many of the dynamic and innovation oriented industries. Furthermore, the most distinctive and important competences in these separate scientific disciplines are becoming dispersed over a widening range of countries[5] (i.e. individual countries now offer a limited range of leading edge competences in selected areas of research). Therefore in order to cover the spectrum of basic and applied research inputs that are needed to assemble a coherent precompetitive research program that can incorporate all likely sources of technology relevant to building the knowledge-basis for future major innovations, MNEs operate through a network of IILs. Each of these focuses on precompetitive research in disciplines that reflect distinctive strengths of the host-country science base and which are expected to have a potential to contribute to the long-term technological development of the MNE.

Since IILs build strong individualized research scopes out of the local science base, but aiming to support coherent and interdependent programs of investigation articulated and coordinated at the group level, the parent MNE is expected to be their main source of funding. For institutional and/or accounting reasons other parts of the MNE group may assist in funding IILs, but this would not be with any logical expectation of direct and immediate benefits from individual pieces of work carried out in such a lab. Local (i.e. here UK) producing subsidiaries could provide funding for an IIL, for reasons not inherent to these labs' natural mode of behavior. Firstly, a subsidiary might offer funding to a stand-alone IIL in order to buy-into the prestige of a world class research operation. Secondly, such a production subsidiary might actually want to acquire (in a manner either authorized by the parent or activated in a subversive and covert fashion) a selection of the IIL's current results to support their own product development operations (i.e. for assimilation and use by their own LIL). Eight (16.7%) of the labs only played the IIL role and 12 (25%) more rated it a predominant one. For 11 (22.9%) it was a secondary role, whilst 17 (35.4%) considered it irrelevant.

Sources of funding

Respondents to the survey of laboratories were asked to evaluate the degree of prominence in their budgets of five potential sources of funding. The relevance of these sources of financing are summarized (in terms of average responses) in Table 10.2. Regression tests were run with each of the five sources of funding as dependent variables. The aim of these regressions is not to achieve five separate tests of rigorous hypotheses relating to each funding source. Rather it is to support the primary emphasis on the results of Table 10.2 by looking for *patterns* across the set of regressions that allow us to discern how funding behavior reflects on the interdependencies within an overall MNE R&D strategy that is articulated through different subsidiary laboratory roles. In this vein regression results are discussed, when relevant, as *ad hoc* reflections on the picture derived from Table 10.2 rather than in a self-contained 'results' section.[6] The regressions included dummy variables for the MNE industry (with the miscellaneous 'other' group serving as

Table 10.2 Sources of funding for MNE laboratories in the UK

	Source of funding (Average response)[1]				
	SUBSID	PARENT	GROUP	UK	EU
By industry					
Electronics	2.20	2.18	1.82	1.30	1.20
Pharmaceuticals	1.69	3.18	1.25	1.06	1.00
Chemicals[2]	1.89	2.33	1.89	1.11	1.11
Other	2.00	2.20	1.20	1.10	1.10
Total	1.91	2.53	1.50	1.13	1.09
By home country					
USA	2.18	2.42	1.33	1.27	1.18
Japan	1.74	2.63	1.58	1.05	1.05
Europe	1.93	2.50	1.53	1.13	1.07
Total	1.91	2.53	1.50	1.13	1.09
By laboratory type[3]					
SL1	2.45	2.18	1.45	1.00	1.00
SL2	1.00	3.62	1.62	1.00	1.00
LIL	1.93	2.13	1.33	1.13	1.13
IIL	1.71	2.68	1.56	1.12	1.06

Sources of funding:
SUBSID – funds from an associated UK producing subsidiary.
PARENT – funds from the parent company of the MNE group.
GROUP – funds from elsewhere in the group.
UK – funds from UK government.
EU – funds from EU budget.

Notes:
1. Respondents were invited to evaluate each source of funding as (i) the only source, (ii) a major source, (iii) a supporting source, (iv) not a source. The average response was then derived by allocating a value of 4 to 'only source', 3 to 'major source', 2 to 'supporting source' and 1 to 'not a source'.
2. Includes petrochemicals and petroleum.
3. Result for laboratories that said they were 'predominantly' or 'only' that type. For descriptions of laboratory types see Table 10.1.

the omitted industry) and for its home country (Europe serving as the omitted source location) and with the lab's degree of commitment to each of the four strategic roles as independent variables. The regression results are reported in Table 10.3.

The first source of finance evaluated was funds from an associated UK producing subsidiary (SUBSID). We hypothesized in the previous section that UK subsidiaries were likely to play a very significant role in funding SL1 units (whose role is to help these to apply extant group technologies to their own competitive contexts), but that the alter-

Table 10.3 Regressions with sources of laboratory funding as dependent variable

	Dependant variable (source of funding)				
	SUBSID	PARENT	GROUP	UK	EU
Constant	2.377*	1.019	1.520*	1.266***	1.124***
	(1.79)	(0.74)	(1.69)	(3.21)	(3.25)
Electronics	0.057	−0.013	0.152*	0.088**	0.040
	(0.42)	(−0.10)	(1.75)	(2.17)	(1.13)
Pharmaceuticals	0.028	0.148	−0.001	−0.033	−0.040
	(0.28)	(1.39)	(−0.01)	(−1.07)	(−1.48)
Chemicals	0.062	0.011	0.202*	−0.020	−0.009
	(0.36)	(0.06)	(1.71)	(−0.40)	(−0.19)
USA	0.183	−0.096	−0.154	0.204	0.146
	(0.40)	(−0.22)	(−0.53)	(1.51)	(1.24)
Japan	−0.156	0.181	−0.029	−0.097	−0.027
	(−0.74)	(0.83)	(−0.21)	(−1.55)	(−0.49)
SL1[1]	0.415	−0.192	−0.096	−0.097	−0.076
	(1.48)	(−0.66)	(−0.51)	(−1.16)	(−1.05)
SL2	−0.627**	0.428*	0.147	−0.004	−0.031
	(−2.65)	(1.73)	(0.91)	(−0.05)	(−0.50)
LIL	0.131	0.164	−0.112	0.005	0.057
	(0.51)	(0.62)	(−0.66)	(0.06)	(0.85)
IIL	−0.193	0.182	−0.038	0.032	0.036
	(−0.85)	(0.78)	(−0.25)	(0.47)	(0.60)
R^2	0.323	0.212	0.223	0.290	0.222
F	1.86*	1.10	1.15	1.59	1.11
N	45	47	46	45	45

1. For definitions of laboratory roles (independent variables) see Table 10.1.
*** significant at 1% ** significant at 5% * significant at 1%
n – number of observations.

native positioning of SL2 (to provide similar types of advice and assistance to non-UK producing units) would preclude extensive funding from local subsidiaries. Since we have seen that LILs are motivated to help the product developing subsidiaries that they operate within to enhance their profitability and, crucially, their intra-group status, these subsidiaries will be expected to provide some of the funding for these labs. The subsidiaries will usually be keen to do so in order to stake a claim to the individualized competences generated through the LIL participation. However, in ways that we have seen can be either *ad hoc* or very systematic, the innovations to which LILs contribute extend overall group-level competitiveness and this may also generate some participation of parent funding. We have suggested that the nature of pure-IIL work provides no logical reason for substantial support from a local production subsidiary.

The reported AR for SUBSID, of 1.71, makes it the second most prominent source of funding for UK-based MNE labs. This, however, seems to reflect a rather dichotomous status. Thus 57.8% of labs that evaluated SUBSID said it was no part of their budgets, but where accessed it then tended to be very significant with 15.6% considering it their only source and 17.8% a major one (so that only 21.0% of those that accessed SUBSID felt it was only a supporting source of funds). This may confirm the expectation that use of local subsidiary finance is quite precisely related to the strategic positioning of labs. This emerges most decisively for the SL roles. Here SL1 units are the most strongly supported by SUBSID (the only one of the four roles for which this source of funds records the highest AR) and the relationship between SUBSID and SL1 in the regressions (Table 10.3) is clearly positively signed (though short of statistical significance). No SL2 units recorded any access to SUBSID and the regression relationship is significantly negative as predicted. SUBSID does play the expected substantial, though by no means dominant, role in funding LILs' operations, but the regression result is only weakly positive. Though the regression relationship between SUBSID and IIL is weakly negatively signed (as predicted) the AR (Table 10.2) is by no means negligible, indicating some participation of UK production subsidiaries in funding the precompetitive research in those labs. This may reflect a prestige-related wish to 'adopt' such a laboratory (with which there will be no operative association) or indicate some acquisition, for local development, of the (essentially more group-oriented) results of these units.

Laboratories in electronics MNEs are the strongest users of SUBSID, in terms of the ARs reported in Table 10.2. This clearly reflects the particularly localized orientation of these units, indicated by the notable strength of the SL1 and LIL roles in their operations (Table 10.1). Once these roles are controlled for in the regression (Table 10.3) the dummy for electronics in the SUBSID test is only very weakly positive. US MNEs' labs are the strongest users of SUBSID (though only weakly positive in the regression), which may be indicative of a strong orientation of their UK facilities to secure the effective commercial operationalization, for European markets, of existing or new technology (SL1 adaptation and, most notably, LIL product development).

Next, responding labs were asked to evaluate 'funds from the parent company of the MNE group' (PARENT) as part of their budgets. Since we have perceived the SL1 role as being one that is normally implemented at the discretion of an associated production subsidiary, when it considers that it needs such support to continue to effectively assimilate and activate existing technologies, the participation of parent funding is likely to be limited. The most plausible exception is likely to be during the establishment of a new subsidiary, when SL1 work might be vital to building the foundations of its successful initial positioning but cannot be funded in-house until adequate profitability is generated. By contrast we noted in the previous section that MNE parent funds are one of the two most logical inputs to the budgets of SL2 units. Though LILs directly support product development in a particular subsidiary we have previously noted the strong potentials for their success in this role to also provide significant spillover benefits to overall group competitiveness. Thus we have predicted some degree of parent funding for such labs. However, the need of IILs to generate significant individualized competences but then to exercise them in a decisively interdependent way in pursuit of group-defined objectives, means these are the type of labs likely to be most strongly dependent on parent MNE funding.

Funding from the MNE emerged as by far the most pervasive source available to MNE labs in the UK. Thus 25.5% of respondents who evaluated PARENT said it was their only source of funding, another 29.8% rated it a major source and 17.0% more a secondary one. PARENT was therefore the only one of the sources available to over half the labs, with only 27.7% not making any use of it. PARENT emerges most decisively as a source of funding for SL2 labs, for which it is overwhelmingly the dominant budgetary input (Table 10.2). The significant positive relationship between SL2 and PARENT in the regression (Table 10.3) mirrors the negative one between SL2 and SUBSID. This is clearly in line with the fact that SL2 work supports other (non-UK) subsidiaries of the MNE, but also indicates that labs playing this role usually do so in a way that is systematically recognized (and therefore funded) centrally by the parent group, rather than representing a series of mainly *ad hoc* transactions with other parts of the group.

As predicted PARENT emerges as clearly the leading source of funding for IILs, though in the regression the positive relationship is only a very weak one. Again in line with previous discussion PARENT clearly shares with SUBSID the main responsibility for funding LIL operations. Perhaps the most surprising result here is the relatively prominent position of

PARENT in funding SL1 facilities (though the regression does still produce a very weak, negative sign). We suggested earlier that this could derive from a need for such external funding to help set up an SL to, in turn, help its new associated production subsidiary to itself begin effective operations around use of established technologies of the MNE group. We will note below that this may be especially associated with the recent expansion of Japanese subsidiaries and laboratories in the UK.

Pharmaceuticals emerges as emphatically the industry where UK-based labs tended to depend most strongly on PARENT and, at the same time, were least reliant on SUBSID. This clearly reflects the strategic positioning of pharmaceutical labs (Table 10.1), which are vastly the most likely to be IILs and equally the least likely to take any of the other three forms (though in the regression for PARENT the pharmaceutical dummy is still quite strongly positive after controlling for lab roles).

Japanese MNEs' laboratories in the UK are somewhat the most likely to use sources of parent funding, a position emphasized by their complementary status as the least likely to have access to local subsidiary funds. This may mainly reflect the newness of the Japanese labs and, indeed, of their production operations in Europe. Thus PARENT may be particularly relevant in the early life of these Japanese facilities, partly because their initial role is the transfer of established (and so far centrally-controlled) technology into the new environment and partly because the UK-based production subsidiaries do not yet have either the independent financial scope or the in-house creative momentum to support labs properly. At the early stage it is the home-country HQs in Japanese MNEs that seem to drive, and therefore to fund, decentralized R&D (even though this is mainly related to local application of existing technology) despite its positioning within UK-based production subsidiaries. Subsequently the subsidiaries are likely to broaden their laboratories' aims and make funding them more their own responsibility.

The last intra-MNE source of finance that labs were asked to evaluate was 'funds from elsewhere in the MNE group' (GROUP). The strongest hypothesis that we have derived with regard to the origins of such funding is to pay for SL2-type support. We also suggested that IILs might receive some funding of this type, simply because of expectation that ultimately the benefits of their work can diffuse throughout the group. Whilst SL1 provides no logical reason for such funding we hypothesize that it is least likely for LILs, since the latter work explicitly enables one subsidiary to assert its individualized competitiveness against 'rival' subsidiaries of the group in seeking the product development role. Overall 63.0% of responding labs considered that none of their budget derived from this source, and only 10.9% rated it as more than a supporting one.

As Table 10.2 shows SL2 units are modestly the most likely to receive funding of this type, but much less than from PARENT. This again underpins the view of SL2 as a centrally-authorized and quite systematically-interdependent form of laboratory positioning. In the regression of GROUP SL2 is the only positively signed laboratory role, though well short of significance. IIL units are also slightly above average in terms of GROUP finance and SL1 perhaps stronger than logically anticipated. As predicted GROUP is weakest in terms of finance for LILs. Chemicals and electronics labs stand out in terms of this type of funding from sister subsidiaries. For chemicals this is clearly compatible with the strong role for SL2 in this industry (though the dummy variable is still positive in the regression after controlling for role). For electronics the relative strength of GROUP is more enigmatic since SL1 and LIL are the dominant lab roles.

Finally laboratories were asked to evaluate two sources of funding from outside of the group, in the form of 'funds from UK government' (UK) and 'funds from EU budget' (EU). These types of funding would be most likely to be available where spillovers beneficial to the local economy could be most realistically expected. These could occur in the form of new types of scientific knowledge (from precompetitive IIL work) or benefits to competitiveness diffusing into the local economy (e.g. to local input suppliers or users, or to local consumers) from successful product development (in LIL supported mandate subsidiaries). The relevance of such funds was never reported as more than a secondary source, and for both the vast majority of respondents (86.7% for UK and 91.1% for EU) said they were not accessed. As anticipated the very sporadic use of these sources that was reported always related to either LIL or IIL facilities.

Conclusions

The strongest and most pervasive source of funding for MNEs' R&D laboratories in the UK emerged as being from the parent company of the group. This is considered as being powerfully indicative of the manner in which such decentralized operations are now integral with the ways in which these companies seek to apply existing core technologies and to regenerate and broaden the scope of these crucial knowledge competences. Thus our detailed analysis has been based on the conceptualization (through a four-part typology of labs) of the refocusing of decentralized R&D away from the short-term objective of assisting particular subsidiaries to apply existing technologies to their specific competitive situation, towards positions in the more sustained technological and competitive development of the MNE group.

One aspect of this repositioning is that it now usually involves labs in the generation of specific individualized capacities that are built out of particular areas of distinctive knowledge competence available in the local economy. Where such work is aimed at expanding the knowledge base of longer-term competitiveness (rather than applying the existing base more effectively locally) there is, however, an innate riskiness involved. When such an R&D unit operates within a manufacturing subsidiary (as an LIL) that production unit is likely to also be competing for status within its group (as well as for final markets) through cost effective (directly profitable) supply. Unilateral subsidiary-level funding (i.e. exclusive local bearing of the risk) of the more speculative aspects of the generation of individualized competences cannot be expected. Where MNE groups understand the benefits of decentralized knowledge generation and product development they also accept the need for significant central financial participation, and therefore of centralized strategic validation, as a facilitating and motivating sharing in the perceived risk of co-opting potentially valuable but notably specialized dispersed capacities.

The second crucial implication of the generation of specialized scopes within MNEs' labs is that this is expected to provide substantial externalities, in the form of systematic spillover group-level benefits. However decisively a lab focuses specific local scientific attributes on a particular problem the ultimate expectation is that it does not aim to fully co-opt the results to a distinct and isolated competitive context, but instead seeks to secure all available synergistic potentials with other group activities. This is most obviously the case with the systematic interdependency of the IIL type of precompetitive work. However, a comparable openness in the product development work of LILs also needs to be inculcated. Not only may the results of LILs have alternative applications elsewhere in the MNE but introverted isolationism in such units can damage their own success and the coherent evolution of group competitiveness. Just as LILs' work can provide positive spillovers to other elements of group technological progress, their own activity may benefit from supportive imports of other facets of group knowledge. Where an LIL-supported subsidiary does make substantial self-contained product development progress this may ultimately distort the group's technological evolution (through lack of supportive complementarities) and be perceived as an inappropriate and disruptive act of competitive aggression within the MNE's strategic overall development. Once again central financial participation in the funding of laboratories can be seen as crucial in developing the necessary interdependencies between decentralized R&D units, and in securing the cohesive growth of intra-group knowledge flows.

The contemporary MNE is increasingly concerned with the sustained evolution of its technological trajectory (Pearce, 1999b). This technological trajectory needs to be continually enriched from a range of scientific sources that are operationalized through decentralized R&D units. But this can only be done in a cohesive and coherent fashion if these dispersed labs can be induced to open themselves fully to an appropriate range of interdependencies and intra-group knowledge flows. Central funding, alongside a range of supporting sources, seems to play a crucial role in securing these strategic aims of decentralized R&D.

Notes

1 Within the wider strategic repositioning of decentralized R&D in MNEs (Pearce, 1999a) a crucial point of emphasis has been the increased relevance of supply-side influences (Florida, 1997; Cantwell, 1991; Cantwell and Janne, 1999; Kuemmerle, 1999a; Granstrand, 1999). Thus distinctive and high-quality local scientific capabilities and technological inputs allow MNEs' R&D labs to generate new knowledge which often flows outwards to support activity elsewhere in the group.
2 Analysis of patterns and organization of networking and interdependence of dispersed R&D in MNEs has been an influential element in the developing understanding of the processes of technological decentralization in the companies (Håkanson and Laage-Hellman, 1984; De Meyer and Mizushima, 1989; Håkanson, 1990; Howells, 1990a; De Meyer, 1991, 1993).
3 The typology of laboratory roles derives from the earlier formulations of Hood and Young (1982), Haug et al. (1983), Pearce (1989, 1997).
4 For reviews see Pearce (1989, pp. 121–32; 1992). More formal investigation of the systematic positioning of PMs in the modern MNE can be found in Roth and Morrison (1992), Birkinshaw and Morrison (1995), Birkinshaw (1996), Papanastassiou and Pearce (1997a).
5 This to some extent reflects forces of agglomeration and the building of regional knowledge clusters (Cantwell and Iammarino, 1998).
6 The overall indecisiveness of the regressions preclude this, of course, but the sense of the results does point towards the key themes of interdependency and centralized supervision (especially manifest in funding sources for the SL1 and SL2 roles) and seem worthy of *ad hoc* comment.

11
Globalization of Technology and the Movement of Scientific Personnel in Multinational Enterprises in Europe

Marina Papanastassiou, Robert Pearce and
George Anastassopoulos

Introduction

In this chapter we examine the movement of scientific personnel involved in Research and Development (R&D) within Multinational Enterprises (MNEs). Traditional theories on Foreign Direct Investment (FDI) and the MNE view, in general, any transfer of any form of knowledge as a one way centrifugal movement (Dunning, 1988). Thus knowledge is centrally created (within the headquarters of a limited number of home countries) and then is transferred to the periphery of MNE groups (i.e. subsidiaries) in order to assist in the realization of production and marketing plans of MNEs. Pioneering work by Ronstadt (1977, 1978) and Behrman and Fischer (1980a, b) and some recent research has shown that this trend in MNEs is more or less obsolete (Papanastassiou and Pearce, 1996b, 1997a; Chapter 7). Papanastassiou and Pearce have shown in previous work that MNEs have a globalized perspective on technology which is closely related to the different roles of MNE subsidiaries. Although MNEs try to internalize most of their creative resources through the development of internal linkages many external linkages are also developed in order to make more efficient the creation and spread of these assets. In this chapter we examine some aspects of the generation of internal linkages in the creation and transmission of technology within MNE groups.

Competitive demands and the so called globalization of production has urged a parallel trend in the globalization of R&D and technology (Dunning, 1994b). MNE groups are not viewed as monolithic organizations but as complex networks where different parts assume different responsibilities. R&D and technology contribute to this complexity which in turn affects the decentralization and networking of technology

(Bartlett and Ghoshal, 1990). Adopting some of the well established terminology on the different roles of overseas R&D laboratories we discern the following: Support Laboratories (SLs), Locally Integrated Laboratories (LILs) and Internationally Interdependent Laboratories (IILs). Another – and in many cases complementary – potential source of innovation can come from the host-country environment, i.e. from universities, other firms, research institutes, etc. Different views on the orientation and form of strategic positioning of R&D can determine different roles for overseas subsidiaries. In the case of centralization of R&D capacity subsidiaries are usually involved in the production of mature and standardized goods. This type of subsidiary is called a Truncated Miniature Replica (TMR). Another type of subsidiary related with the centralization of R&D is the Rationalized Product Subsidiary (RPS) which is involved in the production of intermediary goods. The final type of subsidiary is the World or Regional Product Mandate (WPM/RPM) which is related with genuine decentralization of technology as it is involved in the production of new innovative products using its own R&D laboratory, usually an LIL.

In this chapter we will present some evidence on MNE operations in four European countries, i.e. Belgium, Greece, Portugal and the United Kingdom (Papanastassiou, 1995). Data on these subsidiaries were obtained through postal questionnaire survey research conducted in 1993–94. The number of questionnaires sent was 533. Out of the 145 responses received 99 were in the UK, 16 in Greece, 20 in Belgium and ten in Portugal. The data are presented in the from of frequencies, which give us the differences among industries, home countries and host countries, and average response rates which give us degree of importance.

Results

In analyzing the movement of scientific personnel within MNE groups we accept that this movement will be from and towards the center as an effective response to the pressures of globalization of production (Pearce and Singh, 1992a; Haug *et al.*, 1983).

Movement and roles of scientific personnel

Questions in the survey tried to capture the quantitative aspect of the movement of scientific personnel, in terms of percentages, and then to provide some qualitative elements with regard to what the personnel does. We would expect that following the tradition of a product cycle model (Vernon, 1966), foreign companies involved in FDI will 'export' their personnel in key positions at least for a certain amount of time.

But as subsidiaries gain deeper roots in their host economies this commitment would be diminishing as well. According to our sample we would also expect that high-technology industries would require parent company scientific personnel more often than medium-technology and low-technology industries, and also that subsidiaries in Other Europe (i.e. Greece, Belgium and Portugal) would be more likely to make frequent use of such home-country personnel in scientific operations.

In investigating the roles of such home-country scientific personnel three potential roles were identified: (a) managerial, (b) scientific and (c) a combination of both scientific and managerial duties. Participation in scientific roles was more prevalent with 46 replies, whilst managerial followed with 43 replies and participation in both roles with 40 replies. The findings, in Table 11.1, show that by sectoral grouping, medium- and low-technology industries have little difference in the use of home-country personnel in the scientific work of the laboratory, but both were

Table 11.1 Proportion of scientific personnel of subsidiary laboratories that come from home country of MNE

	Home country personnel in laboratory employment			
	0%	1%–49%	50% and over	Total
Sector				
High-technology industries[1]	33.3	33.3	33.3	100.0
Medium-technology industries[2]	50.0	18.8	31.3	100.0
Low-technology industries[3]	60.0	10.0	30.0	100.0
Total	43.2	24.7	32.1	100.0
Home country				
USA	53.7	4.9	41.5	100.0
Japan	10.0	80.0	10.0	100.0
Europe[4]	31.0	34.5	27.6	100.0
Total	43.2	24.7	32.1	100.0
Host country				
UK	44.6	28.6	26.8	100.0
Other Europe[5]	40.0	16.0	44.0	100.0
Total	43.2	24.7	32.1	100.0

1. Covers, telecommunications, scientific instruments, electronics and electrical appliances, automobiles and pharmaceuticals.
2. Covers, rubber, petroleum, food and drink and industrial chemicals.
3. Covers, building materials, mechanical engineering, metal manufacture and products and other manufacturing.
4. Covers subsidiaries of European MNEs in countries other than the home country.
5. Covers subsidiaries in Belgium, Greece and Portugal.

Table 11.2 Roles of home-country scientific personnel in MNE subsidiary laboratories

	Roles of home-country personnel											
	To mainly organize the laboratory's programme of work			To mainly participate in the scientific work of the laboratory			To participate in both the roles		
	less than 10%	10% to 49%	50% and over	less than 10%	10% to 49%	50% and over	less than 10%	10% to 49%	50% and over
Sector									
High-technology industries[1]	69.6	13.0	17.4	45.8	12.5	41.7	52.2	13.0	34.8
Medium- and low-technology industries[2]	65.0	5.0	30.0	50.0	13.6	36.4	64.7	7.5	35.3
Total	67.4	9.3	23.3	47.8	13.0	39.1	57.5	7.5	35.0
Home country									
USA	52.6	15.8	31.6	36.8	15.8	47.4	58.8	5.9	35.3
Japan	88.9		11.1	88.9		11.1	44.4	11.1	44.4
Europe[3]	73.3	6.7	20.0	47.8	16.7	44.4	64.3	7.1	28.6
Host country									
UK	75.0	7.1	17.9	51.7	6.9	41.4	64.0	4.0	32.0
Other Europe[4]	53.3	13.3	33.3	41.2	23.5	35.3	46.7	13.3	40.0

1. Covers, see Table 11.1.
2. Covers, see Table 11.1.
3. Covers subsidiaries of European MNEs in countries other than the home country.
4. Covers subsidiaries in Belgium, Greece and Portugal.

somewhat below the high-technology grouping. Using home-country personnel to organize the laboratory's program of work may be somewhat more prevalent in medium- and low-technology than high-technology sectors. Participating in both roles is somewhat more common in high-technology sectors. Perhaps the nature of the roles in high-technology industries (more integrated within the group and with local science) makes it somewhat less desirable, less necessary or less feasible to separate the managerial and bench-research roles. On a home-country level USA firms tend to either employ home personnel more often or not at all in their overseas scientific operations, especially when focusing on the managerial role (Table 11.2).

Other results in Table 11.2 show that Japanese firms tend to have a continuous presence of home personnel abroad and particularly in playing both roles. This may be associated with the fact that Japanese subsidiaries are relatively new, so they may need parent supervision and, therefore, with the less deep overseas technological tradition of these subsidiaries. On a host-country level, the Other Europe group presents a stronger presence of home-country personnel than the UK (Table 11.1), with a stronger result in the 'over 50 per cent' category. In the Other Europe group, the key role of home-country personnel is to organize the laboratory's program of work (Table 11.2), indicating that less actual pure scientific work needs to be done in the laboratories of these subsidiaries and more concern is placed on how to integrate these laboratories effectively with other local operations.

Three types of movement of host-country personnel were examined; (a) to the parent, (b) to another R&D laboratory of the MNE group and (c) to another host-country R&D facility (Haug *et al.*, 1983). For all industries host-country scientific personnel is moved to the parent quite extensively (Table 11.3), with pharmaceuticals, food and drink, petroleum and other manufacturing showing above the total average response. Movement to other MNE laboratories also appears as a strong choice, showing the networking of scientific linkages not only from and towards the parent but also from and towards the other parts of the 'periphery' of the MNE group. Thus peripheral R&D linkages are also important in the decentralization of R&D as they promote a more genuine version of technological internationalization. Pharmaceuticals and the food and drink sector tend to be more sensitive to this option. Though movements of personnel to host-country laboratories are rare they are again of above average relevance in pharmaceuticals, food and drink and petroleum. This suggests that the intra-group linkages of these laboratories complement linking into the local science base. Our

Table 11.3 Frequency of movement of host-country personnel to other scientific laboratories

	Average response		
	Parent (i.e. home-country laboratories)	Other MNE group laboratories	Other host-country R&D facility
Industry			
Food and drink	2.12	2.00	1.29
Industrial and agricultural chemicals	1.83	1.47	1.21
Pharmaceuticals and consumer chemicals	2.21	2.07	1.33
Electronics and electrical appliances[2]	1.69	1.50	1.27
Mechanical engineering	1.57	1.33	1.00
Metal manufacture and products	1.75	1.75	1.25
Petroleum	2.00	2.00	1.33
Automobiles	1.60	1.44	1.33
Other manufacturing[3]	2.00	1.67	1.19
Home country			
USA	1.77	1.71	1.24
Japan	1.82	1.33	1.29
Europe[4]	2.03	1.76	1.28
Host country			
UK	1.76	1.56	1.22
Other Europe[5]	2.09	1.88	1.32
Total	1.86	1.66	12.5

1. Respondents were asked to evaluate movement of personnel to each type of facility as occurring frequently, occasionally or never. The average response was then calculated by allocating responses of frequently the value of 3, occasionally the value of 2 and never the value of 1.
2. Includes computers and telecommunications.
3. Includes building materials, instruments, rubber, miscellaneous.
4. Covers subsidiaries of European MNEs in countries other than the home country.
5. Covers subsidiaries in Belgium, Greece and Portugal.

view of a fully-global technological strategy would imply this course of action. Automobiles have above average local-institution personnel links, though relatively few within the group, and mechanical engineering has a limited movement of personnel in general. European firms opt for the peripheral movement slightly more often than USA MNEs and clearly more than Japanese companies. The above average movement of US laboratories' personnel to 'other MNE laboratories' could indicate a European strategy and consequently the treatment of Europe as a separate region with distinct demand and supply conditions.

The strong average response of European MNEs regarding their movement towards the parent suggests a centripetal strategy with less evident signs of a genuine decentralization strategy. Japanese firms also seem to depend technologically on the skills developed in central laboratories. On a host-country level it is obvious that the diversified technological dependence of laboratories located in the Other Europe group contrasted with the stronger technological position of R&D laboratories located in the UK. The fact that the movement of scientific personnel towards host-country facilities is limited could indicate the internationalization of R&D and the 'elimination' of geographical boundaries, could enable firms to emphasize the transfer of their scientific personnel in their world-wide operations (Pearce and Singh, 1992a).

Explaining the intra-firm movement of scientific personnel

The following four possibilities were examined as reasons behind the movement of host-country personnel: (a) training, (b) improvement of knowledge of existing MNE technology, (c) participation in the R&D program in another MNE laboratory and (d) part of an exchange program. We could associate (a) with basic skill needs but also, in the long run, with less dynamic subsidiaries and with either strong centralized R&D creation or with the presence of other strong peripheral R&D centers. Option (c) could be strongly explained as a genuine part of R&D internationalization, where a final high-technology product is achieved as a group-level effort in which subsidiaries play substantial integrated roles supported by personnel movement. On the other hand choice (b) may suggest technological dependence of the subsidiaries in question. Finally, (d) may suggest the existence of adoption of initiatives developed outside the MNE group such as government intervention, etc.

The most prominent reason is found to be (b) with 38.5% of the total replies. The fact that (c) is the second most important factor (32.2%) indicates more clearly that subsidiaries are going through a creative transition. Training comes third with 23.1% of all replies indicating that once parents establish subsidiaries, and as subsidiaries assume more complicated roles than those in the past and as the infrastructure in the host-economies improves (e.g. education), they do not need to transfer personnel so extensively. The most distinctive results for home country are for Japan, especially the very high value of the transfer of personnel for improvement on the knowledge of existing MNE-group technology.

Taken with their low valuation of personnel transfer to participate in group R&D programs, this suggests the Japanese subsidiary laboratories are still more locked into current technology, and less likely than US labs, in particular, to be supporting their subsidiaries aim in creative transition. Subsidiaries in industries like food and drink, industrial chemicals, electronics and other manufacturing are clearly in a creative transition. Pharmaceuticals and automobiles seem to be also in a clear evolutionary process, whilst mechanical engineering and petroleum have a more traditional attitude towards transfer of personnel with training retaining a strong position. European companies and those in Other Europe, weigh more significantly reason (d); this can perhaps be explained as partly due to the European Union (EU) initiatives which support these companies and countries. Subsidiaries in the UK are more involved in group technology (either acquiring it (b), or helping especially to create it (c)) through personnel exchange than those in Other Europe. Subsidiaries in Other Europe have more need to transfer personnel for scientific training. This reflects the UK's stronger scientific background generally and also the more creative roles of subsidiaries in the UK.

Econometric tests of the movement of scientific personnel

The movement of scientific personnel was investigated in regression tests. Two parallel sets of regressions were run, one including the roles of laboratories amongst the independent variables and the second including the sources of technology used in subsidiaries' operations. The set of independent variables include industry and country dummies, those that indicate roles of laboratories, i.e. ADAPT (indicating an SL role), DEVEL (indicating an LIL role) and GROUPRAD (indicating an IIL role), those that show sources of technology, i.e. IMPTECH (for imported technology), HOSTTECH (for technology created in the host country) and SUBRAD (for technology created in the subsidiary) and finally a set of quantitative variables including SALES (representing the absolute size of a subsidiary in terms of the $million value of its sales), RELSIZE (indicating the relative size of a subsidiary in the form of its share of total MNE-group sales), EXPRAT (the percentage of a subsidiary's production that is exported), INTRAEXP (the share of a subsidiary's exports that go to another part of its own MNE group) and finally INTEREXP (the share of a subsidiary's exports that comprise intermediate products).

As an econometric technique OLS is used, although the dependent variable was a qualitative one. In theory, the PROBIT estimation method is a more appropriate technique because it provides more accurate estimates of probability values which is useful for prediction purposes.

Table 11.4 Reasons for movement of host-country scientific personnel to other institutions

	Reasons (percentage[1])			
	A	B	C	D
Industry				
Food and drink	21.4	42.9	35.7	
Industrial and agricultural chemicals	27.8	27.8	33.3	11.1
Pharmaceuticals and consumer chemicals	23.1	42.3	23.1	11.5
Electronics and electrical appliances[2]	17.9	39.3	35.7	7.1
Mechanical engineering	37.5	25.0	37.5	
Metal manufacture and products		50.0	50.0	
Petroleum	37.5	25.0	25.0	12.5
Automobiles	25.0	50.0	25.0	
Other manufacturing[3]	20.0	40.0	36.0	4.0
Home country				
USA	21.5	36.9	36.9	4.6
Japan	17.6	52.9	23.5	5.9
Europe[4]	27.6	36.2	27.6	8.6
Host country				
UK	19.8	39.5	38.3	2.5
Other Europe[5]	27.4	37.1	24.2	11.3
Total	23.1	38.5	32.2	6.3

Reasons for movement of scientific personnel:
A – predominately to train them for the work in the host-country laboratory.
B – to improve their knowledge of the existing MNE technology.
C – to participate in the R&D programme in the other MNE group laboratories.
D – part of an exchange programme with other scientific organizations.
1. Respondents were asked to tick the most relevant case.
2. Includes computers and telecommunications.
3. Includes building materials, instruments, rubber, miscellaneous.
4. Covers subsidiaries of European MNEs in countries other than the home country.
5. Covers subsidiaries in Belgium, Greece and Portugal.

However, as the basic reason for these econometric estimations was to test the degree of significance of the independent variables on the dependent and not to make predictions, the OLS method is preferred (Casson *et al.*, 1991). Preliminary calculations using PROBIT showed almost identical results to the OLS case.

The first dependent variable was movement of personnel to the parent laboratory. This is strongly positively related (Table 11.5) to situations where the R&D laboratory role is either SL involved in adaptation (ADAPT), or an IIL involved in pre-competitive research (GROUPRAD). In the first case the laboratory will probably seek the parent's expertise to

Table 11.5 Regressions with movement of scientific personnel as dependent variables (only significant results are presented)

	Personnel moved to parent		Personnel moved to other group lab		Personnel moved to host-country institutions	
Intercept	0.7841 (1.42)	2.5252*** (4.31)	1.1309* (1.98)	1.9845*** (3.77)	0.2100 (0.35)	1.5582** (2.66)
Electronics and electrical engineering	−0.6852** (−2.44)	−0.7255** (−2.65)		−0.6095** (−2.51)		
Industrial and agricultural chemicals				−0.3484* (−1.72)		
Pharmaceuticals and consumer chemicals						
UK		−0.4117* (−1.92)		−0.4385** (−2.23)		
Japan						0.5531** (2.05)
SALES					0.005** (2.25)	
RELSIZE			0.0104* (1.73)			
EXPRAT			−0.0066** (−2.39)	−0.0067** (−2.47)		
INTRAEXP			0.0078*** (2.91)	0.0071*** (2.91)		
ADAPT	0.2805** (2.46)		0.3143** (2.56)			
GROUPRAD	0.4187*** (4.06)		0.3107*** (2.98)		0.3066*** (2.77)	
HOSTECH				0.1925** (2.07)		
SUBRAD				0.2121** (2.38)		
R^2	0.6040	0.3837	0.6203	0.5496	0.5071	0.2810
F	2.36**	1.46	2.61***	2.75***	1.39	0.80
n	52	68	53	66	48	62

*** significant at 1%   **significant at 5%   *significant at 10%

increase familiarity with the product technology that needs to be adapted. In the second case the laboratory belongs more to a basic research network where obviously the parent laboratories are central, so that personnel movement is crucial to the effective integration of the network's research operations and concerns. The positive strong results on these two variables endorse the previous arguments.

The second dependent variable tested was movement of scientific personnel to other (i.e. non-parent) group laboratories. This test is very significant because it tells about the technological boundaries in MNE groups, and shows the end of a dominance for the one-way parent subsidiary transfer, with movements around the periphery becoming very important and showing the existence of creative group networks in science. The positive sign on RELSIZE shows that laboratories from the relatively large subsidiaries are most involved in this type of 'peripheral movement', probably connecting with similar R&D laboratories in complementary programs and/or assisting the operations of weaker laboratories in the region. The presence of this type of movement is negatively related to the subsidiaries' degree of export orientation (EXPRAT) but positively related to the proportion of those exports which do occur that are traded intra-group (INTRAEXP).

The negative sign on EXPRAT suggests rationalized product (RP) operations do not need to support their use of existing technology by movement of scientific personnel and that RPM/WPM subsidiaries do not need to transfer personnel to gain assistance for their efforts. Once this is taken into account, however, group interdependency does surface in the fact that intra-group exports are more likely to generate such movement than extra-group (positive sign on INTRAEXP). Against that background the positive sign on ADAPT is likely to imply support for the adaptation of product/processes to host-country (rather than export) markets.

The positive sign on GROUPRAD again (as for the first dependent variable) shows high movement of personnel in labs playing a role in group research programs. By source of technology used in subsidiaries, scientific personnel movement is strongest in these using host-country technology and their own R&D results. Thus the movement reflects the possession of knowledge already in the subsidiary and may therefore be motivated by the transfer of it to other subsidiaries, which may be technologically weaker or may possess complementary knowledge. These results would certainly suggest that movement of personnel 'to improve their knowledge of existing group technology' is more as a complement to their own creative efforts than an attempt to absorb it in a submissive (dependent) manner.

Finally the last regression investigates movement of personnel to host-country scientific institutions as a dependent variable. As this type of movement has been seen as relatively weaker, so the regressions are less able to reveal strong factors behind it when it does occur. Once again labs involved in group-level (basic) research programs (GROUPRAD) are most likely to do it, as are laboratories associated with large subsidiaries.

Conclusion

Overall the results support the view that technology creation and use in MNEs is now very much associated with integrated scientific networks supported by multi-directional personnel movement. MNEs use extensively their internalized channels in order to create and distribute technological inputs throughout their operations. In the case of transfer of the human capital input its roles vary according to the level and type of technological independence of the overseas subsidiary. Thus some of this personnel movement is associated with adaptation where this is necessary (i.e. ADAPT is significant for the first two dependent variables in the regressions, but not the third), suggesting some personnel movements may help to adapt for the local market technology from elsewhere in the group. There is also a clear suggestion that it often occurs from a position of creative strength. Thus personnel movement is not generally associated with the issue of imported technology (IMPTECH is always negative signed in the regressions), but more often positively associated with technological capability and ambition in the subsidiary (notably the persistent positive significance of GROUPRAD in the regressions).

These results, in turn, indicate the need to accept a new theoretical perspective regarding the creation and transmission of technology which contradicts the centralized view advocated in theoretical models such as the Product Cycle. To be more precise, theories of industrial organization in combination with strategic approaches to the MNE (as outlined in this chapter) can provide a sound theoretical background in the understanding of the current and future issues involved in the globalization of production. Finally, following Dunning's Investment Development Path theory (Dunning and Narula, 1996) it is evident that such movement of scientific personnel is associated with the ownership advantages of foreign firms which in turn provide a potential framework for the upgrading of the location advantages of host-economies. If the desired goal of governments is to 'help' their countries to promote the development of *created assets* then one way of doing this is to encourage FDI that is associated with genuine technology creation.

12
Multinationals and Economic Development in the Era of Globalization

Robert Pearce and Marina Papanastassiou

The processes of globalization, within which the strategic evolution of MNEs analyzed in earlier chapters has occurred, involves not only increased integration between national economies but also an increasingly systematic policy emphasis on generating those individualized characteristics that define them. This then points again to the role of the generation and progression of differentiated sources of competitiveness at the core of national development strategies. Deriving from this another crucial factor of recent decades has been the increased commitment to technological change as a source of growth and development, for both firms and national economies. Here we can see an analogy for the process of creative transition, within the competitive evolution of MNE subsidiaries (see Chapter 2), operating at the level of national economic development. Thus, at early stages of their pursuit of industrialization as a source of development, countries may possess potential sources of competitiveness (latent static comparative advantages) which local enterprise lacks the capacities to operationalize effectively. Then inward technology transfer can provide the firm-level competences to secure early growth. But eventually policy will need to target indigenously generated sources of the firm-level drivers of competitive individualization and sustainable development. Building local technological change as an impetus to growth has resulted in the generation of national systems of innovation (see Chapter 8) and the pursuit of dynamic comparative advantage.

These points suggest that national economies that pursue sustainable development in an era of globalization and open-market competition need to be aware of their positioning in terms of both *spatial* and *temporal* heterogeneity. Here spatial heterogeneity represents those differentiating attributes of an economy through which it, at a point in time, asserts its international competitiveness. The concern with temporal heterogeneity then acknowledges the acceptance of the dynamic aspects of competitiveness, and thus the continual need to revitalize and reposition through time, a country's sources of spatial heterogeneity.

Here we can see a country's sources of immediate international competitiveness (i.e. its current positioning in global spatial heterogeneity) as deriving from an attempt to secure an optimized match between the inputs that define its static comparative advantage and the most appropriate accessible technologies and production processes to use them. At an early stage of industrialization, we have suggested, the most effective sources of these technologies are likely to be external, i.e. secured through MNEs' technology transfer. Since these MNEs usually have a wide range of locations in which they could apply their technologies (at least those mature and standardized ones that are embodied in currently competitive goods) the choice of the particular economy indicates that, at that stage, the *national* source of *international* competitiveness primarily derives from its inputs. Thus positioning in spatial heterogeneity would here derive from these inputs and their capacity to attract the externally originated means to operationalize them.

This then implies two, ultimately closely interdependent, facets to differentiating an economy's sources of competitiveness over time. The first of these is to upgrade the efficiency and distinctive capacities of the inputs that comprise its static comparative advantage. But for this to be useful as a source of renewed competitiveness (i.e. to become an operative component of spatial heterogeneity) it will need to be combined with similarly higher-grade technologies. This then leads to the second necessary element in temporal heterogeneity, in the form of more advanced technologies embodied in the supply of higher-quality goods and services. Once again a very plausible potential for this can simply be access to more advanced parts of MNEs' extant competitive scopes. But as an economy develops it would normally become an increasingly relevant aspect of national ambitions to escape from these knowledge dependencies and to generate internally these new ways of utilizing its enhanced input resources. In this way the national aspiration to a 'creative transition' eventually leads to the generation of a distinctive science-base and research agenda, with an increasing encouragement of inventive initiative and risk-orientation in human capital (managerial, marketing, engineering, etc). We can note here, and elaborate later, that this indigenization of the pursuit of new sources of competitiveness does not exclude a continued role for MNEs. Indeed it may now benefit from tapping into these firms' experience and competence in creation and innovation, rather than, as before, merely benefiting dependently on their earlier successes. But now some components of MNEs' innovation result in new sources of competitiveness that can be localized in a particular contributing economy. A process of *strategic internalization* (see Chapter 3) is shared between MNE subsidiaries and the creative scopes of its host economy.

The preceding discussion provides us with the *a priori* bases of an argument for the potential for the modern heterarchical MNE to operate as an embedded component of a country's development process; both contributing to and benefiting from the necessary changes in the resource-base and competitive attributes of the economy. To elaborate on these potentials we have distinguished between three levels or types of host-country resource (Pearce and Zhang, 2008). These are essentially differentiated by the extent of their renewability and their capacity to drive sustainability in a country's economic development.

In our typology of development-oriented resources we can start with natural or primary endowments, in the form of extracted minerals or agriculture and forestry. Though not central to our analysis of MNEs' strategic reconfiguration in the last decades of the 20th century these type-1 resources had played a very prominent role in the FDI of the 'first' era of globalization (up to 1914). Thus many of the 'proto-MNEs' of that era operated in primary commodity sectors, with the type-1 natural resources serving as the attracting location advantages (LAs) and the firms' appropriate skills and techniques (as well as access to capital) comprising the relevant ownership advantages (OAs). This *resource-seeking* motivation does, of course, retain clear contemporary relevance; notably when it provides the foundation for a vertically-integrated MNE, whose OAs may now derive more from technical strengths in later stages of the chain or from an organizational ability to coordinate (and gain power from) the integrated sequence.

We can, however, discern two significant constraints with regard to such type-1 primary resources as a basis for sustainable development. Firstly, many of these resources are either totally non-renewable (fossil fuels and other minerals) or can only be renewed over periods that are too long and uncertain to serve as a reliable basis for sustainability (forestry). Secondly, development that is generated from a narrow commodity base will be very structurally limited and vulnerable. The immediate policy implication of this is then that where a strength in primary resources does provide a decisive basis for the *initiation* of a significant developmental process its sustainability will need to be secured through prompt broadening or diversification.

A much discussed potential for broadening the basis of resource-driven development has been to add value before export, by localizing further stages in the processing or refining chain. Clearly vertically-integrated MNEs who already control, and have expertise in, these following stages can be targeted for this role. However, the skill and other input needs (e.g. energy) of these subsequent value-adding stages may not be reflected in the current competitive attributes of the resource-rich economy. Attraction of these operations (with the implication of productive inefficiency) may then require aggressive bargaining by the host government (e.g. leveraging access to the primary resource itself) or some form of subsidization.[1]

Alternatively the revenue and foreign-exchange strength that derives from type-1 resources can be invested into other sectors, where so far unrealized potentials may exist. Here, for example, if a government seeks to diversify into the initiation of a manufacturing sector (perhaps, but not necessarily, related to its particular type-1 resources) it may be able to subsidize MNE entry (in a sense buying access to their OAs) from resource-generated financial strength.

Once a country does embark on industrialization as a basis for sustainable development the alternative resources placed at the center of this are those we here designate as type-2. These are considered to be standardized inputs into mature and successful production processes. The most obvious type-2 resource is, of course, labor. But other supporting aspects of the economy, such as energy supply and infrastructure, also play a type-2 resource role in facilitating industrialization. A crucial characteristic of type-2 resources are that they are renewable, in the sense that they can be upgraded within the development process itself. Thus an existing labor force can be retrained to higher levels of skill, whilst new entrants to the labor force can, as a result of improved education standards, possess higher levels of productivity from the commencement of their employment. Energy supply can also be enhanced as part of the development process, both in terms of reliability and price. Similarly the capacity of many aspects of infrastructure, notably transport systems, ports and airports, IT and communications, should be routinely upgraded to support industrialization.

However, another crucial aspect of these type-2 resources is that they do not themselves have the capacity to help define the role they play. The technologies they work with and the production processes they become part of are determined independently. Whilst the upgrading of type-2 resources is necessary for development it will not be sufficient. The scope to secure improved value from enhanced type-2 resources will depend on access to new opportunities opened up by new technologies and new sources of technical progress. We have suggested that it is limitations of local enterprise in this respect that provides a strong potential for MNE participation in the early stages of industrialization. Thus we can see MNEs transferring relevant OAs to these countries in the expectation of obtaining a boost to profits from responding to the potentials of particular LAs.

To maximize the benefits it gets from its initial entry into a new economy an MNE will seek to address possible limitations from 'inappropriate' technology transfer by improving the match between its OAs and the LAs that have attracted their application. This may well involve some refinements to the resources to be used, most notably some commitment to the training of labor. Such training (and any similar adjustments to other type-2 inputs) would be context specific, with the precise aim of improving the ability of the labor to perform the tasks that are defined by the requirements of the OAs applied by the MNE. Alternatively, the MNE might secure rewards from minor adaptations to its own product or process technologies if this can improve the benefits it secures from host-country LAs. These adjustments then target the objective of moving as close as possible to a static optimization of the benefits from combining the MNE's OAs and the economy's current LAs.

However, as already emphasized, industrialization and development cause and require changes in LAs, in terms of the efficiency and availability of type-2 resources. Negative interpretations of this indicate that movement towards full employment would put upward pressure on wage rates, whilst high rates of growth may lead to increased unreliability in energy supply and further emphasize endemic deficiencies in infrastructure. The alternative positive perspective, however, suggests a sustained policy commitment to the development process, in the form of persistent reinvestment (in the bases of type-2 assets) that can not only alleviate the constraints but interject renewed and upgraded potentials into the economy.

This means that, for the MNEs, properly articulated policy support for the renewal of host-country resources and characteristics, within the development process itself, should result in a positive view of the changes in LAs. So, whilst the loss of the LAs that originally attracted MNE entry might indeed lead to a 'footloose' migration of part of its supply profile to a new lower-cost location, this by no means implies inevitable closure. Instead a subsidiary's production responsibilities can be restructured so as to take positive benefit from upgraded type-2 resources. Thus the MNE would transfer to the subsidiary a new more advanced subset of its OAs to underpin production of a more technically-sophisticated and higher-value-added part of the existing product range. The enhanced LAs central to this would certainly be expected to include improved labor-force productivity, reflecting an ability to work with more complex but more productive technologies. This would derive from both better educated new entrants to the labor force and improved (probably subsidized) access to reskilling programs to support labor market flexibility. Also important will be improved reliability of energy supply and enhanced provision of aspects of infrastructure that are particularly relevant to MNEs' needs, such as roads, ports, airports and international communications.

As at the original entry MNEs would then continue to seek to secure the most effective match between future waves of newly committed OAs and the upgraded LAs that attract them. Once again this could involve in-house training of labor in technology-specific procedures that are defined by new OAs and/or minor adaptations to these new products or processes. This restructured combination of host-country type-2 resources and MNE competitive capabilities therefore targets a new, significantly upgraded, 'static equilibrium'. This allows us to see the MNE as potentially embedded in the development of a host economy through a persisting sequence of 'comparative static' reconfigurations of its subsidiary's operations. Here the MNE is contributing in an 'arms length' way to the country's development, by using upgraded type-2 resources as they become available. But this process is not, in itself, part of the dynamics of sustainable development. The OAs committed by the MNE are parts of its existing mature competitive capabilities seeking to use new input and environmental potentials (i.e. renewed LAs) of the host, whose newly enhanced capacities it had not directly influenced.

Of the range of strategic motivations now available to MNEs the one that provides us with the template for the supply-oriented optimizing scenarios just outlined is that of *efficiency-seeking* (ES). Thus the ES subsidiary is allocated responsibility for cost-efficient supply of a selected part of its parent MNE's product range, as a component of the group's integrated international supply network. Historically, in fact, the move towards export-oriented strategies as a means of building industrialization into early phases of economic development was substantially codeterminous with MNEs' organizational restructuring from multi-domestic hierarchy to network hierarchy (see Chapter 1). The use of the increasingly free-trade environment implied by emerging globalization was, of course, a vital driver of both these strategic reconfigurations.

As we have indicated the source of efficiency that underpins the role of an ES subsidiary derives from matching the process technologies of the goods to be supplied with the type-2 resources that define a location's sources of static comparative advantage. The efficiency secured through this static (or comparative static) optimizing location decision is then augmented by two further benefits. These derive from the subsidiary's position in the group's competitive supply networks. Firstly, the export-market orientation of the ES operation means it will normally be able to fully achieve available economies of scale in its supply. Secondly, for the subsidiary to sustain or improve its position in the inherently flexible and internally-competitive environment of the network hierarchy leaves no room for X-inefficiency. The subsidiary will be strictly judged on its ability to fully secure the potentials of the OAs transferred to it and the host-country resources (LAs) that it accesses. Such judgments, however, not only reflect on current subsidiary-level proficiency, but also inform the inevitable competitive restructuring within an evolving network hierarchy. Thus, as we have already emphasized, it will be the natural objective of a confident and successful supply subsidiary, embedded effectively in the input capacities of its host location, to negotiate itself an upgraded status and higher-value-added responsibilities when similarly upgraded type-2 resources can be projected to merit this.

If we model (see Chapter 1) the network hierarchy as for many MNEs having superseded an earlier multi-domestic hierarchy structure, we then recognize the presence of an alternative strategic motivation that nevertheless also involves the transfer of mature and standardized sources of competitive advantage to subsidiaries. Thus *market-seeking* (MS) subsidiaries are likely to produce a wider part of the parent MNE's product range, but do so for almost exclusive supply to the host country market. The traditional positioning of MS subsidiaries in the multi-domestic hierarchy had reflected a pervasive global protectionist environment. This included, for many countries seeking to initiate a systematic development process, the trade restraints central to an import-substitution industrialization policy. Under these circumstances the potential profitability of a market and related trade restrictions provide a different configuration of LAs to determine the need for local supply. Though the general lowering of trade barriers, and the concomitant transition to export-oriented development strategies, removed much of the original context for MS it does in fact seem to have retained a, perhaps more *ad hoc*, positioning amongst the strategic options of the contemporary MNE. At the core of this appears to be the competitive value of the responsiveness to distinctive tastes and needs of a local market that can be secured most effectively through embedded production.

If the MS role does persist in MNE subsidiaries as host economies grow this means that their increasingly individualized sources of competitiveness will represent response to local *demand* patterns. Any influence on the evolving role of MS subsidiaries that derives from upgrading of type-2 *supply* resources will therefore be secondary and, explicitly, not oriented towards improved *international* competitiveness. This is clearly alien to the comparative static optimization objectives of ES subsidiaries' participation in export-oriented industrialization. However, the seeds of a rather different, intuitively dynamic, developmental potential may be present if an MS subsidiary remains embedded in its host-country's growth. Thus persisting interaction with the demand and, in a perhaps less systematic way, supply changes implicit in the economy's growth generates an increasing degree of subsidiary-level distinctiveness. These localized learning processes may, when host-country characteristics reach a level to support it, allow the subsidiary to accede to more ambitious creative roles in the parent MNE's global innovation and knowledge-generation programs. This will become most viable and systematic when the host-country has itself achieved significant strength in what we can now delineate as type-3 resources.

Thus type-3 resources become the essence of sustainable dynamism in national economic development by opening up the new competitive opportunities that provide the scope to benefit fully from the potentials of upgraded type-2 inputs. Type-3 resources, therefore, have no association with the current supply of standardized goods and services, but instead address the complementary competitive imperative of defining future generations of goods and services based on new technological potentials. A country's growth achieves a fully *dynamic* core when it encompasses the institutional mechanisms to secure both the continual upgrading of type-2 resources and the, effectively interrelated, generation of new internationally-competitive uses for these resources through the innovations of type-3 resources. The embedded investigations of type-3 resources drives temporal heterogeneity that then underpins the competitive spatial heterogeneity of type-2 inputs.

Type-3 resources are manifest in the form of technology, skills, inventiveness and imagination that is embodied in individuals, teams, firms, knowledge support infrastructure and technology policies. The generation and effective application of this ever-evolving nexus of creative inputs and learning processes mediated by appropriate institutional structures is the ultimate aim of national systems of innovation (NSI). The institutions generated for and around type-3 resources then include the education system, research laboratories (private; public; university), innovation-oriented enterprises and government support policies.

It is then the normal aim of an NSI, and its constituent type-3 resources, to generate the knowledge-based potentials for inculcating evolutionary path-dependent sustainability into a country's development. Two interrelated but distinctive levels of output from an NSI then serve to drive competitive renewal as the basis of sustainable development.

The first of these is to provide the inputs into the next generation of firm-level innovations that will secure the immediate developmental impetus for the economy. The type-3 resources that drive this include new technologies, that are emerging for commercial application from antecedent scientific research; scientists who can mediate these technologies to business; high-quality market researchers; inventive engineers and ambitious entrepreneurial management. Innovations that emerge will then respond most clearly to the needs of sustainable development if they take account of the need to use type-1 and type-2 resources in more effective ways. This would involve using scarce type-1 resources as sparingly as possible and seeking roles for type-2 resources that build on their potentials for upgrading and higher productivity usage.

The second aim of the NSI is then to reinforce its core stock of scientific knowledge, from which new competitive technologies can eventually emerge for implementation in subsequent rounds of innovation. The pre-competitive research programs targeting this address issues that are, at that stage, of purely scientific interest. The hope is, indeed, to find viable commercial applications within the output of these pure research programs, but there is no perception of the form these will take when projects are formulated. The agendas for these basic research programs are then most logically and effectively articulated around issues that reflect the core scientific specialisms and strength of the current NSI, and the questions it raises for those scientists presently working with it. This again suggests a dominant path-dependency in the scientific progress at the core of the NSI's progression. This then implies that when elements of this scientific knowledge does feed into future innovations the new technologies that fuel this are likely to have their roots in those that were central to earlier product generations. This should then impart an evolutionary logic to the progress of successive generations of products, in a way that provides a coherence to an economy's competitive development and thereby its sustainability.

The purpose of generating type-3 resources and building them into a well-integrated NSI with a coherent sense of its objectives is, of course, to generate locally the dynamic knowledge-related sources of persisting competitive development of the national economy. But the aim of generating and utilizing these resources locally does not preclude the possibility of constructive participation of MNEs in the process. The key manifestation of success of type-3 resources will be renewal of the technological bases of the economy's sources of competitiveness (i.e. reinforcement of its position in spatial heterogeneity). But in the contemporary global economy the ultimate realization of competitiveness is through firms, and in many sectors the most internationally successful of these firms are MNEs. This, much recent research shows, reflects the ability of modern MNEs to not only *be* competitive in many different economies but to derive the sources of their competitiveness *from* the differences between these economies. The *knowledge-seeking* (KS) objective in MNEs, we emphasize, feeds off the technological- and market-heterogeneity of national economies. However, the aim of many facets of KS behavior by MNEs is to generate new core competences (scientific, technological, marketing, engineering) that can be operationalized in any (or many) locations and which, therefore, do not in any way automatically improve the performance of an individual NSI from which they are generated.

One key aspect of this issue (see Chapter 8) is that different phases of an MNE's *global* innovation strategy will tap into different facets of individual *national* systems of innovation. Then successes that an MNE secures at one stage of an NSI need not inevitably strengthen that NSI overall, or necessarily actually enhance competitiveness of the national economy. We can see this precisely in terms of the two particular aims of an NSI (and type-3 resources) noted earlier.

Here the aim of providing firms with new products that add significant dimensions to competitiveness is the one addressed by MNEs through their product mandate (PM) subsidiaries. An MNE locates a PM within a particular NSI because it expects to co-opt local type-3 resources (in a process of strategic internalization – see Chapter 3) that can help it achieve a distinctive addition to its product range. Here the PM expects to feed off those elements of technological- and market-heterogeneity that will have emerged in a strong NSI to generate new goods with unique characteristics that add effectively to the MNE's internationally competitive product scope. But to be able to do this successfully the PM will also build on its positioning in the current technological scope and market objectives of its parent group. Thus the PM's capacity to discern the specific creative potentials that it hopes to derive from local type-3 resources, and the ability to then draw these into effective subsidiary-level development projects, reflects those existing in-house competences it derives from its MNE group. This clearly reflects the process of interdependent individualism (see Chapter 7), where the PM generates distinctive individualized competitive capacities that derive from its host NSI, but does so in ways that also both draw on and contribute to the knowledge and creative attributes of the wider MNE group.

By the same token, then, the PM adds new dimensions to its host NSI by bringing in complementary technologies, providing new types of creative expertise and by positioning its developmental ambitions in the alternative context of the global competitive needs of an MNE. Though a successful PM can be seen to be adding to the immediate competitiveness of both its MNE and host economy[2] there remain issues about its reliability as an agent of sustainability in development. Thus a PM is a high-fixed cost operation that will be persistently under pressure to sustain its position in its company's innovation network. Several sources of vulnerability can threaten a PM's survival and thereby question the sustainability of its position in the host NSI and the country's competitive evolution. Poor performance of the established leadership of the PM may weaken its ability to get full value from the synergies of its position in the technological communities of both its group and the host NSI. Weakening of either of these sources can also threaten the PM's survival. Poor performance in other components of its MNE's global knowledge network may either isolate a PM from that part of its creative inputs and innovation impetus or simply lessen the group's ability to sustain as many of these high-cost high-risk operations. Similarly if the host country fails to sustain developmental scopes of its NSI, from which PMs need to feed, then one prompt result of this growing weakness would probably be closure of these subsidiaries. A key component of that, we suggested earlier, is the commitment to reinforcing the scientific foundations of the NSI's distinctiveness through a strong basic research agenda.

This too, we then argue, has the potential to benefit from MNE participation. Indeed the first phase of MNEs' global innovation strategy is built around a geographically dispersed, but scientifically interdependent, network of precompetitive research laboratories seeking to discover the knowledge cores of future innovations. This component of

KS then embeds itself in the science-bases of particular countries through stand-alone MNE laboratories (internationally interdependent laboratories – IILs) or through collaborative associations with local laboratories and research institutions (see Chapter 9). The choice of locations for these laboratories or collaborations does then reflect the expectations of very specific contributions that will reflect distinctive elements of the scientific agendas and technological trajectories of the attracting NSI. But the projects generated in these MNEs' operations (i.e. the questions asked of the host science-base) will also reflect an expectation of these laboratories' or collaborations' ability to contribute to the wider research agenda of the group. They will be part of R&D networks with an innate commitment to generation of interdependencies and synergies through persistent exchanges of knowledge and questions (see Chapters 10 and 11).

A positive view of this positioning of a precompetitive laboratory's operation in the wider MNE investigative context is that it can enrich and diversify the scope of basic research in the science-base, without diluting or weakening its distinctive strengths. Bringing in additional and complementary technological perspectives, along with new scientific research issues, can provide a vital way of extending and expanding the momentum of the distinctive research agendas that are defined by the particular core knowledge capacities of the NSI. The alternative perspective that then derives from this interactive positioning is that the most likely context for understanding and further development of results from this work is the broader technological community of the MNE. Good research and exciting results are likely to have their greatest perceived value outside the host NSI. In particular when new technologies to which these results have contributed feed into actual competitive innovations of the MNE there is no presumption that these will occur in, or otherwise benefit, the original host economy. The trade-off here may then be that MNE participation may add to the distinctive strengths of the precompetitive stages of the NSI[3] whilst, at the same time, weakening the internal cohesion between that stage and later developmental possibilities.

In this chapter we have focused on what is, in effect, an aspect of the political economy of MNEs. This accepts that in the era of globalization the growth and development of the international economy still depends on how individual national economies pursue and achieve their own competitive progress. However, the way such national development is formulated does become inevitably conditioned by, and responsive to, a positioning in an increasingly strident international competitive environment. We have investigated here the varied ways in which MNEs, as the most innately *globalized* of competitive institutions, can operate as influential agents in the articulation of the manner in which the changing resource- and knowledge-attributes of an economy can become the bases of sustainable competitiveness and development. The detailed analyses of this chapter demonstrate not only the range of potentials that MNEs' commitment can bring to these processes, but also the compromises and qualifications that securing these benefits may involve.

Beneath these detailed arguments this final chapter also seeks to exemplify a subtext reflecting our view of the positioning and value of such analyses of international business strategy. The first aspect of this is a point that should be routinely obvious, but which still eludes many economists and much of received theorizing in international economics.[4] This is that to understand the essence of the global economy, whose evolution has progressed around increased freedoms of international transactions and transfers, it is necessary to fully comprehend the agent that *organizes*, at the center of its own competitive operations, a vast proportion of these transfers; of goods (final and intermediate products and raw materials), finance and human capital, and of technology and increasingly of scientific research agendas. That is the multinational enterprise. Secondly, that understanding the MNE as a basis for addressing wider issues in economics and public policy cannot proceed realistically without full recognition of its strategic diversity; how it pursues its global competitiveness by responding to both the differences between the current capacities of locations (spatial heterogeneity) and the ways these locations are seeking sources of renewal and differentiation of these capacities (temporal heterogeneity). Ultimately, to comprehend the current efficiency and future progress of the global economy, we need to understand the MNE as an integrating organization that pursues a range of different but complementary objectives, in a range of different locations, in response to a range of distinctive but ever evolving attributes of these locations.

Notes

1 This could involve allowing an MNE that localizes processing or refining to pay less per unit of raw material than it would have been required to do if bought as an export.
2 Assuming that, at least in the short-run, the MNE's PM has made more effective use of local type-3 resources than would a possible alternative – 'crowded-out' – local enterprise. This counter-factual situation cannot, of course, be fully resolved, but here we assume the ability of the PM to recruit the local resources reflects its ability to make more creative use of them.

3 Since scientific results at the precompetitive stage can take on the character of 'public goods' within the MNE their transfer and use elsewhere will not lessen their availability to the creating laboratory and NSI. Thus, providing the laboratory or collaboration remains in place and retains access to its own generated base of knowledge, this can still drive its own further agendas and progress.
4 In this vein John Dunning (2002, 2008) notes his disappointment at the inability to persuade colleagues in economics 'to appreciate fully the relevance of international business research to an understanding of their own lines' of scholarship and 'to acknowledge the uniqueness of IB as a subject area'.

References

Allred, B.B. and Swan, S., 'Contextual influences on international subsidiaries' product technology strategy' (2003), retrieved from http://www. sbm,fitemple.edu/ibrf2003.

Almeida, P., 'Knowledge sourcing by foreign multinationals: patent citation analysis in the US semiconductor industry', *Strategic Management Journal*, 17 (1996) 155–65.

Almeida, P. and Kogut, B., 'Localization of knowledge and the mobility of engineers in regional networks', *Management Science*, 45/7 (1999) 905–17.

Almeida, P., Song, J. and Grant, R.M., 'Are firms superior to alliances and markets? An empirical test of cross-border knowledge building', *Organizational Science*, 13 (2002) 147–61.

Alvarez, M., 'Espana y la senda le desarroelo de la inversion directa: una aproximacin'. Iet document de treball, Institut d'Economia de Barcelona (2001) (abstract only in English).

Andersson, U. and Forsgren, M., 'In search of centres of excellence: network embeddedness and subsidiary roles in multinational corporations', *Management International Review*, 40 (2000) 329–50.

Asakawa, K., 'Evolving headquarters – subsidiary dynamics in international R&D: the case of Japanese multinationals', *R&D Management*, 31(1) (2001) 1–14.

Balasubramanyam, V.N. and Balasubramanyam, A., 'The software cluster in Bangalore', in Dunning, J.H. (ed.) *Regions, Globalization and the Knowledge-based Economy* (Oxford: Oxford University Press, 2000) 349–63.

Barrell, R. and Pain, N., 'An econometric analysis of US foreign direct investment', *Review of Economics and Statistics*, 78 (1996) 200–7.

Barrell, R. and Pain, N., 'Foreign direct investment, technological change, and economic growth within Europe', *The Economic Journal*, 107 (1997) 1770–86.

Barrell, R. and Pain, N., 'Domestic institutions, agglomerations and foreign direct investment in Europe', *European Economic Review*, 43 (1999a) 925–34.

Barrell, R. and Pain, N., 'Trade restraints and Japanese direct investment flows', *European Economic Review*, 43 (1999b) 29–45.

Bartlett, C.A. and Ghoshal, S., 'Tap your subsidiaries for global reach', *Harvard Business Review* (1986) 87–94.

Bartlett, C.A. and Ghoshal, S., *Managing Across Borders: The Transnational Solution* (London: Hutchinson Business Books, 1989).

Bartlett, C.A. and Ghoshal, S., 'Managing innovation in the transnational corporation', in Bartlett, C.A., Doz, Y. and Hedlund, G. (eds) *Managing the Global Firm* (London: Routledge, 1990) 215–55.

Behrman, J.N., *Industrial Policies: International Restructuring and Transnationals* (Lexington, Mass: Lexington Books, 1984).

Behrman, J.N. and Fischer, W.A., *Overseas R&D Activities of Transnational Companies* (Cambridge, Mass: Oelgeschlager, Gunn and Hain, 1980a).

Behrman, J.N. and Fischer, W.A., 'Transnational corporations: market orientations and R&D abroad', *Colombia Journal of World Business*, XV (1980b) 55–60.

Bellak, C., 'The investment path of Austria', Working Paper series, Department of Economics: Vienna University of Economics (2000).
Birkinshaw, J.M., 'Approaching heterarchy: a review of the literature on multinational strategy and structure', *Advances in International Comparative Management*, 9 (1994) 111–44.
Birkinshaw, J.M., 'How subsidiary mandates are gained and lost', *Journal of International Business Studies*, 27(3) (1996) 467–95.
Birkinshaw, J.M., 'Entrepreneurship in multinational corporations: the characteristics of subsidiary initiatives', *Strategic Management Journal*, 18(3) (1997) 207–29.
Birkinshaw, J.M., 'Foreign-owned subsidiaries and regional development: the case of Sweden', in Birkinshaw, J. and Hood, N. (eds) *Multinational Corporate Evolution and Subsidiary Development* (London: Macmillan, 1998a) 268–98.
Birkinshaw, J.M., 'Corporate entrepreneurship in network organizations: how subsidiary initiative drives internal market efficiency', *European Management Journal*, 16(3) (1998b) 355–64.
Birkinshaw, J.M., *Entrepreneurship in the Global Firm* (London: Sage, 2000).
Birkinshaw, J.M. and Hood, N., 'An empirical study of development processes in foreign-owned subsidiaries in Canada and Scotland', *Management International Review*, 37(4) (1997) 339–64.
Birkinshaw, J. and Hood, N., 'Multinational subsidiary evolution: capability and charter change in foreign-owned subsidiary companies', *Academy of Management Review*, 23(4) (1998) 773–95.
Birkinshaw, J. and Hood, N., 'Characteristics of foreign subsidiaries in industry clusters', *Journal of International Business Studies*, 31(3) (2000) 141–57.
Birkinshaw, J., Hood, N. and Jonsson, S., 'Building firm-specific advantages in multinational corporations: the role of subsidiary initiative', *Strategic Management Journal*, 19 (1998) 221–41.
Birkinshaw, J. and Morrison, A., 'Configuration of strategy and structure in subsidiaries of multinational corporations', *Journal of International Business Studies*, 26(4) (1995) 729–54.
Birkinshaw, J., Nobel, R. and Ridderstrale, J., 'Knowledge as a contingency variable: do the characteristics of knowledge predict organizational structure?', *Organizational Science*, 13(3) (2002) 274–89.
Bonin, B. and Perron, B., 'World product mandates and firms operating in Quebec', in Etemad, H. and Séguin Dulude, L. (eds) *Managing the Multinational Subsidiary* (London: Croom Helm, 1986) 161–76.
Braunerhjelm, P. and Svensson, R., 'Host country characteristics and agglomeration in foreign direct investment', *Applied Economics*, 28 (1996) 833–40.
Buckley, P.J. and Artisien, P., 'Policy issues of intra-EC direct investment', in Dunning, J.H. and Robson, P. (eds) *Multinationals in the European Community* (Oxford: Blackwell, 1988) 105–28.
Buckley, P.J. and Casson, M.C., *The Future of the Multinational Enterprise* (London: Macmillan, 1976).
Buckley, P.J. and Casson, M.C., 'Organising for innovation: the multinational enterprise in the twenty-first century', in Buckley, P.J. and Casson, M.C. (eds) *Multinational Enterprises in the World Economy* (Aldershot: Elgar, 1992).
Buckley, P.J. and Casson, M.C., 'Models of the multinational enterprise', *Journal of International Business Studies*, 29(1) (1998) 21–44.

Cantwell, J., *Technological Innovation and Multinational Corporations* (Oxford: Blackwell, 1989).
Cantwell, J.A., 'The international agglomeration of R&D', in Casson, M.C. (ed.) *Global Research Strategy and International Competitiveness* (Oxford: Blackwell, 1991) 104–32.
Cantwell, J., 'The globalization of technology: what remains of the product cycle model?', *Cambridge Journal of Economics*, 19(1) (1995) 155–74.
Cantwell, J., 'Innovation and information technology in the MNE', in Rugman, A.M. and Brewer, T.L. (eds) *The Oxford Handbook of International Business* (Oxford: Oxford University Press, 2001) 431–56.
Cantwell, J. and Iammarino, S., 'MNCs, technological innovation and regional systems in the EU: some evidence in the Italian case', *International Journal of the Economics of Business*, 5(3) (1998) 383–408.
Cantwell, J. and Janne, O., 'Technological globalization and innovative centers: the role of corporate technological leadership and locational hierarchy', *Research Policy*, 28(2–3) (1999) 119–44.
Cantwell, J. and Mudambi, R., 'MNE competence-creating subsidiary mandates', *Strategic Management Journal*, 26(12) (2005) 1109–28.
Casson, M.C., 'Introduction to The large multinational corporation' (by S. Hymer), in Casson, M.C. (ed.) *Multinational Corporations* (Aldershot: Elgar, 1990).
Casson, M.C., 'International comparative advantage and the location of R&D', in Casson, M.C. (ed.) *Global Research Strategy and International Competitiveness* (Oxford: Blackwell, 1991) 68–103.
Casson, M., Pearce, R. and Singh, S., 'Business strategy and overseas R&D', in Casson, M. (ed.) *Global Research Strategy and International Competitiveness* (Oxford: Blackwell, 1991) 213–49.
Castro, F.B., 'Foreign direct investment in a late industrialising country: the Portuguese IDP revisited', FEP Working Paper 147. Universidade do Porto, Faculdade de Economia do Porto (2004).
Caves, R.E., 'International corporations: the industrial economics of foreign investment', *Economica*, 38 (1971) 1–27.
Caves, R.E., *Multinational Enterprise and Economic Analysis* (Cambridge: Cambridge University Press, 1982).
Chandler, A.D. and Redlich, F., 'Recent developments in American business administration and their conceptualisation', *Business History Review*, Spring (1961) 103–28.
Chakrabarti, A., 'The determinants of foreign direct investment: sensitivity analysis of cross-country regressions', *Kyklos*, 54 (2001) 89–114.
Chatterji, D., 'Accessing external sources of technology', *Research and Technology Management* (1996) 48–56.
Chesnais, F., 'Technical cooperation agreements between firms', *STI Review*, 4 (1988) 51–120.
Chiesa, V., 'Global R&D project management and organisation: a taxonomy', *Journal of Product Innovation Management*, 17(5) (2000) 341–59.
Clegg, J. and Scott-Green, S.C., 'The determinants of new foreign direct investment capital flows into the European Community: a statistical comparison of the USA and Japan', *Journal of Common Market Studies*, 37(4) (1999) 597–616.
Cohen, W.M. and Levinthal, D.A., 'Innovation and learning: the two faces of R&D', *Economic Journal*, 99 (1989) 569–96.

Cohen, W.M. and Levinthal, D.A., 'Absorptive capacity: a new perspective on learning and innovation', *Administrative Science Quarterly*, 35 (1990) 128–52.
Collinson, S.C., 'Knowledge management capabilities in R&D: a UK-Japan company comparison', *R&D Management*, 31(3) (2001) 335–47.
Conner, K.R. and Prahalad, C.K., 'A resource-based theory of the firm: knowledge versus opportunism', *Organisation Science*, 7(5) (1996) 477–501.
Cordell, A.J., *The Multinational Firm, Foreign Direct Investment and Canadian Science Policy*, Science Council of Canada, Special Study No. 22 (Ottawa: Information Canada, 1971).
Cordell, A.J., 'Innovation, the multinational corporation: some implications for national science policy', *Long Range Planning*, 6(3) (1973) 22–9.
Crookell, H. and Morrison, A., 'Subsidiary strategy in a free trade environment', *Business Quarterly*, Autumn (1990) 33–9.
Culem, G.G., 'The locational determinants of direct investment among industrialised countries', *European Economic Review*, 32 (1988) 885–904.
Cushman, D.O., 'The effects of real wages and labor productivity on foreign direct investment', *Southern Economic Journal*, 54 (1987) 174–85.
D'Cruz, J., 'Strategic management of subsidiaries', in Etemad, H. and Séguin Dulude, L. (eds) *Managing the Multinational Subsidiary* (London: Croom Helm, 1986) 75–89.
De Meyer, A., 'Techtalk: how managers are stimulating global R&D communication', *Sloan Management Review*, 11 (1991) 49–58.
De Meyer, A., 'Management of an international network of industrial R&D laboratories', *R&D Management*, 23 (1993) 109–20.
De Meyer, A. and Mizushima, A., 'Global R&D management', *R&D Management*, 19 (1989) 135–46.
Dimitropoulou, D. and Pearce, R., 'Foreign direct investment flows into an integrating Europe: MNE strategy and location decisions, 1981–2001', in Fai, F.M. and Morgan, E.J. (eds) *Managerial Issues in International Business* (London: Palgrave, 2006) 180–94.
Dimitropoulou, D., *Multinational Enterprises and the Location Choice: FDI Determinants in the EU 15*. PhD dissertation. University of Reading (2007).
Dimitropoulou, D., Pearce, R. and Papanastassiou, M., 'The locational determinants of foreign direct investment in European Union core and periphery: the influence of multinational strategy', in Dunning, J.H. and Gugler, P. (eds) *Foreign Direct Investment, Location and Competitiveness* (Amsterdam: Elsevier, 2008) 51–79.
Dunning, J.H., 'Trade, location of economic activity and the multinational enterprise: a search for an eclectic approach', in Ohlin, B., Hesselborn, P.O. and Wijkman, P.M. (eds) *The International Allocation of Economic Activity* (London: Macmillan, 1977) 395–418.
Dunning, J.H., 'Explaining the international direct investment position of countries: towards a dynamic or developmental approach', *Weltwirtschaftliches Archiv*, 117 (1981) 30–64.
Dunning, J.H., *Explaining International Production* (London: Unwin Hyman, 1988).
Dunning, J.H., *Multinational Enterprises and the Global Economy* (Wokingham: Addison-Wesley, 1993a).
Dunning, J.H., *The Globalisation of Business* (London: Routledge, 1993b).

Dunning, J.H., 'Re-evaluating the benefits of foreign direct investment', *Transnational Corporations*, 3(1) (1994a) 23–52.
Dunning, J.H., 'Multinational enterprises and the globalisation of innovatory capacity', *Research Policy*, 23 (1994b) 67–88.
Dunning, J.H., 'The geographical sources of competitiveness of firms: some results of a new survey', *Transnational Corporations*, 5(3) (1996) 1–30.
Dunning, J.H., 'Location and the multinational enterprise: a neglected factor?', *Journal of International Business Studies*, 29(1) (1998) 45–66.
Dunning, J.H., 'The eclectic paradigm as an envelope for economic and business theories of MNE activity', *International Business Review*, 9(2) (2000) 163–90.
Dunning, J.H., 'Perspectives on international business research: a professional autobiography – 50 years researching and teaching international business', *Journal of International Business Studies*, 33(4) (2002) 817–35.
Dunning, J.H. and Lundan, S.M., *Multinational Enterprises and the Global Economy* (second edition) (Cheltenham: Edward Elgar, 2008).
Dunning, J.H. and Narula, R., 'The R&D activities of foreign firms in the United States', *International Studies of Management and Organisation*, 25(1–2) (1995) 39–73.
Dunning, J.H. and Narula, R. (eds) *Foreign Direct Investment and Governments: Catalysts for Economic Restructuring* (London: Routledge, 1996).
Dunning, J.H. and Narula, R., 'The investment development path revisited: some emerging issues', in Dunning, J.H. and Narula, R. (eds) *Foreign Direct Investment and Governments: Catalysts for Economic Restructuring* (London: Routledge, 2000) 1–41.
Dunning, J.H. and Rugman, A.M., 'The influence of Hymer's dissertation on the theory of foreign direct investment', *American Economic Review: Papers and Proceedings*, 75(2) (1985) 228–32.
Durán, J. and Úbeda, F., 'The investment development path: a new empirical approach and some theoretical issues', *Transnational Corporations*, 10(2) (2001) 1–35.
Durán, J. and Úbeda, F., 'The investment development path of newly developed countries', *International Journal of the Economics of Business*, 12(1) (2005) 123–37.
Etemad, H., 'Industrial policy orientation, choice of technology, world product mandates and international trading companies', in Etemad, H. and Séguin Dulude, L. (eds) *Managing the Multinational Subsidiary* (London: Croom Helm, 1986) 112–35.
Etemad, H. and Séguin Dulude, L. (eds) *Managing the Multinational Subsidiary* (London: Croom Helm, 1986).
Filippaios, F. and Papanastassiou, M., 'The geography of US outward foreign direct investment within the OECD: a cross-regional empirical analysis'. Mimeo paper, Athens University of Economics and Business (2001).
Filippaios, F., Kottaridi, C., Papanastassiou, M. and Pearce, R., 'Empirical evidence on the strategic behaviour of US MNEs within the framework of dynamic differentiated networks', in Muchielli, J-L. and Mayer, T. (eds) *Multinational Firms' Location and the New Economic Geography* (Cheltenham: Elgar, 2004) 178–204.
Florida, R., 'The globalisation of R&D: results of a survey of foreign affiliated R&D laboratories in the USA', *Research Policy*, 26 (1997) 85–103.
Fors, G., *R&D and Technology Transfer by Multinational Enterprises* (Stockholm: The Institute for Economic and Social Research, 1996).

Foss, N.J. and Pedersen, T., 'Building a MNC knowledge structure: the roles of knowledge sources, complementarities, and organizational context', paper prepared for the LINK workshop, 'Governing Knowledge Processes' Copenhagen, September 7–8 (2001).

Gassman, O. and Von Zedtwitz, M., 'Organization of industrial R&D on a global scale', *R&D Management*, 28(3) (1998) 147–61.

Ghoshal, S. and Bartlett, C.A., 'Creation, adoption and diffusion of innovations by subsidiaries of multinational corporations', *Journal of International Business Studies*, 19(3) (1988) 365–88.

Ghoshal, S. and Nohria, N., 'Internal differentiation within multinational corporations', *Strategic Management Journal*, 10(4) (1989) 323–37.

Giddy, I.H., 'The demise of the product cycle model in international business theory', *Colombia Journal of World Business*, 13(1) (1978) 90–7.

Görg, H. and Ruane, F., 'European integration and peripherality: are there lessons from Ireland', Technical Report, 1999.

Granovetter, M., 'Economic action and social structure: the problem of embeddedness', *American Journal of Sociology*, 91(3) (1985) 481–510.

Granstrand, O. and Sjolander, S., 'Internationalisation and diversification of multi-technology corporations', in Granstrand, O., Håkanson, L. and Sjolander, S. (eds) *Technology Management and International Business* (Chichester: Wiley, 1992) 181–207.

Granstrand, O., Håkanson, L. and Sjolander, S., 'Internationalisation of R&D: a survey of some recent research', *Research Policy*, 22 (1993) 413–30.

Granstrand, O., 'Internationalisation of corporate R&D: a study of Japanese and Swedish corporations', *Research Policy*, 28(2–3) (1999) 275–302.

Gupta, A.K. and Govindarajan, V., 'Knowledge flows and the structure of control within multinational corporations', *Academy of Management Review*, 16(4) (1991) 768–92.

Gupta, A.K. and Govindarajan, V., 'Organising for knowledge flows within MNCs', *International Business Review*, 3(4) (1994) 443–58.

Gupta, A.K. and Govindarajan, V., 'Knowledge flows within multinational corporations', *Strategic Management Journal*, 21(4) (2000) 473–96.

Hagedoorn, J., 'Understanding the rationale of strategic technology partnering: inter-organisational modes of cooperation and sectoral differences', *Strategic Management Journal*, 14 (1993) 371–85.

Håkanson, H. and Laage-Hellman, J., 'Developing a network R&D strategy', *Journal of Product Innovation Management*, 4 (1984) 224–37.

Håkanson, L., 'Organization and evolution of foreign R&D in Swedish multinationals', *Geografiska Annaler*, 63B (1981) 47–63.

Håkanson, L., 'International decentralisation of R&D – the organisational challenges', in Bartlett, C.A., Doz, Y. and Hedlund, G. (eds) *Managing the Global Firm* (London: Routledge, 1990) 256–78.

Håkanson, L. and Nobel, R., 'Foreign research and development in Swedish multinationals', *Research Policy*, 22 (1993a) 373–96.

Håkanson, L. and Nobel, R., 'Determinants of foreign R&D in Swedish multinationals', *Research Policy*, 22 (1993b) 397–411.

Håkanson, L. and Nobel, R., 'Technology characteristics and reverse technology transfer', *Management International Review*, 40 (2000) 29–48.

Håkanson, L. and Nobel, R., 'Organisational characteristics and reverse technology transfer', *Management International Review*, 41 (2001) 395–420.

Han, A. and Hausman, J., 'Flexible parametric estimation of duration and competing risk models', *Journal of Applied Econometrics*, 5 (1990) 1–28.

Harzing, A.W., 'Response rates in international mail surveys', *International Business Review*, 6(6) (1997) 641–65.

Haug, P., Hood, N. and Young, S., 'R&D intensity in the affiliates of US-owned electronics companies manufacturing in Scotland', *Regional Studies*, 17 (1983) 383–92.

Hedlund, G., 'The hypermodern MNC: a heterarchy?', *Human Resource Management*, 25 (1986) 9–35.

Hedlund, G., 'Assumptions of hierarchy and heterarchy, with applications to the management of the multinational corporation', in Ghoshal, S. and Westney, E. (eds) *Organisation Theory and the Multinational Corporation* (London: Macmillan, 1993) 211–36.

Hedlund, G. and Rolander, D., 'Action in heterarchies – new approaches to managing the MNC', in Bartlett, C.A., Doz, Y. and Hedlund, G. (eds) *Managing the Global Firm* (London: Routledge, 1990) 15–46.

Hennart, J-F., 'Transactions cost theory and the multinational enterprise', in Pitelis, C.N. and Sugden, R. (eds) *The Nature of the Transnational Firm* (London: Routledge, 2000) 72–118.

Hirsch, S., *The Location of Industry and International Competitiveness* (Oxford: Oxford University Press, 1967).

Hood, N. and Young, S., 'US multinational R&D: corporate strategies and policy implications for the UK', *Multinational Business*, 2 (1982) 10–23.

Hood, N. and Young, S., 'Inward investment and the EC: UK evidence on corporate integration strategies', in Dunning, J.H. and Robson, P. (eds) *Multinationals and the European Community* (Oxford: Blackwell, 1988) 91–104.

Hood, N., Young, S., and Lal, D., 'Strategic evolution within Japanese manufacturing plants in Europe: UK evidence', *International Business Review*, 3(2) (1994) 97–122.

Horaguchi, H. and Toyne, B., 'Setting the record straight: Hymer, internalization theory and transaction cost economics', *Journal of International Business Studies*, 21(3) (1990) 487–94.

Howells, J., 'The internationalisation of R&D and the development of global research networks', *Regional Studies*, 24(6) (1990a) 495–512.

Howells, J., 'The location and organisation of research and development: new horizons', *Research Policy*, 19 (1990b) 133–46.

Howells, J., 'Innovation and technology transfer within multinational firms', in Michie, J. and Grieve Smith, J. (eds) *Globalisation, Growth and Governance* (Oxford: Oxford University Press, 1998) 50–70.

Howells, J., 'Regional systems of innovation', in Archibugi, D., Howells, J. and Michie, J. (eds) *Innovation Policy in a Global Economy* (Cambridge: Cambridge University Press, 1999) 67–93.

Howells, J. and Wood, M., *The Globalisation of Production and Technology* (London: Belhaven Press, 1993).

Hymer, S.H., 'The efficiency (contradictions) of multinational corporations', *American Economic Review: Papers and Proceedings*, LX(2) (1970) 441–8.

Hymer, S.H., 'The multinational corporation and the law of uneven development', in Bhagwati, J.N. (ed.) *Economics and World Order. From the 1970s to the 1990s* (London: Macmillan, 1972a) 113–40.

Hymer, S.H., 'The internationalization of capital', *The Journal of Economic Issues*, 6(1) (1972b) 91–111.
Hymer, S.H., *The International Operations of National Firms: A Study of Direct Investment*. PhD Thesis, MIT Cambridge, MA. Published (Cambridge, Mass: MIT Press, 1960/1976).
Hymer, S.H., *The Multinational Corporation – A Radical Approach* (papers by Stephen Herbert Hymer) Cohen, R.B., Felton, N., Nkosi, M. and Van Liere, J. (eds) (Cambridge: Cambridge University Press, 1979).
Hymer, S.H., 'The large multinational "corporation": an analysis of some motives for the international integration of business', *Revue Economique*, 19(6) (1968) 949–73. Translated in Casson, M.C. (ed.) *Multinational Corporations* (Aldershot: Elgar, 1990) 3–31.
Hymer, S.H. and Resnick, S.A., 'International trade and uneven development', in Bhagwati, J.N., Jones, R.W., Mundell, R.A. and Vanck, J. (eds) *Trade, Balance of Payments and Growth* (Amsterdam: North-Holland Publishing Co., 1971) 473–505.
Hymer, S.H. and Rowthorn, R., 'Multinational corporations and international oligopoly: the non-American challenge', in Kindleberger, C. (ed.) *The International Corporation* (Cambridge, Mass: MIT Press, 1970) 57–91.
Ivarsson, I. and Jonsson, T., 'Local technological competence and asset-seeking FDI: an empirical study of manufacturing and wholesale affiliates in Sweden', *International Business Review*, 12 (2003) 369–86.
Jarillo, J.C. and Martinez, J.I., 'Different roles for subsidiaries: the case of multinational corporations in Spain', *Strategic Management Journal*, 11 (1990) 501–12.
Johanson, J. and Vahlne, J.E., 'The internationalization process of the firm – a model of knowledge development and increasing market commitments', *Journal of International Business Studies*, 8 (1977) 23–32.
Kiefer, N. and Skoog, G., 'Local asymptotic specification error analysis', *Econometrica*, 52 (1984) 873–85.
Kim, C. and Mauborgne, R.A., 'Implementing global strategies: the role of procedural justice', *Strategic Management Journal*, 12 (1991) 125–43.
Kim, C. and Mauborgne, R.A., 'Procedural justice, attitudes and subsidiary top management compliance with multinationals' corporate strategic decisions', *Academy of Management Journal*, 36(3) (1993) 502–26.
Kogut, B., 'The network as knowledge: generative roles and the emergence of structure', *Strategic Management Journal*, 21 (2000) 405–25.
Kogut, B. and Chang, S.J., 'Technological capabilities and Japanese foreign direct investment in the United States', *Review of Economics and Statistics*, LXXIII (1991) 401–13.
Kogut, B. and Zander, U., 'Knowledge of the firm and evolutionary theory of the multinational corporation', *Journal of International Business Studies*, 24 (1993) 625–45.
Kojima, K., *Direct Foreign Investment: A Japanese Model of Multinational Business Operations* (London: Croom Helm, 1978).
Kotabe, M. and Murray, J., 'Linking product and process innovation and modes of international sourcing in global competition: a case of foreign multinational firms', *Journal of International Business Studies*, 21(3) (1990) 383–408.
Kotabe, M., Srinivason, S. and Aulakh, P., 'Multinationality and firm performance: the moderating role of R&D and marketing capabilities', *Journal of International Business Studies*, 33(1) (2002) 79–97.

Kuemmerle, W., 'Building effective R & D capabilities abroad', *Harvard Business Review* (1997) 61–70.

Kuemmerle, W., 'The drivers of foreign direct investment in research and development: an empirical investigation', *Journal of International Business Studies*, 30(1) (1999a) 1–24.

Kuemmerle, W., 'Foreign direct investment in industrial research in the pharmaceutical and electronics industries: results from a survey of multinational firms', *Research Policy*, 28(2–3) (1999b) 179–93.

Lundvall, B.A. (ed.) *National Systems of Innovation: Towards a Theory of Innovation and Interactive Learning* (London: Pinter, 1992).

Luo, Y., 'Determinants of local responsiveness: perspectives from foreign subsidiaries in an emerging market', *Journal of Management*, 27 (2001) 451–77.

MacDougall, G.D.A., 'The benefits and costs of private investment from abroad: a theoretical approach', *Economic Record*, 36 (March) (1960) 13–35.

Manea, J. and Pearce, R., *Multinationals and Transition* (London: Palgrave, 2004).

Minbaeva, D., Pedersen, T., Bjorkman, I., Fey, C. and Park, H.J., 'Knowledge transfer, subsidiary absorptive capacity and HRM', *Journal of International Business Studies*, 34 (2003) 586–99.

Molero, J. and Buesa, M., 'Multinational companies and technological change: basic traits and taxonomy of the behaviour of German industrial companies in Spain', *Research Policy*, 22 (1993) 265–78.

Molero, J., Buesa, M. and Casado, M., 'Technological strategies of MNCs in intermediate countries: the case of Spain', in Molero, J. (ed.) *Technological Innovation, Multinational Corporations and New International Competitiveness* (Luxembourg: Harwood Academic Publishers, 1995) 265–91.

Murphy, A., 'Simple LM tests of mis-specification for ordered logit models', *Economic Letters*, 52 (1996) 137–41.

Murray, J.Y., Wildt, A.R. and Kotabe, M., 'Global sourcing strategies of US subsidiaries of foreign multinationals', *Management International Review*, 35(4) (1995) 307–24.

Narula, R., *Multinational Investment and Economic Structure: Globalisation and Competitiveness* (London: Routledge, 1996).

Narula, R. and Dunning, J.H, 'Industrial development, globalization and multinational enterprises: new realities for developing countries', *Oxford Development Studies*, 28(2) (2000) 141–69.

Nelson, R.R. (ed.) *National Systems of Innovation: A Comparative Study* (Oxford: Oxford University Press, 1993).

Neven, D. and Siotis, G., 'Technology sourcing and FDI in the EC: an empirical evaluation', *International Journal of Industrial Organisation*, 14 (1996) 543–60.

Niosi, J., (ed.) 'The internationalisation of industrial R&D' (special issue), *Research Policy*, 28(2–3) (1999).

Osterloh, M. and Frey, B., 'Motivation, knowledge transfer and organizational forms', *Organizational Science*, 11(5) (2000) 538–50.

Papanastassiou, M., *Creation and Development of Technology by MNEs' Subsidiaries in Europe: The Cases of UK, Greece, Belgium and Portugal*. Thesis submitted for the degree of Doctor of Philosophy, University of Reading (1995).

Papanastassiou, M., 'Technology and production strategies of MNE subsidiaries in Europe', *International Business Review*, 8(2) (1999) 213–32.

Papanastassiou, M. and Anastassopoulos, G., 'Aspects of Greek inward and outward foreign direct investment. The case of the food and drink sector', *Development & International Cooperation*, XIII(24–25) (1997) 349–74.

Papanastassiou, M. and Pearce, R., 'Host-country determinants of the market strategies of US companies' overseas subsidiaries', *Journal of the Economics of Business*, 1(2) (1994) 199–217.

Papanastassiou, M. and Pearce, R., 'The internationalisation of research and development by Japanese enterprises', *R&D Management*, 24(2) (1994) 155–65.

Papanastassiou, M. and Pearce, R., 'The creation and application of technology by MNEs' subsidiaries in Europe', in Burton, F., Yamin, M. and Young, S. (eds) *International Business and Europe in Transition* (London: Macmillan, 1996a) 207–30.

Papanastassiou, M. and Pearce, R., 'R&D networks and innovation: decentralised product development in multinational enterprises', *R&D Management*, 26(4) (1996b) 315–33.

Papanastassiou, M. and Pearce, R., 'Technology sourcing and the strategic roles of manufacturing subsidiaries in the UK: local competences and global competitiveness', *Management International Review*, 37(1) (1997a) 2–25.

Papanastassiou, M. and Pearce, R., 'Cooperative approaches to strategic competitiveness through MNE subsidiaries: insiders and outsiders in the European market', in Beamish, P.W. and Killing, J.P. (eds) *Cooperative Strategies: European Perspectives* (San Francisco: The New Lexington Press, 1997b) 207–30.

Papanastassiou, M. and Pearce, R., *Multinationals, Technology and National Competitiveness* (Cheltenham: Elgar, 1999).

Patel, P. and Vega, M., 'Patterns of internationalization of corporate technology: location versus home country advantages', *Research Policy*, 28(2–3) (1999) 145–55.

Pavitt, K., 'What do we know about the strategic management of technology?', *Strategic Management Journal*, 32(3) (1990) 17–26.

Pearce, R., *The Internationalisation of Research and Development by Multinational Enterprises* (London: Macmillan, 1989).

Pearce, R., 'World product mandates and MNE specialisation', *Scandinavian International Business Review*, 1(2) (1992) 38–58.

Pearce, R., *The Growth and Evolution of Multinational Enterprises* (Aldershot: Elgar, 1993).

Pearce, R., 'The internationalization of research and development by multinational enterprises and the transfer sciences', *Empirica*, 21 (1994) 297–311.

Pearce, R., *Global Competition and Technology* (Basingstoke: Macmillan, 1997).

Pearce, R., 'Decentralised R&D and strategic competitiveness: globalised approaches to generation and use of technology in multinational enterprises', *Research Policy*, 28(2–3) (1999a) 157–78.

Pearce, R., 'The evolution of technology in multinational enterprises: the role of creative subsidiaries', *International Business Review*, 8(2) (1999b) 125–48.

Pearce, R., 'Multinationals and industrialisation: the bases of inward investment policy', *International Journal of the Economics of Business*, 8(1) (2001) 51–73.

Pearce, R., 'National systems of innovation and the international technology strategies of multinationals'. Paper presented at the European International Business Academy Conference, Athens (2002).

Pearce, R., 'Globalisation and development: an international business strategy approach', *Transnational Corporations*, 15(1) (2006) 39–74.
Pearce, R. and Papanastassiou, M., *The Technological Competitiveness of Japanese Multinationals: The European Dimension* (Ann Arbor: University of Michigan Press, 1996a).
Pearce, R. and Papanastassiou, M., 'R&D networks and innovation: decentralised product development in multinational enterprises', *R&D Management*, 26(4) (1996b) 315–33.
Pearce, R. and Papanastassiou, M., 'Overseas R&D and the strategic evolution of MNEs: evidence from laboratories in the UK', *Research Policy*, 28(1) (1999) 23–41.
Pearce, R. and Singh, S., *Globalising Research and Development* (Basingstoke: Macmillan, 1992a).
Pearce, R. and Singh, S., 'Internationalisation of R&D among the World's leading enterprises: survey analysis of organisation and motivation', in Granstrand, O., Håkanson, L. and Sjolander, S. (eds) *Technology Management and International Business* (Chichester: Wiley, 1992b) 137–62.
Pearce, R. and Zhang, S., 'Multinationals' strategies for global competitiveness and the sustainability of development in national economies', paper presented at annual conference of Euro-Asia Management Studies Association (EAMSA), Kyoto, December (2008).
Peng, M.W. and Wang, D.Y., 'Innovation capability and foreign direct investment: toward a learning option perspective', *Management International Review*, 4(1) (2000) 79–93.
Phene, A. and Almeida, P., 'How do firms evolve? The patterns of technological evolution of semi-conductor industries', *International Business Review*, 12(3) (2003) 349–67.
Pitelis, C.N., 'Stephen Hymer: life and the political economy of multinational corporate capital', *Contributions to Political Economy*, 21 (2002) 9–26.
Porter, M., *Competitive Advantage* (New York: Free Press, 1985).
Porter, M.E., 'Competition in global industries: a conceptual framework', in Porter, M.E. (ed.) *Competition in Global Industries* (Boston: Harvard Business School Press, 1986) 15–60.
Porter, M., *The Competitive Advantage of Nations* (New York: Free Press, 1990).
Porter, M.E., *On Competition* (Boston: Harvard Business School Press, 1998).
Porter, M., 'Winning strategies and country competitiveness in difficult times', presentation in Athens, May 8th (2003).
Poynter, T.A. and Rugman, A.M., 'World product mandates: how will multinationals respond?', *Business Quarterly*, 47(3) (1982) 54–61.
Randøy, T. and Li, J., 'Global resource flows and MNE network integration', in Birkinshaw, J.N. and Hood, N. (eds) *Multinational Corporate Evolution and Subsidiary Development* (London: Macmillan, 1998) 76–101.
Ronstadt, R.C., *Research and Development Abroad by US Multinationals* (New York: Praeger, 1977).
Ronstadt, R.C., 'International R&D: the establishment and evolution of R&D abroad by seven US multinationals', *Journal of International Business Studies*, 9 (1978) 7–24.

Rosenberg, N. and Nelson, R.R., 'American universities and technical advance in industry', *Research Policy*, 23 (1994) 323–48.
Roth, K. and Morrison, A., 'Implementing global strategy: characteristics of global subsidiary mandates', *Journal of International Business Studies*, 23(4) (1992) 715–36.
Rugman, A.M., 'Multinational enterprises and world product mandates', in Rugman, A.M. (ed.) *Multinationals and Technology Transfer – The Canadian Experience* (New York: Praeger, 1983) 73–90.
Rugman, A.M., 'Regional strategy and the demise of globalization', *Journal of International Management*, 9 (2003) 409–17.
Rugman, A. and Bennett, J., 'Technology transfer and world product mandating in Canada', *Colombia Journal of World Business*, 17 (1982) 58–62.
Rugman, A.M. and Douglas, S., 'The strategic management of multinationals and world product mandating', *Canadian Public Policy*, 12(2) (1986) 320–8.
Saez, C., Marco, T.G. and Arribas, E.H., 'Collaboration in R&D with universities and research centers: an empirical study of Spanish firms', *R&D Management*, 32(4) (2002) 321–39.
Souitaris, V., 'Firm-specific competences determining technological innovation: a survey in Greece', *R&D Management*, 32(1) (2002) 61–76.
Taggart, J.H., 'Multinational manufacturing subsidiaries in Scotland: strategic role and economic impact', *International Business Review*, 5(5) (1996) 447–68.
Taggart, J.H., 'An evaluation of the integration-responsiveness framework: MNC manufacturing subsidiaries in the UK', *Management International Review*, 37(4) (1997a) 295–318.
Taggart, J.H., 'Autonomy and procedural justice: a framework for evaluating subsidiary strategy', *Journal of International Business Studies*, 28(1) (1997b) 51–76.
Taggart, J.H., 'Complexity in UK subsidiaries of manufacturing multinational corporations', *Technovation*, 17 (1997c) 73–82.
Taggart, J.H., 'Identification and development of strategy at subsidiary level', in Birkinshaw, J.N. and Hood, N. (eds) *Multinational Corporate Evolution and Subsidiary Development* (London: Macmillan, 1998) 23–49.
Taggart, J.H., 'US MNCs' subsidiaries in the UK: characteristics and strategic roles', in Burton, F., Chapman, M. and Cross, A. (eds) *International Business Organisation* (London: Macmillan, 1999a) 29–46.
Taggart, J.H., 'MNC subsidiary performance, risk and corporate expectation', *International Business Review*, 9(2) (1999b) 233–55.
Tallman, S. and Fladmoe-Lindquist, K., 'Internationalization, globalization and capability-based strategy', *California Management Review*, 45(1) (2002) 116–35.
Tavares, A.T., *Systems, Evolution and Integration: Modelling the Impact of Economic Integration on Multinationals' Strategies*. PhD dissertation. University of Reading, 2001.
Tavares, A.T. and Pearce, R., 'The industrial policy implications of the heterogeneity of subsidiaries' roles in a multinational network', *L'Institute* – Discussion paper 5, Universities of Birmingham, Ferrara and Wisconsin – Milwaukee (1999).
Teece, D.J., *The Multinational Corporation and the Resource Cost of International Technology Transfer* (Cambridge, Mass.: Ballinger, 1976).

Teece, D.J., 'Technology transfer by multinational firms: the resource cost of transferring technological knowhow', *Economic Journal*, 87 (1977) 242–61.

Teece, D.J., 'The market for know how: the efficient international transfer of technology', *Annals, AAPSS*, 458 (1981) 81–96.

UNCTAD, *World Investment Report* (New York and Geneva: United Nations, 2002).

Vernon, R., 'International investment and international trade in the product cycle', *Quarterly Journal of Economics*, 88 (1966) 190–207.

Vernon, R., 'The product cycle hypothesis in a new international environment', *Oxford Bulletin of Economics and Statistics*, 4 (1979) 255–67.

Verspagen, B. (ed.) *Technology, Economic Integration and Social Cohesion: The Policy Challenges*. Technical Report, Targeted Socio-Economic Research, European Commission (1999).

Veugelers, R., 'Locational determinants and ranking of host countries: an empirical assessment', *Kyklos*, 44 (1991) 363–82.

Wheeler, D. and Mody, A., 'International investment location decisions: the case of US firms', *Journal of International Economics*, 33 (1992) 57–76.

White, R.E. and Poynter, T.A., 'Strategies for foreign-owned subsidiaries in Canada', *Business Quarterly*, 48(4) (1984) 59–69.

White, R.E. and Poynter, J.A., 'Organisation for world-wide advantage', in Bartlett, C.A., Doz, Y. and Hedlund, G. (eds) *Managing the Global Firm* (London: Routledge, 1990) 95–113.

Williamson, O.E., *The Economic Institutions of Capitalism: Firms, Markets, Relational Contracting* (New York: The Free Press, 1985).

Yamin, M., 'Determinants of reverse transfer: the experience of UK multinationals', in Schiattarella, R. (ed.) *New Challenges for European and International Business*. Proceedings of European International Business Academy Conference, Urbino (1995).

Yamin, M., 'An evolutionary analysis of subsidiary innovation and "reverse" technology transfer in multinational companies', in Burton, F. Chapman, M. and Cross, A. (eds) *International Business Organisation* (Basingstoke: Macmillan, 1999) 67–82.

Yamin, M., 'A critical re-evaluation of Hymer's contribution to the theory of the transnational corporation', in Pitelis, C.N. and Sugden, R. (eds) *The Nature of the Transnational Firm* (London: Routledge, 2000) 57–71.

Yamin, M. and Forsgren, M., 'Hymer's analysis of multinational organization: power retention and the demise of the federative MNE', *International Business Review*, 15(2) (2006).

Young, S. and Hood, N., 'Designing developmental after-care programmes for foreign direct investors in the European Union', *Transnational Corporations*, 3(2) (1994) 45–72.

Young, S., Hood, N. and Dunlop, S., 'Global strategies, multinational subsidiary roles and economic impact in Scotland', *Regional Studies*, 22(6) (1988) 487–97.

Zander, I., 'Whereto the multinational? The evolution of technological capabilities in the multinational network', *International Business Review*, 8(3) (1999a) 261–91.

Zander, I., 'How do you mean "global"? An empirical investigation of innovation networks in the multinational corporation', *Research Policy*, 28(2–3) (1999b) 195–213.

Zander, I. and Zander, U., 'Sweden: a latecomer to industrialisation', in Dunning, J.H. and Narula, R. (eds) *Foreign Direct Investment and Governments – Catalysts for Economic Restructuring* (London: Routledge, 1996) 101–41.

Zayas, J.M., 'Multinational and national firms in the process of technology internationalisation: Spain as an intermediate case', Documentos de trabajo del Instituto de Anlisis Industrial y Financiero. Complutense University of Madrid (1998).

Index

absorptive capacity, 65
after care programmes, 42
agglomeration, 85, 95, 152, 203
Allred, B.B., 59
Almeida, P., 60, 64–5, 72
Alvarez, M., 89
Anastassopoulos, G., 43
Andersson, U., 60, 70
Artisien, P., 80
Asakawa, K., 57, 60
Asia, 19, 190
Austria, 86, 88
autonomy, 4, 11, 13, 48–50, 74, 108

Balasubramanyam, A., 109
Balasubramanyam, V.N., 109
Barrell, R., 44, 81, 83–4
Bartlett, C., 40, 57, 62, 73, 136, 184, 205
Behrman, J.N., 21, 79, 108, 204
Belgium, 86, 88, 97, 205–6
Bellak, C., 88
Bennett, J., 62, 114
Birkinshaw, J.M., 40, 42, 45–6, 50, 57, 59, 60, 62, 74, 107, 111, 114, 144, 163, 184, 203
Bonin, B., 45
Braunerhjelm, P., 81, 84
Buckley, P.J., 3, 20, 43–5, 54–6, 59, 80, 98, 134, 183
Buesa, M., 136

Canada, 114, 189
Cantwell, J.A., 45, 55, 58, 60, 73, 109, 163, 177, 184, 203
Casson, M.C., 3, 20, 43–5, 54–6, 59, 98, 134, 183, 212
Castro, F.B., 89
Caves, R.E., 3, 69
centres of excellence, 62
Chandler, A.D., 99
Chakrabarti, A., 81
Chang, S.J., 44

Chatterji, D., 57
Chesnais, F., 42, 171
Chiesa, V., 57
Clegg, J., 88–9
clusters, 75, 109, 162, 184, 203
Coase, R., 98
Cohen, W.M., 58, 183
coherence, 13–15, 34, 39, 42, 110–11, 117–18, 133, 135, 153, 194–5, 202–3, 225
cohesion, 14, 20, 42, 110, 119, 135, 153, 203, 227
Cohesion fund (of EU), 86
Collinson, S.C., 70
Connor, K.R., 58
comparative advantage, 1, 2, 4, 7, 8, 21, 40, 48, 54, 59, 159, 216–17, 222
competitive advantage, 1, 3, 5, 6, 12, 43–4, 59, 60, 73, 103, 105, 113, 134, 222
component parts, 21, 27, 38, 49–51, 54, 62, 119, 122, 129
coordination, 2, 9, 14, 16, 109–10, 155, 164–5, 187, 191, 195, 218
Cordell, A.J., 184
'core' (countries in Europe), 78, 81–97
cost-effective supply, 5–8, 19, 21, 27–8, 48–9, 82, 94–5, 102–4, 119, 140, 146, 148–9, 202, 221
created comparative advantage, 22, 27, 29, 55
creative transition, 14, 15, 17, 20–42, 46, 59, 60, 106–7, 109, 114, 124, 210–11, 216–17
Crookell, H., 52, 62, 114
crowding-out effect, 95, 150, 161, 228
Culem, G.G., 81, 83
Cushman, D.O., 83

D'Cruz, J., 44, 114
De Meyer, A., 203
Denmark, 88

Dimitropoulou, D., 80–5, 90
Douglas, S., 114
Dunning, J.H., 1, 2, 20–1, 42, 57–8, 60, 72, 79, 87, 102, 112–13, 136, 171–2, 204, 215, 229
Durán, J., 88–9
dynamic differentiated network (MNE as), 23, 25, 28, 39, 78

economic development, 2, 8, 15, 21, 29, 39, 49, 161, 216, 218–24, 228
economies of scale, 5, 8, 25, 73, 83, 159, 222
education, 10, 22, 108, 110, 150, 210, 221, 224
engineering unit, 15, 28–9, 32, 34, 38, 47, 166, 176, 181, 184, 189–90, 224–5
entrepreneurship, 22, 25, 27, 29, 50, 107, 110, 113, 184, 224
Etemad, H., 45, 184
Europe, 6, 19, 51, 54, 56, 58, 70, 78–97, 104, 119, 125, 137, 161, 164, 169, 172, 187–8, 190–1, 198, 200, 209–11
European Union, 16, 58, 61, 70, 73, 78–97, 172, 201, 211
export orientation, 6, 19, 25, 70, 82, 91, 104, 113, 140, 221–3

Filippaios, F., 44, 81, 83
Fischer, W., 108, 204
Finland, 87–8
Fladmoe-Lindquist, K., 59, 74
Florida, R., 163, 203
footloose behaviour, 15, 19, 21–2, 27, 38, 40, 49, 55, 104, 108, 160, 220
foreign direct investment (FDI), 3, 16, 19, 43–4, 75, 78–97, 112, 138, 204–5, 215, 218
 trade creating FDI, 19, 40, 159
 trade destroying FDI, 19, 80, 159
Fors, G., 136, 185
Forsgren, M., 60, 70, 107, 114
Foss, N.J., 74
France, 86, 88, 96
Frey, B., 75

Gassman, O., 57
Germany, 86, 88
Ghoshal, S., 40, 57, 62, 73, 136, 184, 205
Giddy, I.H., 161
global innovation strategy, 17–18, 42, 138–45, 147, 149, 152–61, 166, 175, 190, 225–6
globalization, 1, 3, 6, 9, 56–7, 108, 159, 188, 205, 215–16, 218, 222, 227
Görg, H., 89
governments, 8, 11, 18, 42, 56, 120, 160–1, 182, 201, 210, 215, 219, 225
Govindarajan, V., 57–8, 186
Granovetter, M., 62
Grandstrand, O., 60, 161, 163, 203
Greece, 15, 58, 61, 63–5, 70, 72–4, 85–8, 205–6
Gupta, A.K., 57–8, 186

Hagedoorn, J., 42, 64, 171
Håkanson, H., 203
Håkanson, L., 44, 59, 60, 64, 70, 136, 162, 185–6, 203
Han, A., 67
Harzing, A.W., 61
Haug, P., 108, 161, 203, 205, 208
Hausman, J., 67
headquarters (HQ), 12–14, 20, 49, 60–1, 70, 74, 100, 110, 144, 189, 200, 204
Hedlund, G., 40, 60, 73, 110–11, 144, 163
hegemony, 6, 13, 16
Hennart, J-F., 98
heterarchy, 11–18, 40, 107–8, 110–13, 144, 163, 184, 218
heterogeneity, 1, 2, 7, 11, 13, 17, 78, 109, 117, 119, 182, 216–17
 see also market heterogeneity; technological heterogeneity
hierarchy, 4, 9, 11, 14, 16, 26, 43, 48, 74, 98–101, 103, 105, 107, 109–13, 144, 146
 see also multidomestic hierarchy; network hierarchy

hinterland, 104
Hirsch, S., 134
home country (of MNE), 3, 4, 6, 9, 13, 56, 59, 60, 72, 99, 138–9, 200, 204–8
Hood, N., 41–2, 46, 55, 62, 108, 114, 136, 161, 203
Horaguchi, H., 98
horizontal organization, 40, 184
horizontally-integrated MNE, 3, 43, 47, 54
host country, 1, 2, 5, 8, 10, 12, 14–16, 21–4, 28, 32, 39–40, 42, 44, 46, 49, 54, 60, 63, 73, 107–9, 127, 135, 151, 159, 163, 173, 180, 195, 205, 208, 210, 214, 220–3, 226–7
Howells, J., 44, 109, 136, 184, 186, 203
human capital, 10, 19, 40, 81, 84, 108, 151, 161, 215, 217, 228
Hymer, S.H., 3, 16–17, 43, 59, 98–114, 133, 144

Iammarino, S., 109, 184, 203
imports, 5, 6, 8, 82, 139, 162
import substitution, 4, 6, 25, 82, 102, 104, 222
individualism, 1, 2, 4, 8, 10–15, 19, 22, 28–31, 40, 48–50, 110, 114, 116–22, 124, 129, 135, 145, 161, 167, 176, 182–4, 187–9, 192, 197, 199–202, 216, 226
industrial revolution, 99
infrastructure, 86, 100, 161, 210, 219–21
innovation, 2, 4, 9–15, 17, 19–24, 29, 44, 59, 60, 63–4, 72, 74–5, 78, 83–4, 96, 103–9, 112, 115, 134–45, 148, 151, 155–7, 159, 161–3, 166, 169–73, 181, 183, 185, 192–4, 197, 205, 223–7
inputs, 5, 7, 8, 21–2, 26–7, 29, 40, 46, 49, 55, 59, 74, 83, 145, 149, 159, 171, 217, 219, 221–2
interdependence, 2, 9, 12–14, 18–19, 59, 107, 110, 116–18, 122, 124, 129, 133, 135, 144, 152, 161, 164, 167, 171–2, 187–92, 202–3, 214, 217, 227

interdependent individualism, 11, 13, 115–37, 161, 164, 226
'intermediate' countries (in EU), 85–9, 90–7
internalisation, 3, 10, 12, 22, 43, 45–6, 50, 55, 98, 110–11, 113, 134, 146, 155, 177, 183, 204
international competitiveness, 4, 5, 8–10, 159, 217, 223
investment development path, 87–9, 96, 215
Ireland, 85–7, 89, 96
Italy, 87–8
Ivarsson, I., 59, 60

Janne, O., 60, 163, 203
Japan, 15–16, 19, 51, 54, 61, 70, 79, 80, 90, 92–7, 104, 125, 127, 129, 137, 164, 170, 187–8, 190, 200, 208–11
Jarillo, J.C., 41, 57, 62
Johanson, J., 59
Jonsson, S., 59, 60

Kiefer, N., 70
Kim, C., 114, 161
Kogut, B., 44, 58, 64, 75
Kojima, K., 19, 40, 80, 102, 158–9
Kotabe, M., 58, 60
Kuemmerle, W., 44, 57, 60, 163, 184, 203

Laage-Hellman, J., 203
Lal, D., 65
Levinthal, D., 58, 183
Li, J., 70, 185–6
licensing, 43
location, 1–3, 7–9, 16, 20, 25, 40, 44, 81, 83–5, 106, 138, 148, 217, 222, 227–8
location advantage, 1–3, 6, 8, 10, 15, 19, 43, 78–9, 87–8, 215, 220–22
Lundan, S.M., 1, 2, 20, 79
Lundvall, B.A., 161, 182
Luo, Y., 61
Luxembourg, 86, 88, 97

MacDougall, 112
management, 4, 8, 16, 21, 48, 74, 100–1, 107–8, 110, 112, 114, 133, 136, 165, 206, 208, 217
Manea, J., 79, 102
market heterogeneity, 10, 17, 60, 102, 135, 141, 225
market research, 10, 25, 28–9, 32, 102, 106, 142, 144–8, 155, 161–2, 166, 176, 181, 189–90, 224–5
Martinez, J.I., 41, 57, 62
metropolis, 100, 104
Mauborgne, R.A., 114, 161
Minbaeva, D., 58
Mizushima, A., 203
Mody, A., 81, 83–4
Molero, J., 136
Morrison, A., 45, 57, 62, 72, 111, 114, 136, 184, 203
Mudambi, R., 45
multidomestic hierarchy, 3–6, 8, 19, 200, 222
multidomestic strategy, 10, 17, 60, 102, 135, 141, 225
Murphy, A., 70
Murray, J.Y., 57, 60

Narula, R., 87, 89, 136, 215
national system of innovation, 1, 10–13, 15, 17, 18, 20, 84, 94, 96, 109, 139, 142, 146–61, 182–4, 188, 216, 223, 225–9
Nelson, R.R., 161, 182, 185
Netherlands, 86, 88
network hierarchy, 8, 9, 20, 221–2
Neven, D., 44, 81
new product concept, 142, 144–8, 155, 157, 160, 162, 166, 173, 175, 190
Niosi, J., 41
Nobel, R., 44, 60, 64, 70, 136, 162, 185–6
Nohria, N., 184

oligopoly, 99, 104–5, 108
OECD, 90, 97
organisational structures (of MNE), 1, 2, 6, 9, 11, 16, 54, 74, 98, 101, 107, 109, 111, 113, 141, 218, 221

Osterloh, M., 75
Ownership advantage, 2, 3, 5–9, 19, 57, 88, 105, 111, 113, 215, 218–22

Pain, N., 44, 81, 83–4
Papanastassiou, M., 19, 24, 38, 41–5, 55, 59, 64–5, 102, 108, 110, 114, 124, 136, 142, 144, 151, 161, 164, 171–2, 185, 190–1, 203–4
parent company, 2–4, 8, 10, 13, 18–19, 24, 46, 101, 164, 171, 176, 190, 193, 199, 201, 205, 208, 210
patents, 84, 95
Patel, P., 60, 185
Pavitt, K., 59–75
Pearce, R., 9, 19, 23–4, 38, 41–2, 44–7, 50, 55–6, 59, 60, 62, 64–5, 79–83, 102, 108, 110, 112–14, 116–18, 124, 130, 136–8, 142, 144, 151, 159, 161–2, 164, 171–2, 184–5, 190–1, 203–5, 210
Pederson, T., 74
Peng, M., 57
periphery countries (in Europe), 58, 73, 78, 81–9, 90–7
Perron, B., 45
Phene, A., 60, 72
Pitelis, C., 98
policy, 1, 18, 40, 54–5, 82, 85, 151, 160, 216, 218, 220
Porter, M., 4, 25, 60, 72, 75, 82, 184
Portugal, 85–9, 205–6
Poynter, T.A., 19, 24, 40, 44, 62, 73, 114, 184
Prahalad, C.K., 58
process,
  adaptation of, 4, 5, 19, 30, 34, 47, 115, 127, 134, 149, 158–9, 165–6, 176, 191, 214, 220–1
products,
  adaptation of, 4, 18–19, 30, 34, 41, 47, 64, 115, 127, 129, 134, 147, 158–9, 164–6, 175–6, 179, 191, 213–14, 220–1

248 *Index*

products – *continued*
  development of, 15, 17–18, 22, 27–30, 32–3, 38–9, 44, 46, 49, 50, 54–5, 64, 84, 106, 108, 111, 115–19, 124, 127–30, 135, 139–40, 145–9, 154–7, 159, 160, 163, 165–6, 169, 171, 173–6, 179, 181–4, 187, 189–90, 192–3, 195, 197, 201–3
product cycle model, 3, 4, 7, 138–41, 144–6, 161, 200, 215
profitability, 5, 6, 75, 80, 103, 141, 222
protectionism, 3–8, 25, 43, 46, 80, 82, 102, 158, 222

Randoy, T., 70, 185–6
Redlich, F., 99
regional integration, 6, 16, 78–97
regulation, 106
research and development (R&D), 4, 10–11, 13, 17–20, 25, 28, 32, 41, 44, 47, 56–7, 60, 78, 84, 94–6, 103–9, 115–20, 125, 127, 129, 131–4, 137, 145, 161, 163, 165, 172–3, 177, 183, 185–8, 192–5, 200–1, 204–5, 208, 210, 214
research,
  types of,
    applied, 116, 133, 144–8, 152–5, 160, 162, 165–7, 169–70, 172–9, 181, 183–4, 193–4
    basic, 11–12, 18, 23, 32, 75, 116, 129, 133, 144–53, 160, 162, 165–7, 169–77, 179, 181, 183–4, 193–4, 212, 215, 224, 226–9
    precompetitive, 11–12, 18, 20, 23, 33, 133, 142, 144, 152, 155–6, 160, 164–7, 169–72, 176–83, 187, 192–3, 195, 198, 201–2, 212, 224, 226–7, 229
R&D collaborations, 10, 15, 18, 20, 29, 32–3, 38, 46, 50, 64, 124, 161, 163–85, 190, 227, 229
R&D funding, 18, 54, 149, 152–3, 173, 179, 186–203

R&D laboratories, 2, 10–15, 17, 18, 20, 29, 32, 38, 40, 46–51, 54–5, 60, 62–4, 70, 115–20, 122–5, 128, 130, 133–5, 142, 149–50, 161–7, 179–80, 183, 187, 200, 202–3, 205–8, 210–12, 214
  types of,
    internationally interdependent lab, 142–4, 149–55, 160, 162, 163, 169–72, 174–5, 177, 179, 181, 183, 193–5, 198–202, 205, 207
    locally integrated lab, 145–6, 151, 155–7, 159, 161–2, 165, 169–71, 174–6, 179, 181, 183–4, 189–92, 195, 197–202, 205, 211
    parent/central lab, 142–4, 153, 161, 164, 173, 190, 210–13
    support laboratory, 64, 146, 159, 165–6, 169–72, 174–6, 179, 182, 188–9, 191–3, 196–201, 203, 205, 211–12
R&D networks, 17, 19, 143, 161, 227
Resnick, S.A., 100
reverse technology transfer, 44, 162, 185–6
Rolander, D., 40, 60, 110–11, 163
Ronstadt, R.C., 108, 184, 204
Rosenberg, N., 185
Roth, K., 45, 72, 114, 136, 184, 203
Rowthorn, R., 98
Ruane, F., 89
Rugman, A., 62, 107, 112, 114

Saez, C., 65
Schumpeter, J.A., 105
science-base, 10–12, 24, 45, 108, 116, 124, 133, 142, 147, 150, 152, 163, 167, 177, 179, 181–3, 188, 195, 208, 217, 227
scientific institutions, 18, 20, 33, 47, 50, 54, 65, 72, 75, 124, 164–70, 172–3, 175–7, 205, 214, 227
scientific personnel movement, 204–15
Scott-Green, S.C., 88–9
Séguin Dulude, L., 184

Singh, S., 56, 60, 116, 136, 162, 185, 205, 210
Siotis, G., 44, 81
Sjolander, S., 161
Skoog, G., 70
Souitaris, V., 72
Spain, 85–9
spillovers, 13, 39, 151, 157, 182, 199, 201–2
strategic competitiveness, 9, 14, 20, 23, 33, 50
strategic internalization, 10, 15–16, 18, 43–56, 183, 218, 225
strategic technology alliances, 42, 171
structural funds (of EU), 86
subsidiaries,
  roles of,
    product mandate, 10–20, 28–30, 32–4, 38–40, 42, 46–5, 50, 54–5, 60, 62, 64, 70, 72–3, 106–7, 109–10, 114, 117, 119–20, 122, 145–6, 155–7, 160–2, 184, 189–90, 192, 201, 203, 205, 214, 225–6, 228
    rationalised product subsidiary, 19, 25–30, 32–5, 38–42, 62, 65, 70, 72–3, 146, 205, 214
    truncated miniature replica, 19, 24–5, 29, 30, 32–5, 39, 41, 62, 64, 70, 72–3, 158–9, 162, 205
  strategic motivations of,
    market seeking, 3–8, 10–11, 14–17, 19, 24–5, 78–84, 90–2, 95, 97, 102, 104, 107, 109, 112, 114, 139, 158, 222–3
    efficiency seeking, 7–11, 14–17, 19–23, 25, 39, 40, 72–3, 78–84, 91, 93–6, 102–4, 106–14, 140, 146, 159, 221–3
    knowledge seeking, 9–16, 18, 20, 22, 25, 28, 38–9, 49, 79, 81, 83–4, 94–6, 102–3, 106, 114, 225, 227
    strategic asset seeking, 20
    natural resource seeking, 102

supply networks, 2, 8, 9, 11, 22, 29, 39, 48, 54, 83, 102–4, 118–19, 140, 159, 191, 221–2
Svensson, R., 81, 84
Swan, S., 59
Sweden, 87–8
synergies, 13, 14, 20, 39, 117, 144, 149, 226–7

tacit knowledge, 15, 19, 23, 34, 38, 48, 51, 55, 64, 72, 191
Taggart, J., 41, 55, 62, 114, 161
Tallman, S., 59, 74
tariffs, 3, 4, 25, 80, 82
tastes, 45, 80–1, 97, 117, 139–40, 142, 145, 149, 159, 161, 166, 190, 223
Tavares, A.T., 45, 55, 62
technological change, 6, 9, 23, 216, 220
technological heterogeneity, 9, 10, 17–18, 60, 102, 135, 141–2, 225
technological trajectory, 12–13, 15, 39, 47, 115–18, 120, 133, 151, 164, 181, 184, 203, 227
technology transfer, 5, 7, 12, 14, 19, 20, 58, 61, 146, 192, 200, 216–17, 220–1
Teece, D., 70, 137
Toyne, B., 98
training, 10, 22, 41, 108, 110, 150, 210, 219–21
transactions cost, 59, 73
transnationals, 40, 184

Ubeda, F., 88–9
UNCTAD, 88, 97
UK, 14–15, 17–18, 23–5, 38–9, 45, 48, 54, 86, 88, 96, 116, 118, 125, 127, 129, 133, 137, 163–5, 167, 169–75, 177, 183, 187–8, 190–1, 193, 195, 197–201, 205, 208, 210–11
USA, 5, 51, 54, 61, 79, 80, 90–1, 93–7, 102, 104, 125, 127, 129, 161, 164, 169, 179, 185, 187–8, 190, 198, 208–9, 211

Universities, 10, 16, 29, 33, 41, 46–7, 50, 56, 65, 72, 124, 151, 167, 169, 172, 176–7, 179–82, 185, 190, 205

Vahlne, J.E., 59
Vega, M., 60
Vernon, R., 3, 7, 19, 59, 134, 138–40, 144, 160–1, 205
Verspagen, B., 89
vertical integration, 21, 218–19
Veuglers, R., 81, 88
Von Zedtwitz, M., 57

Wang, D.Y., 57
Wheeler, D., 81, 83–4

White, R.E., 19, 24, 40, 44, 62, 73, 184
Williamson, O.E., 59
Wood, M., 136

X-inefficiency, 5, 8, 25, 222

Yamin, M., 44, 98, 107, 114, 162, 185–6
Young, S., 41–2, 55, 108, 161, 203

Zander, I., 88, 185
Zander, U., 58, 88
Zayas, J.M., 89
Zhang, S., 218